Must Men Hate?

SIGMUND LIVINGSTON

CRANE PRESS · CLEVELAND · OHIO

Published by CRANE PRESS

CLEVELAND, OHIO

By arrangement with Harper & Brothers

THIRD PRINTING
Revised Edition

Dedicated

to the

sacred memory of my father

MAYER LIVINGSTON

1839–1915

APPRECIATION

To Mr. Richard E. Gutstadt for his consistent encouragement and great assistance; to Mr. Sydney B. Lavine and the research staff of the Anti-Defamation League for factual data; to Mr. Irving Rosenbaum for his work on the Appendix of names; to my secretary, Miss Ethel Hork, for transcribing the manuscript with great care; to Mr. Louis Zara for his critical reading of the manuscript and his constructive suggestions, my sincere thanks.

CONTENTS

For the courtesy of permitting quotation from the publications following, the author expresses his indebtedness and thanks to the authors and publishers:

Over the Teacups, by Oliver Wendell Holmes; Houghton, Mifflin Company, Boston, Mass.

History of Bigotry in the United States, by Gustavus Myers; Random House, New York, N. Y.

Jewish Contributions to Civilization, by Joseph Jacobs; Jewish Publication Society of America, Philadelphia, Pa.

Organized Anti-Semitism in America, by Donald S. Strong; American Council on Public Affairs, Washington, D. C.

Behemoth, by Franz Neumann; Oxford University Press, New York.

A Christian-Jewish Tragedy, by Conrad Henry Moehlman; Printing House of Leo Hart, Rochester, N. Y.

Jews in a Gentile World, by Isacque Graeber and Steuart Henderson Britt, The Macmillan Company, New York.

The Mind in the Making, by James Harvey Robinson; Harper & Brothers, New York.

Why We Behave Like Human Beings, by George A. Dorsey, Harper & Brothers, New York.

The Survey Graphic; The Survey Associates, New York.

Universal Jewish Encyclopedia, New York.

Encyclopædia Britannica, Chicago, Illinois.

Medieval Forgers and Forgeries from "The Collected Papers of Thomas Frederick Tout," Vol. III; The Manchester University Press, Manchester, England.

Shakespeare and the Jew, by Gerald Friedlander; George Routledge & Sons, Ltd., London.

Antisemitism Historically and Critically Examined, by Hugo Valentin; Viking Press, New York.

Jewish Contributions to Civilization, by Cecil Roth; Macmillan & Co., Ltd., London.

'Anti-Semitism Throughout the Ages, by Count Heinrich Coudenhove Kalergi; Hutchinson & Co., Ltd., London.

INTRODUCTION

The conflict between belief and reality has burdened man from the morning hour of civilization. Superstition and bigotry have so long enslaved the mind that even today their shadows darken the truth. Many stubborn delusions and hatreds of the past are important today only as they mark the steppingstones in the history of mankind.

"Reason and humanity have raised their voices in vain—for grey-headed prejudice is deaf." So said Moses Mendelssohn, the "German Socrates," in the closing days of his life, which he had devoted to the war against bigotry, intolerance and inhumanity.

While prejudice is old and deaf and blind, mass reason and the humanities are young and growing. At the time of Mendelssohn, Lessing, Dohm, and Montesquieu, modern science was in its infancy. The intolerance of both the Church and the State would have "exposed" the child, as the Romans did their unwanted offspring. But the new learning survived and grew ever stronger. The world is the richer and the wiser because, in the quiet laboratories of truth, those first men of science fought ignorance and superstition with unrelenting persistence.

But despotism still ruled. The concepts of democracy and freedom of conscience were comparatively new. A great part of mankind could not read and dared not think. It was only "yesterday" in the calendar of civilization that the mass of humanity crossed the threshold of literacy and began to think for itself. Reactionary forces have always impeded the march of progress, but they cannot halt the advance of justice, reason and liberty. Anti-Semitism, which is an all-inclusive hatred of the Jew, as well as antagonism against Judaism, has been nourished only by bigotry, by falsehood, by libels, and by appeals to tne lower instincts of the herd.

I have an abiding faith that religious prejudice and mass hatred will be vanquished, in time, by reason and truth.

America has no history of anti-Semitism. It is a late import from Europe, where it was the poisonous aftergrowth in the jungles of religious fanaticism and superstition. Anti-Semitism can feed only on hatred; it cannot survive without hatred. It has been employed by the political charlatan, by the opportunist, by the witch hunter, and by the frustrated psychopath. Anti-Semitism has been a vicious circle. Anti-Semitism was responsible for repressive legislation and, thereafter, pointed to the effect of this legislation to engender new prejudice and more hatred. It created the laws of Europe which forbade the Jews to cultivate the land, and then charged the Jew with not producing the food which he ate. It enacted the laws which excluded the Jew from the guilds and prohibited him from engaging in handicrafts, and then criticized the Jew for not creating. It wrote laws forbidding the Jew from dwelling near his Christian neighbors and commanding him to live only in the ghetto, and then charged him with being clannish. It restricted his every opportunity to earn a livelihood, except in petty money-lending and the collection of taxes—the two professions most despised by the overburdened masses. It created a stereotype of the ghetto Jew for the public mind, using a superimposed photograph for this purpose, and then urged the masses to hate that stereotype. The masses did not—they could not—know the real Jew. They could see only the false stereotype, the "Shylock." The technique for creating hatred of the Jew was perfect.

Max Nordau said, "Pretexts change, but the hatred remains. The Jews are not hated because they have evil qualities; evil qualities are sought for in them because they are hated." How easy it is to discover evil qualities in any sect or group against which the forces of hatred have been marshaled! If evil qualities do not exist, then hatred demands that they be invented. For hatred has no conscience; it will accuse the hated group of any and all crimes; if there are no crimes, hatred will create them. Among such fictionized crimes were: that the Jews had poisoned the wells of Europe and had caused the epidemic known to history as the Black Death; that the Jews had used the blood of Christian children for ritualistic purposes; that the Jews had an international conspiracy, for which anti-Semitism conveniently invented the fraudulent and often-exposed "Protocols of the Elders of Zion"—to support the contention that such a nefarious conspiracy existed.

Through the ages other sects have suffered in similar degree. Among them were the Cathari, the Huguenots, the Templars, the Catholics, the Albigenses, and others. The struggle against hatred is always difficult, for many individuals actually love to hate. When it conflicts with an established hatred, there is always a strong resistance to reason. Though exposed time and again, libels and fictions which support such hatred refuse to die. The apostles of hate search the dusty records of the past for old libels and fictions and feed them again and again to the credulous public. Whenever expediency seems to require it, scurrilous libels, long buried in the graveyard of past tragedies, are resurrected. The basest of all men is one who invents base libels against any sect or group for the purpose of creating or fostering hatred. Such men wrong not only the present generation but generations yet unborn.

The highest authorities of nearly all Christian denominations have denounced anti-Semitism as unchristian; yet most of the anti-Semites are Christians. Every religious sect or national group, standing before the record of its past, must confess, in the words of the ritual used on the Day of Atonement, "We have sinned, we have transgressed, we have done perversely." If Christians were to be held to account for every inhumanity committed by Christians—recalling for this purpose the cruelty of the Crusaders, the savagery of the religious wars, the sufferings under the Inquisition, and the expulsion of dissidents from their homes—the defense would doubtless be that the acts were unchristian, and that those who were responsible for such deeds had perverted the teachings of Christianity.

The behavior or dereliction of a few Jews supplies the data for a general accusation against an entire people, its

xiii

past, its present, and even its future. To use a similar defense as given above, and reply that the guilty ones perverted Judaism and transgressed Jewish ethics and morality avails nothing, for the reaction is, at once, that Jewry is responsible for the misdeeds of every Jew! Were this same responsibility imposed upon *all* sects and groups, there would surely be less anti-Semitism. The comparative records would silence the accusers.

The tyranny of hatred has ruled the minds of men, not by divine right but by the usurpation of the throne of reason and justice. Hatred is the last stronghold of the forces of evil against the brotherly understanding and tolerance of peoples.

In our American democracy there can be no place for mass hatred against any group of American citizens, whatever their faith, creed or racial origin. Washington, Jefferson, Hamilton, and the other great statesmen, from those who attended at the birth of our government to those who are at the helm of the Ship of State today, have written into our basic laws and traditions that American democracy is to be enjoyed by all its citizens equally, with special rights to none. In such a democracy anti-Semitism cannot function. Should it prevail, it would destroy that democracy.

When many of the Christian denominations declared anti-Semitism unchristian it was a great step forward. But the practical benefits of this pronouncement have not yet been evidenced. The forgeries, libels and calumnies used by anti-Semites to engender hatred against the Jew must be denounced and stigmatized *whenever* and *wherever* they rear their ugly heads. Generalities are of little value in combating deep-seated antagonisms. Pronouncements are not self-executing. Results can be accomplished only by action. The worker in the vineyard does not rid the vineyard of weeds by declaring them to be noxious. He takes a hoe and goes out to uproot the poisonous growth.

As in military warfare the best defense is the offense, so in this age-old warfare against reaction we must launch an offensive of truth against every anti-Semitic citadel of forgery, scurrility, libel, fraud and bigotry. Only thus can we destroy the insidious foe.

In this book I have tried not only to analyze anti-Semitism but to sketch the long development of the hatred against the Jew, and to prove that anti-Semitism is incompatible with reason, and that it is inconsistent with the principles of American democracy and with the ethical basis upon which Christianity stands.

Anti-Semitism is a social problem which affects not only the Jew but also the general public. The Jew and the non-Jew must learn to understand each other. Each must be willing to place himself in the other's position so as truly to know his neighbor. Each must be willing to appreciate the emotion, the spirit, the purpose, and the eternal outlook of the other. We must learn the facts, and we must discard the fictions. The points of accord must be emphasized and the points of differences must be explained. This is the technique for the establishment of an intelligent public opinion.

From my many years of experience and contact with men who expressed anti-Semitic attitudes, I can say, without reservation, that no normal, intellectually honest person, *who is willing to reason,* can fail to arrive at the conclusion that such an attitude is without basis in fact and is socially unsound. Indeed, any person who will try honestly will find real satisfaction, and even exhilaration, in the conquest of these prejudices. The only cure for this age-old social problem is a continuous, consistent, and vigorous educational process supervised by the forces which mold public opinion. *Teach the truth and unmask every falsehood.* The Jew has nothing to fear from the truth, but everything to fear from ignorance. An intellectually honest man, knowing the truth about the Jew, cannot be an anti-Semite.

MUST MEN HATE?

PART ONE

SEEDS SCATTERED UPON VIRGIN SOIL

HATRED is not inherited. It is acquired. Long after its seeds have been planted germination may take place.

Both environment and early teachings may bring hatred and, specifically, hatred of the Jew, into childhood. Often unconsciously, and even unintentionally, the virus of anti-Semitism is injected into the child mind by otherwise well-meaning parents, relatives and instructors who would not willingly teach any other kind of hatred.

The realm of childhood is, by nature, a real democracy. Children do not know the past; they live in the present; they have no anguish of the future. Children glory in imagery and fantasy. Their earliest knowledge of the world of fear comes when they learn of monsters, witches, devils and "the big, bad wolf." The child mind never forgets that which caused it the least pang of fear. Vividly it creates pictures of objectives and of persons it has never seen; graphically it constructs and fills out the details of episodes which it has never witnessed. Many of these impressions, whether of lovable princes who rescue fair maidens, or of detestable rogues and highwaymen who harass peaceful travelers, are lasting and affect future mental attitudes, especially if later experiences recall these pictures from the subconscious regions of the mind. Thus the fears and fantasies of childhood affect future adult attitudes and conduct.

It is for these reasons that the very manner in which the Jew is introduced to the average child mind may prove of serious consequence to that child's development as a completely adjusted adult, tolerant of his fellow citizens.

The ill-considered presentation of the Jew will not itself

influence the child when grown up to be anti-Jewish, or anti-Semitic. But it will condition the mind for the reception of those fictions and libels of the Jew which are the shame of our Western civilization. A mind so conditioned will absorb and will accept without resistance every appalling accusation leveled against a people whom it does not really know. For it is elementary that the mind accepts readily that which it is conditioned to accept and rejects only that with which it is in conflict.

Count Richard Coudenhove-Kalergi, a distinguished student of anti-Semitism, has declared:

> The history of the origin of anti-Semitism leads us to early childhood. Since Freud's discoveries it has been established beyond all doubt that the soul of the child is the retort wherein a great many of the later instincts and sentiments originate. Choked up and buried impressions and prejudices, received and acquired in childhood, sink into the subconscious mind and there turn into instincts.
>
> The anti-Semitic instinct, too, mostly originates in a childish prejudice.[1]

A commonplace introduction of the Jew to the child often occurs somewhat like the following:

"Mother, Tom says Joe is a Jew. Is he?"

"Yes, he is."

"What are Jews?"

"Well, they are *not* like other people. You know, they are not Christians."

Innocent and well-meaning as that mother's reply is, she is already establishing in her child's consciousness that Joe, the Jewish lad, is "not like other people." As her own son accepts that thought he assumes that Joe and all other Jews must be odd, quaint, perhaps weird folks, not merely with different religious ideas but with peculiar ethical ideas as well. In short, the word "Jew" soon stands for

---

[1] *Anti-Semitism Throughout the Ages*, by Count Heinrich Coudenhove-Kalergi, Hutchinson & Co., London, p. 247. Chapter VII, "Jew Hatred Today," from which the above quotation is cited, is by the author's son, Count Richard Coudenhove-Kalergi.

2

everything unusual and undesirable, for the narrow, for the avaricious, and for the untrustworthy.

Another incident illustrates an even more frequent manner in which the Jew is singled out to the child mind. It is another well-meaning mother who speaks thus to her sons and daughters:

"Children," she says, "I don't want you to play with those boys and girls across the street. They are Jews."

Again, in exercising the prerogative of the parent, the mother has drawn an invisible line between her children and Jewish children. She has implied differences no child can understand; she has insinuated qualities that do not exist; she has sown liberally the seeds of apprehension and mistrust. Now to her children Jews will always be different and suspect. "They are Jews," she has said and has provided a category into which to thrust everything and every person who is not like them, or is not liked by them.

Examples could be cited of harsher, cruder statements uttered in lower strata of society. These two are given because their very casualness makes them seem mild and inoffensive. Yet they plainly influence the child mind and prepare it to receive the larger slanders, many of which have been created deliberately to poison and to infect.

Seeds in Juvenile Literature

EVEN the child's first reading inclines his mind to that anti-Jewish bias. A partial survey of juvenile literature reveals the Jew portrayed always as a rascal and a rogue, the eternal villain in a world of good people.

The Mother Goose nursery rhymes are known to every child. Often they are repeated in little songs before the youngster can speak clearly. "Jack and Jill," "Old King Cole," "Little Boy Blue" and several of the other verses are part of nearly every toddler's early education. But the Mother Goose rhymes also contain a reference to the Jew which no child can soon forget. Picture the scene at a children's party with perhaps the eldest girl reading to the children from the following rhyme:

> Jack sold his egg
> To a rogue of a Jew,
> Who cheated him out
> Of half of his due.
>
> The Jew got the goose
> Which he vowed he would kill,
> Resolving at once
> His pockets to fill.[2]

So into the nursery world creeps this hateful image. "A rogue of a Jew!" The child does not reason; he accepts faithfully what his elders teach him. The nouns "rogue" and

[2] This rhyme appeared in an edition of *Mother Goose* published by Thomas Y. Crowell Company until early 1939. The same rhyme was included in *The Big Book of Nursery Rhymes*, McLaughlin Bros., Springfield, Mass. It also appeared in the Book of Knowledge, Vol. XVI, p. 5930 of the Blue Edition, published by the Grolier Society; the publishers have since removed the offensiv passages. Needless to say, the impressions originally made cannot be expunged so easily from the minds of the readers.

"Jew" become synonymous. What a creature this must be who kills the goose solely "His pockets to fill"! Thereafter, the very word "Jew" inspires in the child mind a picture of one who cannot be trusted, one who must be watched constantly. An intelligent adult must reflect that evil has been sown, and nothing but evil may be expected from whatever harvest such impregnation of ideas may bring.

Here is *Grimm's Fairy Tales,*[3] a collection which has amused several generations of children. The story entitled, "The Jew in the Bush," makes a merchant character, a cheat who ends up on the gallows, none other than a Jew. What reaction can the child mind have other than that the Jew, wherever he is, however clothed, wherever he resides, is a mean creature?

The famous story of "Aladdin; or the Wonderful Lamp,"[4] which has been enjoyed by youthful readers for centuries, contained an episode in which the Jew was, by implication, a great rogue "even among the Jews." The child's sympathy for Aladdin naturally makes him abhor any character so delineated. The constant identification of roguery as Jewish cannot but help to make the child despise anyone who is a Jew and to revile anything remotely Jewish.

Even in books where one would hardly assume that such references could be of the least pertinence, the same lack of understanding is often evident. A. Frederick Collins, author of many volumes on a variety of subjects, wrote a book entitled *Fun with Figures*, which consisted primarily of mathematical puzzles. But one puzzle presented a problem of a diamond-studded cross and was called "Outjewing the Jew (It Can't Be Done)." Here again a simple tale which involved an amusing problem contained a vicious barb. Any young student who worked on this puzzle could not help but be affected by the notion that the Jew was

[3] In the Garden City Publishing Company's edition, prior to 1935. Since then the story has been altered to avoid needless prejudice.

[4] In *Fairy Tales Every Child Should Know*, edited by Hamilton Wright Mabie, Garden City Publishing Co., editions prior to September, 1941, when the publisher deleted the objectional references.

5

cunning and not averse to seeking his own advantage to the detriment of his neighbors.[5]

In *A Child's History of Civilization* by Stephen King-Hale[6] the story of the Crucifixion was given without explanatory caution. Because the material is controversial and is especially apt to impress the child that the Jew is unfair and, indeed, even bloodthirsty, it is highly important that every such account be checked carefully. But even a volume entitled *Beautiful Stories of the Bible*[7] erred in this respect. These instances are but a sampling of the many that have appeared through the centuries and have wrought incalculable damage to relations between Christian and Jew by prejudicing the child mind before it has learned to think for itself.

In discussing this subject, Hugo Valentin, lecturer in history at the University of Upsala, said:[8]

> At the same time, as children learn to love Christ, the Saviour and the friend of children, they are naturally seized with indignation against those whom they deem to have hated, tortured and killed Him. When the child hears the word "Jew," he associates this conception with the passion of Christ. This very often has decisive influence on the individual's subsequent attitude toward the Jews. In Christ he does not see a Jew who loved his people and whose whole being bore the stamp of religion and ethical inheritance from his forefathers.

The fair-minded reader may revolt at this point and say, "Those were only the children of the ignorant who reacted so badly. The children of better educated parents and families would not be misled so easily." But Oliver Wendell Holmes, essayist and poet, a practicing physician by profession (and the father of the Oliver Wendell

[5] D. Appleton-Century Company, Inc., New York. This puzzle was revised in August, 1941.

[6] Wm. Morrow and Company, Inc., New York, 1928. Now out of print.

[7] Saalfield Publishing Co., Akron, Ohio. Revised, in this respect, after November, 1936.

[8] *Anti-Semitism*, Victor Gollancz, Ltd., London, 1936, p. 13.

Holmes who became the Great Dissenter and the pride of the United States Supreme Court) confessed:

> I shared more or less the prevailing prejudices against the persecuted race. I used to read in my hymn book,— I hope I quote correctly—"See what a living stone the builders did refuse! Yet God has built His Church thereon in spite of envious Jews." I grew up inheriting the traditional idea that they were a race lying under a curse for their obstinacy in refusing the Gospel. Like other children of New England birth, I walked in the narrow path of Puritan exclusiveness.
>
> In the nurseries of old-fashioned orthodoxy, there was one religion in the world,—one religion, and a multitude of detestable, literally damnable impositions believed in by uncounted millions who were doomed to perdition for so believing. The Jews were the believers in one of these false religions.[9]

But Holmes, fortunately, conquered these early impressions. As he stated himself:

> Recognizing the fact that I was born to a birthright of national and social prejudices against the "chosen people," chosen as the object of contumely and abuse by the rest of the world, I pictured my own inherited feelings of aversion in all their intensity and the strain of thought under the influence of which those prejudices gave way to a more human, a more truly Christian feeling of brotherhood.[10]

However, not every child coming to maturity is able to shed these aversions by the power of reason and the force of logic. Picture the ordinary youngster who reads *The Child's Scripture.*

Question No. One for Sabbath Schools and Private Families:[11]

[9] "At the Pantomime" in *Over the Teacups,* published by Houghton, Mifflin Company, Boston, 1891, pp. 193, 194.
[10] *Ibid.*, p. 194.
[11] Published by the Cumberland Presbyterian Publishing House. See Lesson 37, p. 21.

Q: Who put Jesus to death? *A:* The wicked Jews.
Q: How did they put Him to death? *A:* On the cross.

Every fair-minded observer must be aware of the effect produced in the child mind by the story of the trial and the crucifixion of Jesus, as recited in such staccato style.

Nor are Christian educators unaware of the dangers of such quasi-catechisms. Dr. Conrad Henry Moehlman, outstanding Christian scholar and member of the faculty of Colgate Divinity School, has stated the case admirably:[12]

> Unfortunately Christian religious education, whether of the old or new variety, teaches children many errors regarding the Friday of Passion Week.
>
> A Bible manual in widespread use in the United States contains these statements:
>
> "When Cain heard this sentence of God, he gave way to despair, saying: 'My sin is too great to be pardoned.' So God set a mark upon him, and he went forth, a wanderer and fugitive upon the face of the earth."
>
> "The murdered Abel is a figure of Jesus Christ, while Cain is a figure of the traitor Judas, and the Jewish people, who put our Saviour to death."

Dr. Moehlman quotes from many other books intended for youth which deal with the story of Calvary and malign the Jews, though Jesus was himself a Jew and his Apostles were of the same faith and origin. He concludes:

> Are the Christian boys and girls who taunt innocent Jewish children with being "Christ-killers" more guilty than their elders who permit them to study it in schools of religion?[13]

This question may not be passed over lightly, for truly here the sins of the parents pass unto the next generation as the tide of anti-Semitism mounts higher and higher.

Simple writers, spurred on by religious zeal, are not the

12 *The Christian-Jewish Tragedy*, by Conrad Henry Moehlman, Printing House of Leo Hart, Rochester, N. Y., p. 163. Dr. Moehlman includes quotations from several lives of Christ, which are brutally direct in so dramatizing the Crucifixion that the youthful reader becomes incensed against "the guilty ones."

13 *Ibid.*, p. 168.

only ones who err. Even *The Life of Our Lord* by Charles Dickens, which was written for his children, and countless other books on the Bible, sin grievously by telling the story with appealing embellishments, but without any cautionary explanation. We watch our histories for political and economic references, but on the religious side we let prejudice, rather than modern psychology, prevail.

In these stories the child is not told, nor is it pointed out to his special attention, that the immediate followers of Jesus were Jews, that His disciples were Jews, that Mary, His mother, was a Jewess, and that, in the manner of the flesh, Jesus was Himself an observing Jew.

Neither is the child told that only the few who were officials under Roman rule, and who were, like all Quislings, seeking favor with the Roman conquerors—those officials striving to be even more Roman than the Romans—only those were the guilty accusers of Jesus, and that the great body of Jews throughout Palestine, and throughout the rest of the world, were innocent of the crime of Golgotha. Nor is the child admonished that it would be wrong to blame the Jews now living for any share in this tragedy. Can any true Christian believe that Jesus Himself, were He to tell this story today to the children, would relate it as it is told in these books for children?

The story will be told for ages to come. Would it not better serve the Christian cause, and keep the pliant child mind free from hate and resentment, if the story were so told as to guard against an improper reaction in the child's mind? Doubtless, Charles Dickens, and the authors of these other volumes, did not intend to poison the minds of their own children and the minds of other children against the Jew. But it cannot be denied that the results have been anti-Semitic, rather than Christian, in the truest meaning of that word.

Some years ago Mr. Philip Cowen, publisher of *The American Hebrew*, propounded, to leading clergymen of various faiths, the query as to whether the prejudice against the Jews was not due largely to the religious instruction given by the Church and by Sunday schools throughout the land. This was not only a difficult but an embarrassing question. The question should have been whether these teachings condition the minds to accept readily the standard prejudices against the Jew and those libels which are revived from time to time. Mr. Cowen received many answers.

Mr. Irving Washington Gladden, eminent preacher, replied, "Possibly, in part. I have no doubt that prejudices against the Jew have been raised, unwittingly, by the teachings of Church and Sunday School. Christian teachers of all grades ought to explain more carefully than they sometimes do, that the Jews, with all their prejudice, were the very best people in the world when our Lord came to earth, possessing the purest morality, honoring the family as it was honored by no other nation. We ought to keep it before our children that Jesus Himself was a Jew; that all the Apostles were Jews; that Christianity was planted in Asia and in Europe by Jews."

Reverend R. Heber Newton of New York answered, "Doubtless it has been a serious factor in times past, and may be still a serious factor among the ignorant."

Reverend A. B. Kendig answered, "It grows out of a want of instruction, or grossly perverted instruction."

George William Curtis answered, "I suppose that the feeling against them is founded, first, upon the Christian tradition and teachings that Christ was crucified by Jews, and, second, upon their position as social outcasts in the Middle Ages, which was also due to the Christian tradition and forced them into hostility and revenge."

Margaret Eland, author of *John Ward, Preacher,* answered, "I am inclined to think that the teaching of the Church and Sunday School is largely responsible, but only among the uneducated classes."

Dr. Titus Munson Coan replied, "There is no justification for the prejudice against the Jewish religion, although that undoubtedly exists, and is undoubtedly due in large part to the religious misinstruction that is given by Christians."

Some clergymen replied that the teachings were historic,

and that any misconception was overcome by the teaching of brotherly love. Others said, "No," but limited their reply to their own denomination. However, the nature of the replies was evidence enough that intelligent Christian leaders were themselves troubled at the net effect of such teachings not merely upon the child mind but upon future conduct of those children come to adulthood.

As George A. Dorsey so well said:[14] "Living beings are not elements but reaction systems; their behavior can be molded. Ours is already set; but it is not necessary that we condition our children to the mold in which we hardened."

The adolescent youth reads *The Merchant of Venice* and similar books and plays which depict the Jew unfavorably. Very few ever read Lessing's *Nathan, the Wise* or Eliot's *Daniel Deronda*. Indeed, if the members of the graduating class of any high school were asked to name a Jew in fiction, they would reply in unison, "Shylock!" If they were asked to name a world-renowned scientist or author or musician of Jewish origin, many of these same students probably could not name a single one.

[14] *Why We Behave Like Human Beings*, by George A. Dorsey, Harper & Brothers, 1925, p. 470.

Seeds in Adolescent Education

The Merchant of Venice has had a most disastrous effect upon the good repute of the Jew. Innumerable are the persons who have never known or met a Jew, but who visualize him as a living facsimile of Shylock. The importance of this fictitious character in the history of world anti-Semitism merits an analysis of *The Merchant of Venice*.

William Shakespeare was born in 1564; he died in 1616. There certainly were no Jewish moneylenders in England during his lifetime, for the Jews had been expelled from England in 1290 and did not begin to return until 1655. At most there were only a few Marrano families in the entire kingdom. Shakespeare never knew a Jew personally. As far as the records show,[15] there was only one Jew in England, and he was "imported" from Portugal in 1559. He was Dr. Roderigo Lopez, a converted Jew, who was physician to Queen Elizabeth and was held in high regard by his English colleagues. When the Earl of Essex brought to England Don Antonio, the Pretender to the Spanish throne, Dr. Lopez acted as Don Antonio's interpreter. But a bitter enmity developed between Dr. Lopez and Don Antonio. The Earl of Essex suspected, or merely alleged it, that Lopez was in the pay of Elizabeth's enemies. In any case, Essex charged that Dr. Lopez was conspiring to poison both Queen Elizabeth and Don Antonio. The Queen would not believe the indictment against Lopez, but Essex left no stone unturned until he had persuaded the Queen to sign the death warrant. To accomplish his purpose, Essex pressed into service ancient anti-Semitic, as well as anti-Spanish, prejudices. After the execution of Dr. Lopez, on June 7,

[15] *A History of the Marranos*, by Cecil Roth. Jewish Publication Society, Philadelphia, 1932, pp. 256-257. See also Cambridge Modern History, Vol. III, p. 335.

1594, Queen Elizabeth granted property to his widow and children. This fact is recorded in the Calendar of State Papers for 1595. Evidently the Queen feared that a grave act of injustice had been committed, else she certainly would not have made such gifts to the widow and children of a man who had tried to poison her!

Shakespeare knew Christopher Marlowe's play, *The Jew of Malta*, the central figure of which was named Barabas. Like Dr. Lopez, Barabas was a physician. Marlowe made his character admit that he poisoned wells and killed people. Immediately after the execution of Dr. Lopez, *The Jew of Malta* was staged repeatedly in London. The same year *The Merchant of Venice* was performed for the first time. It is more than coincidental that where the enemy of Dr. Lopez was named Don Antonio, Shakespeare gave to Shylock's foe in *The Merchant of Venice* no other name but Antonio! Thanks to Essex, all England knew that the physician charged with the intended poisoning of the great and good Queen was a Jewish convert. The time was ripe for any dramatist to capitalize on the sensation of the day. Shakespeare catered to this hunger for more sensation by creating his own Shylock.

But the plot of Shakespeare's play was not original. There had been many stories concerned with the pound of flesh. Gregorio Leti, biographer of Pope Sixtus V, gave the following account in his work which was published in Venice in 1587, *eight* years before *The Merchant of Venice* was produced. Leti wrote:[16]

It was reported in Rome that Drake had taken and plundered St. Domingo in Hispaniola, and carried off an immense booty. This account came in a private letter to Paul Secchi, a very considerable merchant in the City, who had large concerns in those parts, which he had insured. Upon receiving this news, he sent for the insurer, Sampson Ceneda, a Jew, and acquainted him with it. The Jew,

[16] Quoted from *Shakespeare and the Jew*, by Gerald Friedlander, George Routledge & Sons, Ltd., London, 1921, pp. 15-17. See also Graetz's *History of the Jews*, Vol. IV, p. 657; see also Jewish Encyclopedia, Vol. XI, p. 317.

whose interest it was to have such a report thought false, gave many reasons why it could not possibly be true; and at last worked himself up into such a passion that he said: "I'll lay you a pound of my flesh it is a lie."

Secchi. who was of a fiery hot temper, replied: "I'll lay you a thousand crowns against a pound of your flesh that it is true." The Jew accepted the wager, and articles were immediately executed betwixt them, that if Secchi won, he should himself cut the flesh with a sharp knife from whatever part of the Jew's body he pleased. The truth of the account was soon confirmed, and the Jew was almost distracted when he was informed that Secchi had solemnly sworn he would compel him to the exact literal performance of his contract. A report of this transaction was brought to the Pope, who sent for the parties, and being informed of the whole affair, said: "When contracts are made, it is just they should be fulfilled, as this shall. Take a knife, therefore, Secchi, and cut a pound of flesh from any part you please of the Jew's body. We advise you, however, to be very careful; for if you cut but a scruple more or less than your due, you shall certainly be hanged. Go and bring hither a knife, and a pair of scales, and let it be done in our presence." Thus far the Italian writer.

Naturally, the Christian desists. The Pope sentences both Jew and Christian to death. This punishment was altered. They were told that they would be sent to the galleys. At the intercession of Cardinal Montalto a substantial fine was subsequently inflicted in lieu of the punishment to which they had been sentenced.

It is only fair to add that the historical accuracy of this story has been questioned. But for the present purpose that is immaterial since we are only concerned with the tracing of the background of the Shylock story. All agree that the story employed by Shakespeare was a fiction. If Shakespeare, however, took the story of *The Merchant of Venice* from Leti's work, then he purposely reversed the parties to the contract, for it was the Christian, and not the Jew, who demanded the pound of flesh. How ironical if this figure of Shylock, which has so long haunted the Jew, were inspired from a tale where not the Jew but the Christian was the mean, cruel figure!

Indeed, it is difficult to believe that Leti's account could be fiction. First, it was incorporated in the biography of a great pope and Leti was himself of the Catholic faith. Second, he probably had access to official records; Sixtus V wore the papal crown from 1585 to 1590. Third, the judgment of Sixtus, as related in the story, is of great credit to him, especially when we remember that he lived in an age when the Jews were bitterly oppressed, were confined to the ghetto, and had few rights. If Leti were indulging in fiction, would he not have had Sampson Ceneda, the moneylending Jew, demand the pound of flesh?

As for Shakespeare's conception of Shylock as he created him in *The Merchant of Venice*, we can say only that he followed the prejudice of his age. He, too, had since childhood been exposed to the same slanders about the Jews. What matter that he had never known a Jew? The public was incensed against a Jewish physician. Marlowe's *Jew of Malta* was receiving acclaim. What was more natural than that Shakespeare should produce his own Jew play? It is a miracle that he put even those stirring speeches of self-defense into Shylock's mouth. Shakespeare's artistry threatened to triumph even over age-old prejudices.

But had Shakespeare ever known Jewish life and lore he would have realized that the Jewish law positively forbade any Jew from mutilating the human body for any purpose. However, the law concerning the cutting of human flesh could be found in the Roman Laws—Decemviral Laws of the XII Tables—where a creditor was empowered to mutilate the body of his debtor, and that without fear of punishment should he cut more or less than the magistrate allowed. The old German law followed the Roman law in this respect. To the Jewish law such an action would have been abhorrent and indefensible.

Needless to say, no one impugns the literary or artistic merits either of *The Merchant of Venice*, or of *The Jew of Malta*, or of any other novel or play which employs the Jew as a whipping boy. But that these perversions of talent are lamentable cannot be denied. The same characterizations could have been as powerful in their rascality without the added cloak and beard of the stage Jew. To say that the audiences would not have been as excited is merely to dwell upon the fact that the dramatists catered to the known passions of their publics.

Moreover, both Shakespeare and Marlowe were the children of their centuries. We can judge the Shylock and Barabas creations only by the conditions existing at the time of their production. Europe was steeped in superstition, fanaticism and bigotry. Witches lurked in every dark corner. The funeral pyres of heretics were still lighting the skies. Judaeophobia prevailed. The Continent was aspiring to civilization, but the mass mind was still steeped in barbarism. It was charged that the Jew was not merely guilty of the Crucifixion, he was not merely a creature who—by decree—wore strange garb and lived in isolated quarters, he was also a vile usurer.

The charge of usury has, alas, survived to our own times. Many have regarded usury as "a Jewish crime." The falsity of such an allegation will be clear to anyone who makes an honest study of moneylending and banking in the past, as well as in the present.

Until the launching of the Crusades the Jews were engaged in as many handicrafts, trades and professions, including agriculture, as their Christian, or their pagan, neighbors. The violently religious emotions stimulated by the Crusades reacted against the Jews, who, of course, took little or no part in these ventures. The crusading fervor turned upon the hapless Jews, and whole communities were slaughtered by the obsessed zealots. Many repressive laws were enacted, restricting the Jews from both the ownership and the cultivation of land. When the Jews were excluded from the all-powerful guilds, they could no longer earn their livelihood by the arts and crafts. Soon they were denied even the privileges of military and civil service.

The walls of the trap were sprung: the Jew had no means by which he could earn his bread, save one channel only—that of petty moneylending. It is a mistake to assume that the Jews were the "bankers" of the Middle Ages. The clergy made many laws, as did the nobles; but families like the Fuggers, the Welsers and the Medicis were the great bankers. Few Jews could achieve any real wealth, for the barons, dukes and kings were ever ready to confiscate large sums. Furthermore, these princes made the Jews their tax collectors, always an unpopular assignment. Under the Roman Empire the Jew had been an ordinary citizen; in the Middle Ages he was no more than the chattel of the princeling within whose city walls he was allowed to make his home. Accepting his fate and serving as faithfully as he could, he was now charged with the accusations, "Moneylender! Tax collector! Usurer!" What a sorry chapter in the cultural history of Europe!

The unlettered masses, always in need of a scapegoat when crops failed, when plagues came, when battles were lost, had a perennial victim in the Jew. Even the educated classes salved their hurts at the expense of those whom they had made outcasts.

Count Heinrich Coudenhove-Kalergi, a devout Catholic and an erudite scholar, said:[17]

I confess that I have myself been a theoretical Anti-Semite. When I was much younger I was even a practical Anti-Semite, and this for excellent reasons, because I had had the most unpleasant experiences imaginable with Jewish usurers. Had I been asked a few years ago, when I decided to study the Jewish question and to write a book on it, whether this work would turn out Anti-Semitic, my answer to this question would most probably

[17] *Anti-Semitism Throughout the Ages*, by Count Heinrich Coudenhove-Kalergi, Hutchinson & Co., Ltd., London, p. 18. On p. 105 the author refers to "Selections from the Best Patristic Works in the German Language," edited by Dr. Valentin Thalhofer, published by Joseph Kosel in Kempten in *eighty* volumes. He points out that having studied the Indexes, which alone take up two volumes, he found no mention whatever of the Jews under "Usury, avarice, cupidity and the taking of interest." He concludes that the Church Fathers knew little or nothing of the charges of Jewish usury, extortion, blood rituals and the like, for had they been aware of these accusations they would surely have recorded them. Apparently, these charges were not current at all in the early centuries of the Christian era.

17

have been in the affirmative. A serious and, as I believe, a thorough study of the subject has set me right.

Few persons, whether farmers, physicians, attorneys, artists or craftsmen, have either the time, the patience, or the inclination to study so involved a question. Yet the reader can quickly ascertain his own attitude by asking in the quiet of his soul, "Who introduced me to such notions as I now have and entertain about the Jews?" Many will come to the realization that years have passed since they first heard those accusations. One can ask further: "Who conditioned the mind to give credence to these slanders without a shred of evidence?"

More than one conscientious man or woman has looked up in dismay and confessed candidly that those notions were buried long ago in the child mind, so long ago, indeed, that they seemed a part of his education and his heritage. Troubled, they have in turn asked, "What makes the average mind so receptive to every anti-Jewish slander and libel? Why does the average mind not resist these horrible vilifications?"

PART TWO

SEEDS SCATTERED UPON FERTILE SOIL

THE modern accusations against the Jew, when analyzed and considered, will be found to be not innocent delusions but pure inventions and fictions, which have been purposely invented to create hatred and disunion.

James Harvey Robinson expressed a thought which has been repeated by many psychologists:[1]

> Few of us take the pains to study the origin of our cherished convictions; indeed, we have a natural repugnance to so doing. We like to continue to believe what we have been accustomed to accept as true, and the resentment aroused when doubt is cast upon any of our assumptions leads us to seek every manner of excuse for clinging to them. *The result is that most of our so-called reasoning consists in finding arguments for going on believing as we already do.*

From childhood to the threshold of maturity the mind has been prepared to receive hospitably every accusation against the Jew. In any event, the mind has *not* been prepared to resist and to reject slanders and libels against the Jew. No wonder then that we have Jew hatred. Every element to promote hatred is supplied, and the hate merchants have been busy selling their wares. When we consider how few individuals really know anything at all about the Jew we might almost say that it is astonishing that we do not have more anti-Semitism. The story is told of Charles Lamb, that he had uttered severe and unfriendly criticisms of another man. A friend remarked, "But, Mr. Lamb, you do

---

[1] *The Mind in the Making*, by James Harvey Robinson, Harper & Brothers, New York, 1921, p. 41. The italics are the author's.

not know him. You never even met him!" The essayist hardly blinked as he stuttered the classic reply, "No, of course, I don't know him. If I had met him I fear that I should like him!"

Even among university graduates it would be a very rare exception to find one who has ever read any post-Biblical Jewish history. They know nothing of the real reasons for the antipathy toward the Jew. They have never heard of the special laws concerning the Jew which—apart from Hitler—existed in many European countries up to recent times. To illustrate, they may observe that the Jew is not, in proportion to his numbers, engaged in agricultural pursuits. But they do not know that, as noted in the preceding chapter, the Jew was forbidden for hundreds of years either to own or to cultivate land, since he could not take a Christian oath of fealty to the feudal lord. They may possibly observe that in his immediate home the Jew is not engaged in the crafts (this subject will be treated more fully later). However, they do not know that the guilds of Europe closed their membership rolls to Jews and that nearly all crafts were controlled by these guilds. They may perhaps feel, even from personal observation, that the Jews are clannish. But do they know that, until recent decades, the Jew was compelled to live in ghettos completely separated from his non-Jewish neighbors, and that these ghettos were guarded and were chained off except for certain hours of the day?

Quite generally, the Jews are classified as foreigners even in this country, notwithstanding the fact that the Jews were early settlers. A Jewish congregation for worship existed in Newport in 1658. There were early settlements in Connecticut, Pennsylvania, Rhode Island and Maryland. The records show that there were Jews in Maryland in 1656. Long before this date they had settled in Mexico and in South America. They took an active part in the defense of the colonies, and participated in the American Revolution.

However, it is not strange that the public at large has had so little knowledge about the Jew. There is so much to

20

study that universal knowledge is not to be expected. Because of this fact, the hate-monger and the professional anti-Semite have found a veritable paradise for their insidious enterprises.

To understand anti-Semitic propaganda, it is necessary to turn back to some of the important accusations which were the foundation stones of modern anti-Semitism. Jew hatred and the persecutions resulting from it date from the period of the Crusades. Before that time, persecution of the Jew was not general, and, indeed, was very rare. It was during the Holy March of the Crusades that the Jews were accused of piercing the Holy Host until it bled. Unquestionably, this was an insane delusion. The little bloodlike stains on certain foods are caused by contact with various bacteria; there was no blood on the wafers. Nevertheless, this accusation against the Jew caused many medieval pogroms. It was a charge sincerely believed by devout Christians of that day, but the effect of this belief was tragic for the Jew.

Merely to enumerate the tragic results of that one accusation, that the Jews had stabbed or desecrated the Host, would fill a volume. A typical case was that of the monk, Johann Capistrano, to whom the Pope granted special plenary powers to supervise the Jews of Germany and Poland. To carry out his mission Capistrano first went to Germany. In 1453 he charged that the Jews in the vicinity of Breslau had desecrated the Host. As a result, all the Jews of Breslau were imprisoned and, of course, their entire property was confiscated. Seventeen Jews at Schweidnitz and forty at Breslau were burned at the stake for this imaginary crime. All children under the age of seven years were taken from their parents and were forcibly baptized. It is hoped that their descendants are good Christians. All others were expelled.

In the twelfth century the Jew was accused of ritual murder, the charge being that he had murdered Christian children in order to use their blood for ritualistic purposes. This tragedy has been repeated in every century since; one of the most recent accusations culminated in the Beilis trial in Russia during 1911-1913. It is strange, but curiously

21

interesting, that this accusation of ritual murder is the identical charge made by the Romans against the Christians in the early Christian centuries. Although this charge of ritual murder has been branded absolutely false by several popes and by a number of the outstanding Protestant historians and ministers, yet it is repeated by the Nazi propagandists, even to this day.

The next accusation was made during the fourteenth century—to the effect that the scourge of the Black Death was due to the poisoning of the wells of Europe by the Jews. The fact that the Jews drank the *same* water did not appease the superstitious masses. The people were whipped into so violent a fury by the religious fanatics that many Jewish communities were wiped out and thousands met with cruel death. So universal was this accusation in Europe that Pope Clement VI, in a bull published in 1348, sought to expose the foolishness of the charge that the Jews were responsible for the Black Death. His bull, however, fell upon deaf ears.

These delusions, which poisoned the mind of Christian Europe during the Middle Ages, seem strange and abhorrent to us, but not any more than the delusions of the present will appear to future generation. Even in enlightened America, which was settled by the victims of superstition and persecution, the belief in witchcraft long prevailed. In America, women were convicted in court of the charge of witchcraft and were condemned to death. Parano boasts that in a century and a half the Holy Office had burned at least 50,000 witches "who, if they had been left unpunished, would easily have brought the whole world to destruction." When, in the Rhineland, the winter was prolonged until June, and the vineyard suffered, it was widely believed that this was a curse of witchcraft, and hundreds of innocent men and women were convicted and burned to death. The German court records disclose no less than ten thousand convictions for witchcraft.

Up to recent centuries it was believed in Europe that public calamities could be stopped by driving a nail into a tree or a wall. A Roman law provided that the highest magistrate should drive a nail into a tree or a wall every year on the thirteenth day of September. It is said that in certain parts of Europe, peasants still practice nail driving as a cure for calamities and ills.

There is not a single accusation against the Jew which was not directed against the Christians during the first four centuries of the Christian era.

Tertullian, a church father, declared, "They take the Christian to be the cause of every disaster to the State, of every misfortune of the people. If the Tiber reaches the walls, if the Nile does not reach the fields, if the sky does not move or the earth does, if there is famine, if there is plague, the cry is at once, 'The Christian to the lion!' "

Augustine, a Roman pagan, wrote, "There is a shortage of rain, surely the Christians are the cause of it."

Tertullian defended the Christian from the accusation that he uses human blood for ritualistic purposes:[2] and in *Octavius*, Minucius Felix described the early Christians:

A gang of discredited and proscribed desperadoes band themselves against the Gods. Fellows who gather together, illiterates from the dregs of the populace, and credulous women with the instability natural to their sex, and so organize a rabble of profane conspirators, leagued together by meetings at night and ritual feasts and unnatural repasts, not for any sacred service but for piacular rites, a secret tribe that shuns the light, silent in the open but talkative in hid corners; they despise temples as if they were tombs; they spit upon the Gods; they jeer at our sacred rites; pitiable themselves, they pity our priests; they despise title and robes of honor, going themselves half-naked.

And further, the same author said:[3]

Already—for ill weeds grow apace—decay of morals grows from day to day, and throughout the wide world the abominations of this impious confederacy multiply. Root and branch it must be exterminated and accursed.

[2] *Apologeticus*, Chap. IX.
[3] *Octavius*, Chap. VIII.

They recognize one another by secret signs and marks; they fall in love almost before they are acquainted; everywhere they introduce a kind of religion of lust, a promiscuous brotherhood and sisterhood by which ordinary fornication, under cover of a hallowed name, is converted to incest. And thus their vain and foolish superstition makes an actual beast of crime.

By the same author, the early Christians were accused of worshiping "the head of an ass, the meanest of all beasts; a religion worthy of the morals which gave it birth."

Dr. Conrad Moehlman quoted the following from the Roman accusers of Christianity:

"I hear that they adore the head of an ass. . . . Now the story about the initiation of young novices is as much to be detested as it is well known. An infant covered over with meal, that it may deceive the unwary, is placed before him who is to be stained with their rites: this infant is slain by the young pupil, who has been urged on as if to harmless blows on the surface of the meal, with dark and secret wounds. Thirstily—O Horror! they lick up its blood; eagerly they divide its limbs. By this victim they are pledged together; with this covenant of wickedness the Christians are covenanted to mutual silence. . . . On a solemn day they assemble at the feast, with all their children, sisters, mothers, people of every sex and every age. There, after much feasting, when the fellowship has grown warm, and the fervor of incestuous lust has grown hot with drunkenness, a dog that has been tied to the chandelier is provoked, by throwing a small piece of offal beyond the length of a line by which he is bound, to rush and spring; and thus the conscious light being overturned and extinguished, in the shameless darkness, the connections of abominable lust involve them in the uncertainty of fate."[4]

And then Moehlman comments:

With these accusations of alleged crimes, commercial antagonism should be mentioned as another reason for the discovery of the uniqueness of Christianity on the part

[4] *Christian Jewish Tragedy*, p. 56.

24

of the Roman Empire. The presence of Paul at Ephesus resulted in the burning of books of magic and in an economic riot staged by the silversmith Demetrius because of the loss of revenue from the manufacture of silver shrines of Artemis. And in distant Bithynia, Pliny noticed that his action against the Christians meant a rise in stocks in the cattle market.[5]

It is astounding that anti-Semitism should utilize practically the same charges as were invoked in Rome against the Christians. Just as these charges were inventions intended to produce hatred against the Christians, so today the same charges are used to produce hatred against the Jews. Would any real Christian give credence to the vile accusations against the Jews if he knew that they were merely the repetition of charges made against Christianity by the Romans? Thousands of the early Christians suffered persecution and perished in the arenas of Rome because of these accusations and delusions.

Whenever delusions have captured the mass mind, the progress of civilization has been checked. A delusion, whenever it has saturated the mass mind, becomes a common faith. The denial of that faith is heresy. This is the reason that the delusions of men have been so obstinate and enduring. Those possessed of them always seek converts to their belief. Success in the making of converts strengthens the faith in the delusion. Once they have possessed the mass mind, the destruction of delusions is a slow process. The restoration of reason becomes a creative enterprise.

The fabric of religious and racial prejudices was woven in the morning of our civilization, when man first awakened from the slumber of savagery. The threats of fear, of magic, and of superstition, all the emotionalism which burdened man in his infancy, were woven into this mighty fabric. Humanitarianism and science have here and there changed the design somewhat, but the warp of fear and the woof of hate remain in this tapestry of tradition, ignorance and superstition.

One who will divest himself of his preconceived ideas

[5] *Ibid.*

and his emotionalism, and who will honestly use his mind to determine the real cause for the antipathy against the Jew, will help himself to eradicate that prejudice. Where there is correct thinking, there can be no prejudice.

In this respect every honest man should welcome the opportunity to be disillusioned. No matter what one's religious faith may be, his conscience must command that he shall not bear false witness against his neighbor. Intellectual honesty demands that we seek the truth and that we banish falsehood.

The resistance to such disillusionment is frequently insurmountable. Most people love their hates. For our hates are frequently psychological compensations for our ignorance. Some extreme anti-Semites are paranoiacs, but under our democracy are not restricted by law, although they are a social menace. Many anti-Semites are the victims of mental complexes that reflect their own personal maladjustments and false interpretations of life.

Count Heinrich Coudenhove-Kalergi makes this diagnosis:

> This psychosis, which in the case of many men bears the symptoms of a pathological phenomenon or of a fixed idea, can only be cured by a clear insight into its causes and by a comprehension of its origin. The recognition of a prejudice as such is tantamount to the first step towards a delivery from its power. Only when the educated Anti-Semite will have realized that both individual and historical Anti-Semitism are based upon religious fanaticism and that their scientific convictions are rooted in the religious prejudices of their nurses and nursery governesses—then only will they be able to liberate themselves from their delusions. Just as in the case of psychoanalytical therapeutics, in Anti-Semitism, too, it is a question of recalling into consciousness a hidden event or experience of early childhood in order to effect the liberation from a prejudice which has developed into an instinct.[6]

[6] *Anti-Semitism Throughout the Ages*, by Count Heinrich Coudenhove-Kalergi, p. 248.

Anti-Semitism is based not on fact but upon emotional interpretations. In general, the process of substituting balanced and wholesome attitudes for disordered prejudice requires basic re-education conducted wisely and with patience.

The Ritual Blood Accusation

THE accusation that Jews use Christian blood for ritual purposes dates back about eight hundred years. It was seriously believed to be true by the majority of the people of all the European countries. It was frequently exploited by the local rulers to exact heavy fines from the Jews, or to justify the expulsion of the Jews from their countries. In some instances false confessions were forced from the accused by relentless torture.

But the Jews were not the first to be accused of ritual murder. In Rome the early Christians were accused of committing murder so as to use the blood of Roman pagans in their mystic rituals.

Tertullian complains, "We are called the most villainous of mortals because of the secret practice of killing and eating children." Later the Christians themselves accused the minority Christian sects, who were considered heretical, of this same crime and practice. This accusation was made by the Christians against the Gnostics, and also against the Manichæans; later the Knights Templar, a militant sect, were similarly accused; in 1466 this charge was made against a Christian Italian sect. Later, the Dominicans were accused of the same crime and practice by the Franciscans. One monastic order accused the other of using the blood and the eyebrows of Jewish children for their secret ritualistic purposes!

In China, Christian missionaries were accused of this crime as late as 1870. In Madagascar, in 1891, the foreigners were charged with devouring human hearts. Here the accusations made were so strong that the government authorities, in order to pacify the general population, issued a decree forbidding foreigners, particularly the French and the English, from indulging in such practices.

28

Notwithstanding the fact that this accusation against the Jews was pronounced as without the least foundation, this libel reappeared at different periods and was frequently revived for political expediency.

During the nineteenth century forty-two cases of alleged ritual murder were reported. The bloody Kishinev massacre of 1903 resulted from this charge. During the Nazi propaganda campaign this accusation against the Jews was reiterated constantly. Julius Streicher's *Der Sturmer* devoted a special twelve-page issue to the revival of this old libel, and the Nazi press frequently repeated the sordid details. It was even imported into America. In Quebec two French newspapers tried to arouse the populace by repeating the ritual murder charge, and several of the anti-Semitic publications have repeated it, pursuing the canard to the point where they hinted that the Lindbergh child, kidnapped and murdered by the German, Bruno Hauptmann, was a victim of ritual murder.

Hate-mongers have no conscience, and however heinous an accusation, they will not be deterred from employing it for their purpose, for there are some ready to believe *any* accusation, regardless of how often it has been disproven and branded fraudulent.

One case, which particularly aroused the conscience of the world, occurred in 1913. Upon the accusation that Mendel Beilis, a Russian Jew, had killed a boy so as to use the blood for ritualistic purposes, an actual trial was held. The case was prepared and was presented by the highest state officials of Russia and had the approval of the archimandrite of the Russian Catholic church. Looking back, this event seems like a mirage, or the stage reproduction of a tragedy which might have occurred centuries ago when all the world was steeped in superstition and ignorance.

On the eve of the Russian Easter, a boy, twelve years old, was found murdered outside of the city of Kiev in Russia. A reactionary newspaper made the sensational charge that here was a case of ritual murder by the Jews. The Duma was in session at the time, and immediately an interpellation was made by the government. Nistchuk, the chief of the Kiev secret police, reported after a thorough investigation that the murder had been committed by a notorious band of local criminals. The government, however, disregarded the report and determined that a case of ritual murder must be prepared and tried. At this very time, the Duma was considering a bill to repeal the special laws against the Jews and to grant to them the right to reside outside of the Jewish pale of settlement. The reactionaries had opposed this bill bitterly, and had started an agitation against the Jews, including in their propaganda the accusation that the Jews practiced ritual murder. In the person of Mendel Beilis, superintendent of a brick kiln, the government found a victim to persecute. The accusing witnesses were two habitual drunkards, a lantern tender and his wife.

The entire civilized world was aroused that such a charge could be made officially and be prosecuted by a government in this enlightened age. Representatives of other countries, among them leading intellectuals, were sent to protest to the Czar. From Germany came Gerhart Hauptmann and Friedrich Delitzsch. From France came Anatole France and Henri de Regnier. In England, the leaders sent their protest to the Russian government.

In the United States, seventy-five outstanding Christian clergymen, representing all the Christian denominations, signed a petition to the Czar, in which they protested against the proceedings. Among the signers of the American petition were David H. Greer, Episcopal bishop of New York, William T. Manning, Cardinal Farley, and James R. Day; the other signers were leaders of different Christian churches. The petition is a historic document and deserves to be recorded here:

To His Imperial Majesty, Nicholas II,
Czar of all the Russias
Sire:
As the representatives of various Christian denominations of the United States of America, irrespective of creed, we unite, in the name of our sacred faith, in an appeal to you, that the charge of ritual murder against the Jew, Mendel Beilis, now on trial at Kiev, be with-

drawn, because of the untold evils to the cause of humanity which may follow from its further prosecution.

We are convinced that the blood accusation against the Jews, which has been made sporadically, is as unfounded as was the same accusation which, as history shows, was frequently directed against the early Christians. It has been subjected to the most careful investigation for centuries, and no evidence warranting the slightest credence has ever been discovered, and it has been rejected as unworthy of serious consideration by Church and by State. Bulls were issued by four Popes—Innocent IV, Paul III, Gregory X and Clement XIV—which formally declared this superstition to be a baseless and wicked invention. The genuineness of these pronouncements has been recently officially certified by Cardinal Merry del Val, the Secretary of the Holy See.

Many Sovereigns have in the past forbidden the attribution of religious significance to such accusations, among them the German Emperors Frederick II (1236), Rudolf of Hapsburg (1275), Frederick III (1470) and Charles V (1544); the Bohemian King, Ottocar II (1254); the Polish Kings, Boleslaw V (1264) Casimir III (1334), Casimir IV (1453) and Stephen Bathori (1576).

Emperor Alexander I of Russia issued a ukase on March 18, 1817, by which he prohibited the prosecution of so-called ritual murder cases, for the proclaimed purpose of ending the superstition that the Jews employed Christian blood for ritual purposes. This ukase was confirmed by Emperor Nicholas I on January 13, 1835.

Prince Obolensky, the former head of the Holy Synod of the Russian Empire, has recently declared: "On the strength of all historical and literary materials concerning ritual murders I can say that this accusation against the Jews is just as ill-founded as were the accusations of the same nature directed against the Christians long ago. You must remember that the use of blood is contrary to all the teachings of the Jewish religion."

For centuries, numerous authoritative theological, scientific and historical writers, who have carefully studied the subject, have united in reaching the same conclusion.

Believing that the continuance of the pending prosecution may give rise to acts of violence, as a result of the

31

passions aroused by fanaticism and religious hatred stimulated thereby—consequences which would be deplorable from the standpoint of true religion, of humanity and of civilization, and abhorrent to the spirit of Christianity—as Christians, and for the advancement of our holy cause, we pray that you may avert this grave peril, and that you may forestall the possibility of the imposition of injustice, not only upon the individual who is now on trial, but upon the entire Jewish people, and that to that end you may confirm the ukase of your glorious ancestor, Alexander I, by which he sought for all time to destroy the hideous imputation, that the Jews require Christian blood for ritual purposes.

In full confidence that this appeal will be favorably received by Your Imperial Majesty, and that the motives which have prompted us in presenting it will not be misunderstood, with the utmost esteem and respect we have subscribed these presents, this thirty-first day of October Nineteen hundred and Thirteen.

SIGNED by 75 leaders of Christian denominations.

At the Beilis trial many scholars of Russia and of other lands testified that ritual murder was never practiced or sanctified by the Jews or by Judaism. These scholars were of the Protestant churches, of the Roman Catholic church, as well as of the Russian Catholic church. Several Russian officials who testified against the State were immediately imprisoned by the government. After the trial, Vera Cheberiak, a leader of a band of criminals, confessed that she was guilty of the murder. The trial ended in the acquittal of the defendant, Beilis, but the court rendered a judgment that the murder of the child *was* a ritual murder. It was evident that the latter part of that judgment was forced by the government as a face saver.

No political expediency could ever justify the action of the Russian government in staging this medieval tragedy.[1]

[1] Universal Jewish Encyclopedia, Vol. 2, pp. 139-141.

Libels Concerning the Talmud

No literature in all the world has been so libeled and traduced as the Talmud. Those responsible have been men who have never read any part of it and, in all probability, were unable to do so. Most of its modern critics do not even know what the Talmud is. They have snatched a few libels from the accusations of the past and have publicized them as the products of their own fertile brains.

The fact that the general public is not conversant with this literature is not strange. Recently a professor of science, a Nobel prize winner and a man free from all hatred, inquired of me whether the Talmud is not *part* of the Jewish Bible.

In a recent test high school students were asked to name the Bible of the Christians. All answered, "The New Testament." They were then asked to name the Bible of the Moslems; with very few exceptions they replied, "The Koran." The third question was on the Bible of the Jews, and none of them could answer correctly. Strange that none of this student body should know that the Bible of the Jews is the Old Testament.

The Talmud consists of the writings of various rabbis collected over centuries. The Talmud is not a book but a compilation of writings upon many subjects and of many contradictory opinions. Some of these writings are discussions and dialogues but there are also recorded the sayings of great teachers. The Babylonian Talmud was compiled between the period of 100 B. C. and about 500 A. D. The well-known translation by Soncino consists at present of twenty-four volumes of about three hundred to seven hundred pages each. It was not until the sixteenth century that Joseph Karo wrote a compendium of the Talmud. These writings may be compared with the writings of the Church Fathers.

In general, the accusations and libels have been that the Talmud sanctions a different morality for the conduct between Jew and Christian than it does for the conduct between Jew and Jew, and that, consequently, it does not forbid crimes committed against Christians or the debasement of them. No accusation has ever been so completely without foundation. As a matter of fact, the Talmud consistently emphasizes that all men are brothers and that any person who leads a moral and religious life and worships God in some way, even though his faith differs from the Jewish faith, must in every respect be regarded the same as an Israelite. The Talmud refers to the commandments of Noah as fundamental and binding upon all peoples. One of the imperishable statements of the Talmud is that God caused all mankind to be descended from a single human pair so that no one might be able to say to another, "My father is nobler than thine."

It is not generally understood that only limited numbers among the Jews have ever read the Talmud, or any part thereof. The Talmud is used by Hebraic scholars rather than by the Jewish public. In fact, few are able to read its Hebrew or Aramaic text, which is unvocalized. Of course, there are translations of the Talmud and various books containing Talmudic stories, which are accessible in the larger libraries.

One of the outstanding traducers of the Talmud was August Rohling, a professor at the University of Prague. He was a man without principle or honor, as was afterwards clearly proven. Professor Hugo Valentin says of him that he hated Protestantism as well as Judaism, and attempted to prove that the reformers of the Christian faith were morally defective. It was Rohling who stated:[1] "Wherever Protestantism sets its foot, the grass withers. A spiritual void, the deterioration of holy morals, a terrible desperation of heart

[1] *Der Anti-Christ Und Das Ende Der Welt.*

34

are its fruit. A Protestant who lives according to Luther's precepts is a monster."

In 1882 a revival of the ancient accusation of ritual murder occurred. August Rohling declared that he was able to prove under oath that Jews actually committed ritual murder. This accusation was widely publicized in the Austrian press, and resulted in such bitter feeling against the Jews that many local disturbances broke out.[2] Joseph Samuel Bloch, a rabbi, braved all opposition and, in articles which appeared in the Vienna press, publicly attacked August Rohling, charging him with ignorance, and deliberate falsification, and challenging him to translate any page of the Talmud taken at random. The attack upon Rohling was telling, and members of the faculty of the University of Prague asked him what action he intended to take. He replied that he would not dignify the ravings of this rabbi by any act of his. The faculty, however, demanded that Rohling defend himself and institute a suit for libel against Rabbi Bloch.

Whereupon, a certain Christian lawyer undertook the defense of Rabbi Bloch. This lawyer was so intent on establishing once and for all the falsehood of Rohling and others of his kind that he devoted his entire time to the preparation of the case. He even learned to read the Talmudic texts.

The court of Vienna appointed two outstanding Christian Hebraic scholars to answer a series of questions, each question relating to the accusations of Rohling on the teachings of the Talmud. Their names were Professor Theodor Nöldeke of the University of Strasburg, who was proposed by the German Association of Orientalists, and Professor August Wünsche of Dresden, who was proposed by Hofrat Zschokke, rector of Vienna University and professor of Catholic theology.

The court also appointed, as an expert concerning the writings of the Fathers and the early Christian theologians, the patristic scholar, Professor Pius Knoell, at the suggestion of the Vienna University authorities. He was charged with

[2] Joseph Bloch, *Israel Among the Nations*, Chap. XXXIV, p. 33.

35

the translation of the literature of the Fathers and of these theologians. The court also appointed Franz Weihrich for the translation of the writings of Agobardus of Lyons. The writings of Paolo Medici, having been quoted by Rohling, were also of importance. Since these were in the Italian language the court appointed Dr. Leone Roncali, an official interpreter, to translate for the court.

Perhaps no court ever used greater precaution to be accurately, and completely, informed upon the issues to be tried. It is also noteworthy that the court selected only outstanding Christian scholars as experts in each of the particular fields of inquiry, in view of the fact that the issues in the trial were charges and criticisms of the teachings of Judaism, particularly as contained in the Talmud, by this supposedly Christian scholar, Professor Rohling.

After a year's study the expert witnesses, recognized by the Christian world as outstanding scholars, answered every question propounded to them by the court. In each instance their reply was that Rohling had misquoted the Talmud or had falsely translated it, and that every accusation made by Rohling was false and without any basis in fact. So annihilating was the testimony of these experts that immediately prior to the beginning of the trial, the plaintiff, Rohling, voluntarily dismissed his suit, and the court taxed the costs and expenses against him.[3] The faculty of the University of Prague then demanded his resignation. Later, in 1893, Rabbi Bloch instituted a suit for libel against three publishers who had again revived the Talmud libels, the result of which was that the defendants were punished.

The greatest Christian scholars and theologians in Hebraica and Orientalism have repudiated the accusations time and again. Professor Nöldeke described the libels as "a piece of baseness." The German-Christian scholar, Professor Hermann L. Strack, characterized them as a combination of ignorance, blind hatred and malevolence. Strack, in his work concerning the ritual blood accusation, stated,[4] "I

[3] A full account of all the questions and the answers is contained in Bloch's book, *Israel and the Nations*.
[4] *The Jew and Human Sacrifice*, Bloch Publishing Co., London.

publicly accuse Rohling of perjury and gross falsification."
Professor Franz Delitzsch described these accusations as "a
network of infernal lies" and said, "But the God of truth
still lives, and exalted at his right hand, Christ still lives,
who will know how to defend His honor against the
slanderers of His name . . . . a Rohling and a Justus (who
think they are serving Him with their lies) shall die through
their lies." Professor Strack, who is recognized as a great
Christian Talmudic scholar said,[5] "Judaism does not possess
any written work or oral tradition whatsoever that is in-
accessible to Christians. The Jews are at no pains to conceal
anything from the Christians, nor could they do so. For the
correctness of this statement I pledge my honor as a man
and a scholar."

Notwithstanding these statements by distinguished Christian scholars, whose devotion to the Christian faith no one
has ever questioned and whose sole and only purpose was
truth, their opinions are, even at this stage, swept aside
by irresponsible and ignorant promoters of hatred. The
great tragedy is that people who will read the lying tracts
or will listen to the harangues of hate-mongers never will
read the denunciations of these falsehoods and libels by
the great German scholars, Nöldeke, Wünsche, Strack, Delitzsch, and Reuchlin.

It has been observed that the Talmud is a favorite subject
for diatribes by anti-Semitic agitators. It lends itself to their
purpose admirably because the audience knows nothing
concerning the subject and there is a certain amount of
mysticism about it. At the same time these propagandists
gain some prestige for erudition and scholarship by the very
fact that they are discussing so profound a subject as the
Talmud.

Recently a woman propagandist, in addressing audiences
in various cities throughout the country, told her audiences,
among other falsehoods, that the Talmud teaches Jews to
commit immoral acts with non-Jewish girls "at so tender an
age as three years"!

[5] *Einleitung in Talmud Und Midrasch*, published in 1921.

The astounding fact is not that the speaker would indulge in such nonsense but that the audience would listen
to her. It is not likely that one person in her audiences even
doubted the truth of her statement, but they were, instead,
fortified in their hatred by this new calumny. So has this
propagandist, and many others, for years scattered the seeds
of hatred upon fertile fields.

The Protocols of the Elders of Zion

A LITERARY FORGERY

"The Protocols of the Elders of Zion" is one of the most notorious literary forgeries, frauds and hoaxes to be perpetrated since history began. It first appeared in 1905 in Russia where it was promoted by the Black Hundreds during the reign of Nicholas II. The author, whose name was subscribed to the original editions, was a mediocre lawyer known as Sergei Nilus. Originally, the "Protocols" appeared as an appendix to the second edition of Nilus' book, entitled *The Great in the Little.* In the various succeeding editions Nilus gave conflicting accounts as to how he had procured the original, which he had translated into Russian. Later editions by others also varied in their accounts as to the origin of this fraudulent document. Some of the editions claimed that the "Protocols" was the minutes of the Zionist Convention at Basle, presided over by Dr. Theodore Herzl, who was a leading citizen of Austria. The argument of the fraudulent document was that the Jews were conspiring to control all the governments of the world, to destroy Christian civilization, and to make themselves the world's masters. To accomplish this, malevolently cunning details had been worked out, and these were allegedly given here.

There was never an organization such as the "Elders of Zion," or *The Wise Men of Zion.* Yet it was claimed that these protocols were the proceedings of this organization "of the thirty-third degree," evidently confusing it with that degree in Masonry.

"The Protocols" was first used in Russia to stir up animosity against the Jews. Its immediate purpose was to undermine the political influence and the personal standing

39

of Count Witte, then the most powerful minister in the Russian government. Count Witte was a man of broad understanding. He had the confidence of the Czar, and was ambitious to shape the policy of the Russian government along modern and enlightened paths. Since Witte's wife was an Odessa Jewess, there was a general belief that he was favorably inclined toward the Jews of Russia, who had been oppressed for centuries. The political antagonists of Witte, led by the Grand Duchess Elizabeth herself, did their utmost to discredit him with the ruling class and with the royal family. One of his stanchest antagonists was George V. Butmi de Katzman whose name is connected with the publication of the fraudulent "Protocols."

On the eighth of January, 1935, a Catholic priest personally called upon me in Chicago and delivered to me a written statement to which he had subscribed and sworn. I had previously written a small brochure pointing out the fraudulent character of the "Protocols of the Elders of Zion." This publication was the incentive for his visit.

In his written statement my caller identified himself as Father Gleb E. Werchobsky, a priest of the Roman Catholic church of Slavic and Byzantine rite. He was ordained a Roman Catholic priest in Constantinople on the thirtieth of July, 1914. At one time he had charge of the parish at Woonsocket, Rhode Island. In 1929 he moved to Chicago, devoted himself to religious arts for church decorations, and continued to serve as priest in the Roman Catholic church. He was born in St. Petersburg, Russia, on October 23, 1888. His father was Eugene I. Werchobsky, an architect, and his mother was Mary C. von Stein. George V. Butmi de Katzman, a former lieutenant in the Imperial Guards of Russia, was a friend of the family. Immediately following the Dreyfus affair in France, Butmi went to Paris. Upon his return to St. Petersburg he produced several French manuscripts which he desired to have translated into Russian. The translating was done by Butmi's wife and by the mother of Father Werchobsky. This was the translation which afterwards appeared under the name of "The Protocols of the Wise Men of Zion"!

The name of Butmi's wife was Nadezda Vassilievna. Butmi's residence was 15 Alexandrowski Prospect, Petersbourgskaia, Storona, near the Tutchkov Bridge. When Father Werchobsky visited St. Petersburg, he called at Butmi's home, and received from him a printed copy of his edition of "The Protocols."

In his sworn statement, which he handed to me that day, Father Werchobsky stated that "The Protocols of the Wise Men of Zion" were a fraud and a forgery, and that he had made this statement and had delivered it to me solely in the interest of truth. He further stated that of the group interested in the publication of this fraudulent document, he knew personally Sergei F. Sharapoff, editor of a weekly publication called *Russky Trud*, which paper was particularly antagonistic to Count Witte; Paul V. Oi, S. K. Efron, also known under the pen name of "Litvin"; A. V. Vassiliev; Butmi; and his, Werchobsky's, father. This group and other individuals with whom Werchobsky was not acquainted personally were very militant in their opposition to Count Witte. They fought bitterly the Count's effort to establish a gold standard for Russia for the purpose of encouraging foreign capital for her industrial development; his plan was also opposed by the landowners and by the nobility. Count Witte was strongly inclined to a French alliance. His opponents, particularly the landowners and the nobility, opposed him on that point, too, for they were strongly inclined toward an alliance with Germany. The two factions were bitterly arraigned against each other. Since it was well known that Count Witte desired to ameliorate the conditions of the Jews of Russia, and that he favored the repeal of certain repressive laws, these "Protocols" were used to undermine him with the Czar, with the royal family and with other governmental officials.

Feodor Roditchev, a member of the Russian nobility and a former member of the Duma, said:

"How did Sukhotin (from whom Nilus claimed to have received the documents)[1] get the protocols? An unknown had brought them to him. They were given to him by an unknown lady who had received them from an unknown but energetic participant in the Basle Congress. Was this credible? Well, then, there is another version of the original—intended for the German readers. The Russian government sent a spy to the Basle Congress. He himself did not go to the Congress, but bribed one of the participants. He was carrying the protocols from Basle to Frankfurt to the local masonic organization. He stopped on the way in a little town, and gave the protocols to the spy. He engaged copyists who worked all night and copied the protocols.

In the first Russian version the protocols were supposed to have been brought to Russia from France. According to the German version, the protocols were copied, consequently they were in German.

In Russia the problems of Christianity and Judaism have been studied by such men as Vladimir Solovyov, Professor Troitsky, Professor Kokovtsev, Kartashov, Bulgakov, Berdyayev—men of profound intellect and a living conscience. In them the counterfeit ravings of the ignorant monk, Nilus, evoked but a smile of contempt. The low level of the circle in which men like Nilus moved and worked is only too well known. It was the world of police denunciations, divorce perjuries, monastic servility and feigned, blasphemous piety. In order to attract attention Nilus' *Protocols of the Wise Men of Zion* had to emigrate from Russia and the further away they went the better they fared.

Mr. Lucien Wolf in his article, "The Nonsense of Nilus," stated, concerning the explanation of Nilus as to the authenticity of the instrument published by him as the protocols:

According to one, the protocols came from a deceased friend, unnamed, who received them from a woman also unnamed, who stole them from one of the most in-

[1] In the "program edition" of 1917 Nilus claimed he had received the "Protocols" in 1901 from Alexis Nikolaievich Sukhotin, later Vice-Governor of Stavropol. But Sukhotin was already dead, the technique of referring to witnesses who cannot testify is an old one.

fluential and most highly initiated leaders of Freemasonry * * *, according to the other there was no woman intermediary and no despoiled French Freemason, but the whole business was done by the deceased friend himself, who rifled the safe of the Headquarters Office of the Society of Zion in France * * —In the third and enlarged edition of his work, published in 1911 * * he tells us that the documents came not from France but from Switzerland, that they were not Judeo-Masonic but Zionist and that they were the secret protocols of the Zionist Congress held in Basle in 1897.

No credence to the "authenticity" of the "Protocols" was given to it by enlightened Russian leaders. However, it served its purpose in stirring up animosity against the Jew. It was later translated into various languages and was distributed by anti-Semitic organizations everywhere.

In the year 1921, Philip Graves, a staff member of the London *Times*, who was then in Constantinople, came upon a worn copy of a French novel, *Dialogues of Hell*, which afforded highly interesting data. This story had been written in 1858 by Maurice Joly, a French citizen. The novel was an attack upon Napoleon III in the form of a dialogue between Montesquieu and Machiavelli, and Joly was imprisoned for it for fifteen months. It was a great discovery that Philip Graves had made. On August 16, 17, and 18, 1921, he gave the facts as to the "authenticity" of the protocols in three long articles in the London *Times*. He proved that Nilus had simply plagiarized Joly's *Dialogues* and had altered them to serve his own purpose. (These articles were later published in pamphlet form and were entitled, *The Truth About the Protocols, a Literary Forgery*.)

Many other exposures followed concerning this fraudulent document. In 1933 a comparison was published including paragraphs from the protocols placed side by side with the corresponding parts in Joly's book. The parallel columns occupied forty-two folio pages.[2]

[2] Another comparison of the book appears in the appendices of *Questions and Answers Concerning the Jew*, published by the Anti-Defamation League, 100 North La Salle Street, Chicago.

The fraudulent character of the "Protocols" has been before the courts, and wherever the question of its authenticity has been propounded, the court has declared it an impudent and fraudulent forgery made, decidedly, for anti-Jewish propaganda. In August, 1934, in Port Elizabeth, South Africa, a court decision rendered by Sir Thomas Graham and Justice Jutsche of the Supreme Court stated: "The Protocols are an impudent forgery, obviously for the purpose of anti-Jewish propaganda." In May, 1935, a Swiss court in Berne, in a proceeding where the defendant was charged with distributing seditious literature, said: "I deem the 'Protocols' to be a forgery, a plagiarism, and silly nonsense."

But the Nazi propaganda machine printed the text of the "Protocols" in many languages, and distributed them to the greater part of the world, long *after* their fraudulent character had been exposed. The "Protocols" have also been printed in this country by professional anti-Semites, of course, and have been distributed by the thousands. The American publishers also knew that the fraud had been exposed, but they relied upon the stupidity of their gullible followers to accept as true anything which appeared in print. In addition, they knew that most of their public had never seen and, in all probability, never would see the evidence of the fraud.

After the exposure had proven the "Protocols" a rank plagiarism on the *Dialogues* of Joly, some anti-Semites claimed that Joly was a baptized Jew whose name was Moses Joel, and that, of course, he was a Communist and had been shot in 1871; that he must have been acquainted with the plan for world Jewish conquest; and that it was perfectly natural, therefore, that his book and the "Protocols" agreed! As a matter of fact, the data on Joly reveals that the man was a monarchist and an anti-Semite, and a descendant of a French Catholic family, many members of which had been government officials.

Some anti-Semites also claimed that recent events throughout the world occurred in accordance with the plans contained in the "Protocols." But there is only one place in the world where such nefarious plans have been tried, and that is in Nazi Germany. Furthermore, not the Jews but the Nazis of Germany launched sinister plans for world domination and for the destruction of Christian civilization and of every personal liberty.

Even in this country a very unfortunate circumstance occurred with regard to the "Protocols." Mr. Henry Ford was the owner of the Dearborn *Independent*. Here was published a series of weekly articles entitled, *The International Jew,* which contained most of the accusations from the "Protocols." These articles caused many Americans great anguish. For Henry Ford had been deceived. He had entrusted his publications to men in whom he had confidence. These men themselves were deceived, or else they purposely deceived Mr. Ford. It was Arthur Brisbane, editor of the Hearst newspapers, who convinced Mr. Ford that he had been deceived and was doing a great injustice to innocent people. A libel suit had been instituted against him, and was in progress, when Mr. Ford finally awakened to the fact that he had been made the instrument for the publication of a great fraud. He immediately gave orders to suspend the Dearborn *Independent* and to halt the distribution of the brochures and the pamphlets which were reprints of the articles which had appeared in his weekly paper. He ordered the stock of these pamphlets on hand to be destroyed.

He also made public acknowledgment of his error in a letter to Mr. Louis Marshall, chairman of the American Jewish Committee and a prominent citizen of the State of New York. Mr. Ford's letter read:

For some time past I have given consideration to the series of articles concerning Jews which since 1920 have appeared in the Dearborn *Independent*. Some of them have been reprinted in pamphlet form under the title, *The International Jew*. Although both publications are my property, it goes without saying that in the multitude of my activities it has been impossible for me to devote personal attention to their management or to keep informed as to their contents. It has therefore inevitably followed that the conduct and policies of these publications had to be delegated to men whom I placed in charge of them and upon whom I relied implicitly.

To my great regret I have learned that Jews generally, and particularly those of this country, not only resent these publications as promoting anti-Semitism, but regard me as their enemy. Trusted friends with whom I have conferred recently have assured me in all sincerity that in their opinion the character of the charges and insinuations made against the Jews, both individually and collectively, contained in many of the articles which have been circulated periodically in the Dearborn *Independent* and have been reprinted in the pamphlets mentioned, justifies the righteous indignation entertained by Jews everywhere toward me because of the mental anguish occasioned by the unprovoked reflections made upon them.

This has led me to direct my personal attention to this subject, in order to ascertain the exact nature of these articles. As a result of this survey I confess that I am deeply mortified that this journal, which is intended to be constructive and not destructive, has been made the medium for resurrecting exploded fictions, for giving currency to the so-called *Protocols of the Wise Men of Zion*, which have been demonstrated, as I learn, to be gross forgeries, and for contending that the Jews have been engaged in a conspiracy to control the capital and the industries of the world, besides laying at their door many offenses against decency, public order and good morals. Had I appreciated even the general nature, to say nothing of the details, of these utterances, I would have forbidden their circulation without a moment's hesitation, because I am fully aware of the virtues of the Jewish people as a whole, of what they and their ancestors have done for civilization and for mankind toward the development of commerce and industry, of their sobriety and diligence, their benevolence, and their unselfish interest in the public welfare. Of course, there are black sheep in every flock, as there are among men of all races, creeds and nationalities, who are at times evildoers. It is wrong, however, to judge a people by a few individuals, and I therefore join in condemning unreservedly all wholesale denunciations and attacks.

46

Those who know me can bear witness that it is not in my nature to inflict insult upon and to occasion pain to anybody, and that it has been my effort to free myself from prejudice. Because of that I frankly confess that I have been greatly shocked as a result of my study and examination of the files of the Dearborn *Independent* and of the pamphlets entitled *The International Jew*. I deem it to be my duty as an honorable man to make amends for the wrong done to the Jews as fellowmen and brothers by asking their forgiveness for the harm that I have unintentionally committed, by retracting so far as lies within my power the offensive charges laid at their door by these publications, and by giving them the unqualified assurance that henceforth they may look to me for friendship and good will.

It is needless to add that the pamphlets which have been distributed throughout the country and in foreign lands will be withdrawn from circulation, that in every way possible I will make it known that they have my unqualified disapproval, and that henceforth the Dearborn *Independent* will be conducted under such auspices that articles reflecting upon the Jews will never again appear in its columns.

Finally, let me add that this statement is made on my own initiative and wholly in the interest of right and justice and in accordance with what I regard as my solemn duty as a man and as a citizen.

Henry Ford
Dearborn, Michigan
June 30th, 1927

Long after this occurrence, the German propaganda machine, well knowing all the foregoing facts, continued to print the "Protocols" or *The International Jew* under the imprimatur of Henry Ford. Copies of *The International Jew* and the "Protocols" under the imprimatur of Henry Ford were also published by certain anti-Semitic organizations in Mexico, in South America, and in our own country. All the parties involved knew of the foregoing disavowal.

On January 7, 1942, Mr. Henry Ford addressed a letter to me upon the subject. His letter reads:

47

Ford Motor Co.
Dearborn, Mich., January 7, 1942

Mr. Sigmund Livingston,
Chicago, Ill.
Dear Sir:

In our present national emergency, I consider it of importance that I clarify some general misconceptions concerning my attitude toward my fellow citizens of Jewish faith. I do not subscribe to or support, directly or indirectly, any agitation which would promote antagonism against my Jewish fellow citizens. I consider that the hate mongering prevalent for some time in this country against the Jew is of distinct disservice to our country and to the peace and welfare of humanity.

At the time of the retraction by me of certain publications concerning the Jewish people, in pursuance of which I ceased the publication of the Dearborn *Independent*, I destroyed copies of literature prepared by certain persons connected with its publication. Since that time I have given no permission or sanction to anyone to use my name as sponsoring any such publication or being the accredited author thereof.

I am convinced that there is no greater dereliction among the Jews than there is among any other class of citizens. I am convinced, further, that agitation for the creation of hate against the Jew or any other racial or religious group has been utilized to divide our American community and to weaken our national unity.

I strongly urge all my fellow citizens to give no aid to any movement whose purpose it is to arouse hatred against any group. It is my sincere hope that now in this country and throughout the world, when this war is finished and peace once more established, hatred of the Jew, commonly known as anti-Semitism, and hatred against any other racial or religious group shall cease for all time.

Sincerely yours,
Henry Ford

At about the same time Mr. Ford also caused his personal attorney to address similar letters to Mr. J. A. Colescott, Imperial Wizard of the Ku Klux Klan, and to Senor

Miguel Aleman, Secretary of the Interior of the Republic of Mexico.[3]

It was courageous of Mr. Ford to acknowledge in public statements that he had been imposed upon by men whom he had trusted. Mr. Ford has for many years been a great power in this country. Through his inventive genius and business sagacity he has amassed a fortune which is probably greater than the combined wealth of all American Jewish industrialists. He certainly had never made any pretense of being a student of history or of mass psychology, of the past or the present. He sponsored The Dearborn *Independent* but never wrote a line of it and, according to his own statement, did not know its contents. It is certain that in his manufacturing enterprise he tests every part of a new device in his laboratory. The matters in his publication, however, were not tested for truth. His venture into a field about which he knew nothing was tragic. Are there not many others like Mr. Ford who were deceived and still lend support to causes they know nothing about and, thus, unwittingly contribute to grave social problems because their pride will not permit them to acknowledge their errors?

[3] These are given in Appendix II.

A French Forgery

MANY persons more naïve than worldly may wonder how a forged document could be used so long, be reprinted by various sources, and be given credence so widely. The history of spurious and fraudulent documents which have materially affected nations and peoples of the world testify to the astonishing credulity of the public mind and to the cunning art of the forgers and their sponsors in purveying pure fiction as fact and imaginary episodes as historical events. Many of these spurious documents were conceived and uttered for the specific purpose of creating national hatred and religious antagonism.

Professor T. F. Tout of the University of Manchester said in relation to two of the most notorious forgeries of medieval documents:[1]

> Both of these cases involved not merely the fabrication of a single document. Both are on a scale that in each instance runs to the size of a moderate volume. One is a late 14th Century forgery of an alleged early 12th Century history; and the other is an 18th Century fabrication of an imaginary 14th Century original. Both were generally accepted as authentic; both have been abundantly proved to be absolute and complete fabrications. Yet they have been so long used by numerous writers that a generation ago there was hardly a textbook that did not swallow wholesale the lies of these writers.

Philip the Fair instigated the fabrication of a papal bull designed to hold up the policies of Boniface VIII to popular opprobrium.

Innocent III issued a letter in which he explained an-

[1] *Medieval Forgers and Forgeries*, Manchester University Press, 1920.

other spurious and false papal bull and cautioned against the acceptance of such spurious documents.

In his book on Formosa the famous Psalmanazar attempted to make the Emperor of Japan the victim of world resentment. That book was a fraud from the beginning to the end, yet it was accepted as authentic until the author was finally forced to confess that the greater part of his work was fabulous and that he had planned to leave behind him, to be published after his death, a "faithful account of that unhappy step."

Annius of Viterbo was a most prolific forger. One of his books entitled, *Brevarium de Temporibus by Philo Judaeus* was a forgery conceived by an acute but perverted mind and was accepted by a large part of the public as a newly discovered book written by Philo Judaeus.

James Anson Farrer in his work, *Literary Forgeries*, says: "Annius expresses his wonder that the *Brevarium* had come to be so neglected of theologians and bishops, since it contains so much good material against the Jews; but how could they have neglected what was non-existent?"

The Bertram forgeries are the supposed writings of Richard, a Westminster monk, claimed by Bertram to have been secretly taken from neglected archives by a Mr. Gamm, "now dead," and given by him to Bertram. The fraud was so cleverly conceived that the documents were accepted as authentic by the learned societies of England. The forgery and fraud was completely exposed in the last half century.

So common were forgeries of historic documents that Pope Gelasius published a decree in which he distinguished between authentic documents and fraudulent forgeries.

Bishop Burnet demonstrated the fraud of a French historian Varillas, "who invented facts freely. He endeavored to make them pass for realities by affecting citations of titles, instructions, letters, memoirs and relations; all of them imaginary."

William H. V. Ireland was a famous forger of this class and deceived the English public.

Hilaire Belloc, in an article on "False Documents" in *The New Statesman* of October 8, 1921, said: "I know what

I was talking about because I have myself produced several documents more or less falsified."

Professor Tout, in his treatise added:[2] "Even nowadays historic sanitary science has its work cut out to destroy the extraordinarily tenacious microbes, which breed so readily that they are still liable to infect the pure wells of history."

Our own country recently had an illustration of nefarious forgeries. One of the leading newspaper syndicates of this country was induced to believe authentic certain documents, supposedly of the Mexican government, which related to the disbursement of secret funds to various members of the United States Senate for corrupt purposes; also that the Mexican government was contributing large sums to revolutionists in China and strikers in England to Bolshevize political and economic movements in these countries. These documents were procured for the American newspaper syndicate by John Page, who had paid Miguel Evila $30,000. Fortunately, the United States Senate made a thorough inquiry as to the authenticity of the documents. The purveyor of these documents admitted the forgeries. After a most searching investigation the United States Senate stated: "These papers without exception are fraudulent, spurious and, insofar as they purport to bear the signature of either President Calles or the Secretary of the Mexican Treasury, they are forgeries." Such a fraud, perpetrated on a large, influential American newspaper syndicate, might have proven most serious if the forgeries and the frauds had not been exposed promptly through the investigation of the Senate.

The famous forgery responsible for the conviction of Captain Alfred Dreyfus was one of the most diabolical conspiracies. Here documents were not forged merely to convict Captain Dreyfus but also to stimulate the incipient Jew hatred in France, and to further propaganda against the German government of that period.

In 1894 the French General Staff was definitely anti-Semitic. At the same time France and Germany were bitter

[2] *Medieval Forgers and Forgeries*, Manchester University Press, 1920.

enemies. The French secret service discovered a list of documents which afterwards became famous as "the bordereau." This item was picked out of a wastepaper basket in the office of the German military attaché, Schwarzkoppen, by a French agent. The French General Staff accused Captain Alfred Dreyfus of the authorship of the bordereau and charged that while an officer of the General Staff he had undertaken espionage for the Germans. Hatred of the Jews was enough to pillory Dreyfus for this crime without any real evidence against him. The General Staff reasoned that no French officer of the staff could possibly be guilty of such an offense; therefore, it must have been a Jewish officer! Because Dreyfus had possible access to the information contained in the bordereau, he was held to be the guilty one. Emotions became so aroused that demand was made that *all* Jewish officers of the French army be discharged. The honor of French officers had to be safeguarded; the crime had to be fastened upon a Jew. Dreyfus was examined, and no evidence was discovered to prove his guilt. The experts disagreed on the handwriting of the bordereau.

Libre Parole, a newspaper, started an agitation and the entire nationalist press followed on a violent campaign against Dreyfus as a traitor, and against the Jews, who were assumed to be in alliance with Emperor Wilhelm of Germany. Mercier, the War Minister, was swayed by the public demand. Directed by him, a court-martial was held. Important evidence of forgeries by Major Henry, a member of the General Staff, was purposely kept from Dreyfus and his counsel, and on December 22, 1894, the accused was condemned. The sentence was imprisonment for life and deportation. The ceremony of degradation took place on January 5, 1895. In the presence of his regiment Captain Dreyfus' sword was broken over his head and his military designations were torn from his uniform. Again and again he cried out that he was innocent, saying, "Tell France that I am innocent."

By special law enacted for that purpose Dreyfus was sent to the feared Devil's Island, off the coast of French

Guinea, where the climate was unbearable. There the prisoner was subjected to torture which would have broken the spirit and the mind, as well as the body of an ordinary man. But he was sustained by one sacred hope, that the truth would finally be made known and that his name would be cleared.

Later, Colonel Georges Picquart was appointed chief of the French Intelligence Service. He, too, was an anti-Semite but, also, he was an honest man. In 1896 he discovered that the bordereau was not in the handwriting of Dreyfus but of a Major Count Walsin-Esterházy, a notorious scoundrel in the French army. He made his report to General Gonse, second in command of the General Staff, but he was ordered to be silent. Picquart replied, "I do not intend to take this secret with me to the grave." Hoping that he would never return, his superiors sent Picquart to a frontier post in Tunis.

From that time on the French General Staff determined to protect Esterházy and to prevent the rehabilitation of Dreyfus. They reasoned that it was better that the Jew stay on Devil's Island until death released him from his torture than that the honor of a Christian French officer should be impugned. To support their case they were willing to engage in perjury, forgery, and fraudulent manipulations. But Mathieu Dreyfus, brother of the condemned officer, and other prominent Christians and Jews, moved for a revision of the sentence. The anti-Semitic press of France continued its campaign of hatred. It charged that the Jews were a secret, international, and unpatriotic group in alliance with Germany. Every Christian who favored the revision of the Dreyfus sentence was accused of having accepted a bribe. The royalists and the clerics began an attack not only against the Jews but even against the republic itself, depicting it as corrupt and as a "Jewish republic."

At last Esterházy was charged publicly with the crime for which Alfred Dreyfus had been sentenced. But the trial was a mockery and the court-martial acquitted Esterházy on January 11, 1898. The royalists and the anti-Semitic newspapers and agitators shouted throughout France, "Long live Esterházy! Down with the Jews!"

Finally, on January 13, 1898, that great world figure, Emile Zola, published his brilliant *J'Accuse* letter, in which he challenged the General Staff, the Army, and the entire anti-Semitic group. In this great appeal Zola said, "I have only one passion, the desire for light in the name of humanity, which has suffered so much and has a right to happiness. My burning protest is only a shriek from the heart. Let them dare to hale me before the courts and let the investigation take place in the light of day. I await it." Immediately Zola was attacked bitterly. Hostility against the Jews was rife all over France. In some places pogroms took place. However, two Frenchmen with unusual courage, Jaurés and Clemenceau, supported Zola. For his public denunciation Zola was tried, convicted and sentenced to one year of imprisonment. Then Zola said, "All seem to be against me, the two Chambers, the civil power and the military, the great newspaper and public opinion, which they have poisoned. On my side I have only the ideals of truth and justice, and I am perfectly calm. I shall be victorious. I would not have my country left in the power of lies and injustice. I may be punished here. One day France will thank me for having saved her honor."

Colonel Picquart refused to give false evidence, though he had been threatened and was afterwards arrested.

The issue of the next election in France was whether the candidate would favor revision of the Dreyfus sentence. The result was a defeat for the Republicans and the Democrats; Reinach and Jaurés, pre-eminent members of Parliament, were both defeated. But the crimes of Major Henry, now a colonel, were finally exposed; he had forged an important document in the Dreyfus dossier. Henry promptly committed suicide. The chief of the General Staff resigned. On September 1, 1898, Esterházy fled to England.

During the presidential election of 1899 all France was in a turmoil. Emile Loubet, who was favorable to a revision of the sentence, was elected President, and Dreyfus was brought back from Devil's Island. On the day he arrived, Colonel Picquart was released from prison.

The trial for treason was reopened. All fair-thinking men the world over were shocked when justice was again thwarted and Dreyfus was convicted for "treason in extenuating circumstances" on September 9, 1899. He was sentenced to ten years in prison but, by presidential decree, he was immediately pardoned. (That treason can be committed under "extenuating circumstances" is strange and most likely indicates that it was a judgment for convenience.) Dreyfus, however, was not content with a pardon. He demanded a revision of the entire trial and a full investigation. On July 12, 1906, the *cour de Cassation*, highest court of appeal, declared him innocent, and he immediately reentered the Army and was promoted to the rank of major. He was solemnly rehabilitated and decorated before the same regiment which had witnessed his degradation more than eleven years before.

Perhaps no trials in the history of the world created such profound interest as did these. During the last trial, which was public, the leading metropolitan newspapers of the United States, as well as those of England, Germany and other countries, carried reports of the evidence from day to day. It seemed as if all the Jews, and not merely Alfred Dreyfus, were on trial.

During this twelve-year period the attack by the anti-Semites of France was not merely against the Jews but always against "Jews and Protestants." The Protestants and the Jews were held up to the public as a corrupting influence in France. The combination was referred to almost daily as the "Jewish-Protestant monster." Anti-Semitic pamphlets charged, "It is quite certain that the Jews, the Freemasons and the Protestants have formed an alliance against Catholic nations in order to establish their dominion over the world. The real culprit is Protestantism."

A strange parallel took place in America after the last war. The Ku Klux Klan and other Protestant organizations directed a warfare for public opinion against Jews and Catholics. In fact, this agitation was more bitter against the Catholics than against the Jews. In this allegedly Protestant patriotic agitation the Jews and the Catholics were linked together. In Germany, Hitler and his Nazi party linked the Jews with Masonry and with Bolshevism, and also against all affiliated Christians. They have repeatedly referred to Christianity as Jewish.

Thus, it is seen that the Jews are thrown into partnership with varied groups, according to the purpose and goal of anti-Semitism in each country. In France it was allegedly a co-partnership of the Protestants and the Jews; in the United States it was supposed to be a co-partnership of the Catholics and the Jews; in Germany it was declared to be a co-partnership of the Masons, the Bolshevists, and the Jews. So "the partnership" of the Jews depends entirely upon the whim and the hallucination of the anti-Semites in the several countries.

It is a great advantage to the propagandists of hatred to be able to label as Jewish anything against which their hatred is marshaled. It is an old and ingenious trick.

The Forgery Concerning Benjamin Franklin

No spurious document has been more widely circulated by anti-Semites in this country than the one generally known as the "Benjamin Franklin prophecy." It made its appearance on February 3, 1934, in the *Liberation*, a pro-Nazi periodical published by William Dudley Pelley, now in the penitentiary under a conviction in the Federal court.

"The prophecy" is a fictitious quotation, supposedly from a speech made by Benjamin Franklin before the Constitutional Convention in 1787, warning against the immigration of Jews into this country. It was claimed that this quotation was taken from a diary kept by Charles Pinckney of South Carolina and that the original Pinckney diary was in the possession of the Franklin Institute at Philadelphia. No diary of Charles Pinckney has ever been discovered; in fact, none exists. The historian, Charles A. Beard, an authority on Benjamin Franklin, made a most diligent search for the diary or the journal supposedly kept by Pinckney and was

57

unable to find it or, indeed, any trace of it. In a public statement Professor Beard charged that this fictitious quotation was clearly a literary forgery, invented for the purpose of encouraging anti-Semitism in this country. The Franklin Institute of Philadelphia does not possess this notorious diary, never has possessed it, and has been unable to find any record of such a diary.

James F. Jamison, chief of the Division of Manuscripts of the Library of Congress, made the following statement:

> It is practically certain that the diary alleged to have been kept by Charles Pinckney during the sessions of the Philadelphia Convention in 1787 does not exist and never did exist. That chit-chat is almost certainly imaginary. Anyhow, it is absolutely certain that the speech against the Jews, said to have been delivered by Franklin at that convention, is a clumsy, impudent, and vicious forgery. It is incredible that James Madison, taking notes on every speech, should have failed to show an important speech by Franklin. It is incredible that a man of Franklin's mind and disposition should have made such a speech.

The Franklin Institute of Philadelphia, located at Benjamin Franklin Parkway at Twentieth Street, stated:[3]

> Reports have been widely circulated, for several years, off and on, saying that Dr. Franklin made a speech during the Constitutional Convention against the Jewish race. The purported speech is printed, and said to be quoted in full, from a "private diary" kept by Charles Pinckney of South Carolina, who was a fellow delegate with Franklin at the Convention in 1787. But this private diary has not been produced. Historians and librarians have not been able to find it or any record of it having existed. Historians have said further that some of the words and phraseology used in the quoted speech cast grave doubt on its colonial origin. In plain English, they have claimed it a fake.

The Charles Pinckney "private diary," containing

[3] No. 4 of Vol. 3 of *The Institute News*, August, 1938.

Franklin's vitriolic speech, is now reported to be in the possession of The Franklin Institute.

The truth is, we *do not* possess the notorious diary. In fact, we know no more about its whereabouts than we did before and that was nothing.

Alfred Rigling, librarian for the Franklin Institute, in a letter dated August 12, 1938, said of this journal of Charles Pinckney:

> Neither the original, nor any copy of it, is in the possession of The Franklin Institute. Historians and Historical Societies have endeavored to locate the Pinckney work, but without success. There is no copy in the Library of Congress, or the New York Public Library. Our state Historical Society has made careful investigation and fails to find any information concerning it. On the evening of July 16, a broadcaster from Germany read this fictitious statement, and we have reason to believe now that this is foreign propaganda.

As a matter of fact, Benjamin Franklin was a friend and admirer of the Jews. He signed a petition to citizens of every religious denomination for contributions to the Hebrew Society of Philadelphia when that society wished to build a religious house, namely, a synagogue or place of worship, in Philadelphia. Franklin also contributed to this fund himself.

It has been frequently noted by authorities on the subject that in relating a falsehood the perverted mind will go into detail so as to give credence to misstatements. This very detail often convicts the author of the falsehood. In this instance, the fictitious speech was said to have been taken from the Pinckney journal or diary. There is no such journal or diary. It is also claimed that the original of the journal or diary is in the possession of the Franklin Institute, when, as a matter of fact, neither the original nor any copy thereof has ever been in the possession of the Franklin Institute. It is therefore evident that the perverted mind which invented this fiction, instead of giving it a semblance of credence, defeated its own purpose.

That Communist Charge

ONE of the most widespread aspersions against the Jew is that he is the creator and patron of Communism and Bolshevism. Ever since Hitler coined the term "Jewish Communism" this appellation has been utilized by the professional anti-Semites. An analysis of the charges will reveal the truth to any open mind. It is even a common practice among the cunning, professional anti-Semitic propagandists to declare that the Jews are Communists and at the same time to charge also that the Jews are capitalists. The Jewish international bankers, the Jewish stockbrokers, the Jewish moneylenders, the Jewish industrial empire—these are the bogies held up by these professionals to one stratum of society, while the Jewish Communists and the Jewish Bolsheviks are held up as a threat to the other stratum.

Of course, any sensible person will appreciate at once that Communism and capitalism are diametrically opposed to each other. To claim that the Jew is a vital force in both Communism and capitalism is incongruous. If Jews are capitalists, then certainly out of self-interest they would not encourage Communism; if they are the sponsors and supporters of Communism, then certainly they are opposed to capitalism.

There are some Jews who are Communists. The number is a very small percentage of Jewry. Compared to the total number of Communists throughout the world, the Jewish number is absurdly negligible. . . . The overwhelming numbers who qualify as Communists or Bolshevists are *non-*Jews and stem from Christian homes.

When Hitler assailed Communism as Jewish and the Jews as Communists, he had a double purpose in mind. One was to inspire all people opposed to Communism to also oppose the Jewish people. The other was to influence these people who were already anti-Semitic, or anti-Jewish, and to make them also anti-Communist. The Nazi propaganda organization flooded this country with anti-Semitic propaganda material containing these charges, and the little Hitlers of this country, aided by the German-American Bund and organizations such as the Silver Shirts, the American Vigilant Intelligence Federation, the Christian Front, the National Union for Social Justice, the Defenders of the Christian Faith, etc., carried on the same propaganda.

That the lies were, to a considerable extent, effective cannot be doubted. On this particular point a personal incident is worth relating. A certain metropolitan paper of undoubted journalistic influence and of large circulation printed a statement that Dr. Albert Einstein was a Communist; that he had attended the Third International at Moscow; that for this reason he had to flee Germany; and the immigration authorities were criticized for permitting him to enter this country. The article received editorial notice. Knowing the falsity of the accusation, I personally called upon the editor. As a result that paper interviewed Dr. Einstein. In that interview the scientist stated that he had never been in Russia in his life; that he had never attended a political meeting; that he was not interested in politics or economics; and that he was not a Communist.

This incident gave occasion for more intimate conversations with the editor. During these talks the editor declared that he could not understand why the Jews of Germany had been Communists and thus had strengthened Hitler's efforts to overthrow the German republic and to establish Nazism. I immediately recognized that this editor had himself succumbed to pernicious propaganda. It was amazing that a man whose vocation it was to influence public opinion could have been such an easy victim for false and fraudulent propaganda.

I asked whether he knew the size of the Communist vote of Germany immediately prior to Hitler's rise to power. He answered in the negative, and I informed him that in 1932 the total Communistic vote of Germany was 5,960,240. He was then asked if he knew how many Jews had lived in

Germany. Again he replied in the negative and he was told that there were then only 550,000 Jews in all Germany, including men, women and children. He agreed that of this entire Jewish population certainly not more than 200,000 were voters. Thus if the entire Jewish vote were subtracted from the total Communistic vote, it would still leave 5,760,240 votes! He was informed that the majority of Jews had voted the Social-Democrat ticket and that the number who voted the Communistic ticket was a very small percentage of the entire 200,000 votes, and certainly a negligible amount of the total Communist vote. This editor was quite gracious in his appreciation of the facts and frankly acknowledged his error.

It would make an interesting study in mass psychology if accurate data could be procured of the number of people in this country who have been influenced by the barrage of propaganda upon this specific point. To begin the analysis of this subject, the basic point made by Hitler and the Nazi propaganda machine is that Karl Marx was the founder of Communism and that he was a Jew. It is true that Karl Marx was born of Jewish parents. He was baptized into the Christian faith at the age of six. Long before his birth, his parents were estranged from Jewry, and his father had been baptized into the Christian faith. His education and environment were entirely Christian. He was not taught anything about Judaism. In fact, he became an outspoken antagonist of Judiasm. The mind is shaped by education and environment. It is a social product; birth alone has nothing to do with the mental attitude of the child when he reaches maturity. That a child has been born of Catholic or Protestant parentage is no factor in determining whether such child, when mature, will become a Communist, a Democrat, or a Fascist. Early teachings and associations will influence the young mind. If Karl Marx had been born of Christian parentage and at the age of six had been taken into the Jewish fold and had been taught the principles of Judaism and Jewish ethics, there is no doubt that the charge would have been that he was a Jewish product, notwithstanding the fact that he was of Christian parentage. Furthermore, Frederich Engles, the co-laborer of Karl Marx, was a Teutonic German. The Nazi propaganda machine has rarely mentioned that.

From the same sources it has also been publicized that 90 per cent of the Communist party in Russia in 1918 were Jews. The official records of that period show a total party membership of 124,000 of which 75 per cent were Russians, 10.5 per cent Latvians, 6.3 per cent Poles, 3.7 per cent Esthonians and only 2.6 per cent Jews. Even the anti-Bolshevist paper, *Poslednija Novosti,* published in Paris, gives the percentage of Jews in the party at that time as no more than 4.34 per cent.

It has been likewise repeatedly publicized by these sources that Bolshevism was conceived and created by Jews, and the Russian government has been referred to as "Jewish Bolshevism." The truth is that the great body of Jews *opposed* Bolshevism. Most Russian Jews belonged to the lower middle class of tradesmen and artisans. The intellectuals, known as the Cadet Bloc, were a liberal, democratic group. Among the leaders of this bloc were many outstanding Jews, including Maxim Vanivar, later Foreign Minister in the anti-Bolshevist government of Crimea. Others were Herzenstein, Josef Hessen and Professor Vladimir Hessen. The largest number of the Russian-Jewish population were of the "Mensheviki," the democratic party which was opposed to the Bolshevists. They supported the provisional government of Alexander Kerensky, who was overthrown by the Bolshevik revolution. The three great Jewish workers' organizations were the Serz, the Poalezion, and the League of Jewish Workers. Each of these publicly declared its opposition to Bolshevism.

On March 15, 1918, Lenin's government issued a manifesto *attacking* the Jewish workers for their anti-Bolshevist attitude. (What better proof upon this issue can there be than this manifesto?) In 1918 the Jewish workers had made common cause with the Jewish bourgeois in the Ukraine, and opposed Bolshevism with armed resistance. At that time two-fifths of Russia's Jews were tradesmen, one-third were employed in handicraft, and the Communist movement meant a greater catastrophe for the Jews than for any other group of the Russian people. The establishment of Bolshevism declassed 25 per cent of the Russian Jews, but only 5 per cent to 6 per cent of the non-Jews. The declassed received no bread cards, were denied the right to hold office, to work in factories or to send their children to industrial schools. The distress among the Russian Jews was so great that they would have died of starvation had it not been for the American Jewish relief agencies.

The Russian Bolshevik government dealt blow after blow at Jewry. Synagogues were converted into workmen's clubs. Jewish religious philanthropic organizations were liquidated. Hebrew schools were forbidden and the teaching of the Hebrew language was proscribed. No person under eighteen years of age could be taught religion.

Vladimir Lebedev was Minister of the Navy under the provisional government of Russia and was a co-laborer with Kerensky in setting up a stable government for Russia after the downfall of the Czarist government. When the Bolshevik revolution succeeded in defeating the provisional government he escaped from Russia. He is a Russian of the Orthodox Catholic faith with no Jewish antecedents.

Upon learning of his presence in this country, I addressed a letter to him upon this question. He favored me with the following reply:

Chicago, Ill., April 22, 1938

Dear Mr. Livingston,

Replying to your letter, to your question as to what truth there is in the assertion that "Bolshevism is created by Jews" and that the present government of the USSR is allegedly "a Jewish government," I with pleasure respond to you as follows:

All these and similar assertions are a result of *propaganda inimical to Russia,* and they come, mostly, from the National-Socialist ranks, the aim being concealment of their real plans with regard to Russia.

This propaganda is absolutely *one of lies,* harmful to Russia. It excites racial passions. It is carried on in order to form in Russia and abroad, among the emigrés, anti-

Semitic fascist groups, owing allegiance to the German National-Socialism and able to aid Hitler in case he marches against Russia.

As for the essence of this question I can say the following. The party of Bolsheviks was first formed in 1903, when the Russian Social-Democratic party split into the majority, "Bolsheviks," and the minority, "Mensheviks."

Its creator, theorist and sole dictator was the Russian nobleman, Vladimir Ilyich Lenin (Ulyanov). This party carried on its propagandist activity among the Russian proletariat and Russian intelligentsia, and during the war also in the Russian troops and navy.

Citizens of Jewish origin, equally with other national groups of Russia, were among members of this party. But Jews took part in decidedly *all* Russian political parties, excepting of course anti-Semitic parties.

The program of the Bolshevik party contained nothing specifically Jewish, and it promised the Jews no privileges.

The main mass of the Russian Jewry, like other masses of Russia, remained outside of politics. Being concentrated, mainly within the so-called "pale of settlement," it (the Jewry) in its majority did not even know the Russian language and grouped itself around its social and religious organizations. As for that part of the Jewry, which was united politically *as Jewish* it grouped itself in the only mass-like Jewish party, the Bund. Part (of the Jewry) sympathized with the *Zionists*. The Bund as well as the Zionists have been persecuted by Bolshevism from the *first* days of the October upheaval of 1917 to the present day.

Besides, Jews, in a number *insignificant* when compared with Russians, entered as Russian citizens the other Russian parties as well: The Kadet (liberal-bourgeois, leader P. N. Milyukov) the Socialist-Revolutionary (leader V. M. Chernov), the Bolshevist (leader V. I. Lenin), the Menshevist (leader Plekhanov), etc., etc. But their (the Jews') number was perfectly insignificant when compared with Russians, and these parties were *Russian*.

The Bolsheviks persecute all parties, so that very many Jews, members of these parties, have been *shot*, or linger in prisons and concentration camps, or are exiles abroad. No privileges, in comparison to other nationalities, were given to them by the dictatorship of the Bolsheviks. The law of death and persecution was applied to them as well as to other members of these parties.

Of course, among Lenin's lieutenants there were also Jews, but they entered the party not as Jews (many indeed renounced their Jewishness publicly), but as followers of the Bolshevist doctrine. Lenin promoted some of them to important posts, just as he promoted Russians, Georgians, Letts, Ukrainians, Armenians, Tartars, etc., etc. From these posts they together with others carried out Lenin's teaching, which is not Jewish to any measure at all. The overwhelming majority of them have by now been executed by the present-day government of Stalin, and this again shows that their Jewish origin did not and does not have *any* significance.

However, the fact that in Lenin's party there were *also* Jews gave a pretext for the dishonest and lying propaganda to assert that "Jews created Bolshevism" and that the present-day government of the USSR is "a Jewish government."

As I have already said, this propaganda is being carried on by the enemies of Russia, mainly by the German National-Socialists, who see in anti-Semitism and in racial propaganda a mighty medium of *strategy* for the seizure of power and for war, first of all against Russia.

Lenin's dictatorship guaranteed to Jews *no* privileges. It bankrupted the more or less well-off strata of the Jewry, the strata that either followed mainly the Kadet party or remained orthodox; it destroyed social and religious organizations of the Jewry, and it subjected the Jewry to political violence just as it did other nationalities. And in view of the fact that the Jewry, because of special conditions, was more than other nationalities occupied in petty trade and brokerage, this dictatorship delivered it (the Jewry) a crushing blow.

Such are the facts, refuting the stupid and harmful assertion of Russia's enemies about the alleged Jewish "dominance" in the times of Bolshevism.

Please accept my expression of respect.

(Signature) **V. L. Lebedev.**

Some time thereafter I had an intimate discussion of the same subject matter with Alexander Kerensky, who was the

66

nominal head of the provisional government. In all respects he concurred in the conclusions of Mr. Lebedev. He told me that in fact the majority of Russian Jews were earnest and valuable supporters of the provisional government and did everything possible to support the regime of this government against the demands of the Bolshevik party.

The supreme directing body in Russia is the Politburo. It consists of seventeen members and five candidates, inclusive. These are: Joseph Stalin, Andrew Andreyev, Lazar Kaganovich, Nikolai Bulganin, Georgi Dimitrov, Simyon Timoshenko, Alexei Bodayev, G. M. Popov, Anastas Mikoyan, Klementi Voroshilov, Nikhail Kalinin, Vyacheslav Molotov, Andrey Zhdanov, Lorenti Beria, Nikolai Shevernik, Georgi Malenkov, Alex. Shcherbakov.

Only one is Jewish; namely, Kaganovich.

Of the nineteen commissars, fourteen are Great Russians and Ukranians. One is an Armenian and four are Jews.

During the regime of the czars the lot of the Jew in Russia was most cruel and bitter. There were 650 special anti-Jewish laws. Jews were confined to the pale of Jewish settlements and were prohibited from owning or cultivating land. For many years all the subservient groups strove against the despotism of the tyrants and tried to further democratic government. The erstwhile serfs and peasants suffered under conditions which no other European or American people would endure and the government feared revolution by the masses. The jails were filled by all classes of suspects, and the march over the cruel Siberian snow by men and women in whose hearts burned the desire for liberty and democracy is well-known. There was a continuous effort by the government and by the organization known as the "Black Hundreds" to divert the attention of the people to the Jew. To divert the threat against tyranny, they sought to poison every mind and heart against the Jew. To the ignorant masses the Jew was portrayed as the cause of all their suffering. Their deep religious feeling was flagrantly exploited, for when not interfered with the Russian peasants and the Jews had always lived in harmony, since they suffered alike from their despotic government.

One of the leaflets distributed in 1905 by the Black Hundreds read: "The Cry of 'Down With Autocracy' comes from the blood-suckers who are commonly known as Jews, Armenians and Poles. Beware of the Jews! They are the root of all evil, the sole cause of our misfortunes. The glorious moment is already approaching when there will be an end of all Jews in Russia. Down with the traitors! Down with the Constitution!"

There were hundreds of similar leaflets. These were printed in the police department and were financed by the government purse. Between the eighteenth and twenty-ninth day of October, 1905, 690 pogroms took place. All had been prearranged by government officials.

On Easter Day in 1903, a carefully prepared massacre took place in Kishinev. The defense force of the Jews was disarmed by the police and the mob was let loose. The cruelty perpetrated beggars description. Little children were thrown out of windows. Men and women were blinded, maimed and killed. Plehve had secretly ordered the government of Bessarabia not to use force to suppress the anti-Jewish disturbances. When these facts became known, Count Leo Tolstoy, the great author and humanitarian, openly charged the government with the shameful crime committed at Kishinev.

In 1906, after the pogrom at Bialystok, the Russian Duma adopted a resolution in which the crime of fostering or permitting these pogroms was declared as "unexampled in the history of civilized countries," and the dissolution of the government was demanded. As a result the Czar dissolved the Duma two days later. Prime Minister Stolypin made efforts to persuade the Czar to a reformed policy concerning the Jew. His efforts were useless.

The people of this country were aroused. At the suggestion of President Theodore Roosevelt, a petition, to be signed by American citizens throughout the land, was prepared for submission to the Russian government. This famous document is now known as the Kishinev Petition.

To His Imperial Majesty the Emperor of Russia:

The cruel outrages perpetrated at Kishinev during Easter of 1903 have excited horror and reprobation throughout the world. Until your Majesty gave special and personal directions, the local authorities failed to maintain order or suppress the rioting. The victims were Jews and the assault was the result of race and religious prejudice. The rioters violated the laws of Russia.

The local officials were derelict in the performance of their duty.

The Jews were the victims of indefensible lawlessness.

These facts are made plain by the official reports of, and by the official acts following, the riot.

Under ordinary conditions the awful calamity would be deplored without undue fear of a recurrence. But such is not the case in the present instance. Your petitioners are advised that millions of Jews, Russian subjects, dwelling in Southwestern Russia, are in constant dread of fresh outbreaks.

They feel that ignorance, superstition and bigotry, as exemplified by the rioters, are ever ready to persecute them; that the local officials, unless thereunto specially admonished, cannot be relied on as strenuous protectors of their peace and security; that a public sentiment of hostility has been engendered against them and hangs over them as a continuing menace.

Even if it be conceded that these fears are to some extent exaggerated, it is unquestionably true that they exist, that they are not groundless, and that they produce effects of great importance.

The westward migration of Russian Jews, which has proceeded for over twenty years, is being stimulated by these fears, and already that movement has become so great as to overshadow in magnitude the expulsion of the Jews from Spain and to rank with the exodus from Egypt.

No estimate is possible of the misery suffered by the hapless Jews who feel driven to forsake their native land, to sever the most sacred ties, and to wander forth to strange countries.

Neither is it possible to estimate the misery suffered by those who are unwilling or unable to leave the land of their birth; who must part from friends and relatives who emigrate; who remain in never-ending terror.

Religious persecution is more sinful and more fatuous than war. War is sometimes necessary, honorable and just; religious persecution is never defensible.

The sinfulness and folly which give impulse to unnecessary war received their greatest check when your Majesty's initiative resulted in an International Court of Peace.

With such an example before it, the civilized world cherishes the hope that upon the same initiative there shall be fixed in the early days of the Twentieth Century, the enduring principle of religious liberty; that by a gracious and convincing expression your Majesty will proclaim, not only for the government of your own subjects, but also for the guidance of all civilized men, that none shall suffer in person, property, liberty, honor or life, because of his religious belief; that the humblest subject or citizen may worship according to the dictates of his own conscience, and that government, whatever its form or agencies, must safeguard these rights and immunities by the exercise of all its powers.

Far removed from your Majesty's dominions, living under different conditions, and owing allegiance to another government, your petitioners yet venture, in the name of civilization, to plead for religious liberty and tolerance; to plead that he who led his own people and all others to the shrine of peace will add new luster to his reign and fame by leading a new movement that shall commit the whole world in opposition to religious persecution.

HAY.

This petition, signed by thousands of leading Americans and addressed to the Czar, was forwarded to John Hay, Secretary of State. Hay sent the text to our Minister to Russia, and inquired whether this petition would be received by the Russian government. Our Minister made the necessary inquiries and was informed that the petition could *not* be accepted. Theodore Roosevelt, then President of the United States, thereupon ordered the petition to be placed in the archives of our own country.

PART THREE

SEEDS SCATTERED UPON PLOWED SOIL

UNTIL recent times the incentive for this hate and persecution of the Jew has been, largely, religious. Born in bigotry and superstition, anti-Semitism was sustained for many centuries by religious ardor and conviction. The original purpose was the conversion of Jews to Christianity. Prior to the era of the Crusades, the attempt at such conversion was made through preaching. Groups of Jews were compelled to attend functions at which powerful sermons were delivered in the hope of winning them over to the Christian religion. Now and then, unquestionably, some were converted.

For this purpose, also, rabbis were often commanded to engage in public debate with the Christian theologians. Of course, unless the rabbi wished to invite immediate punishment or death, he had to take the greatest care in his disputation, lest he offend the Church. Frequently rabbis were accused, tried and convicted for statements made in these debates which were construed as insulting to the Church and its doctrines.

Often the populace, in its overzealous religious faith, became enraged against the Jew, but not until the time of the Crusades was an organized, bloody warfare launched against him. This warfare continued unabated, with few breathing spells. The Jews were expelled from one country to another, but generally they were able to find some land willing to give them a brief sanctuary. Yet every one of these expulsions, with its tragic consequences, was prompted by religious ardor and enthusiasm. The expulsion of the Jews from Spain during the reign of Ferdinand and Isabella clearly demonstrates the religious motive at work, since all the

71

Jews were given the opportunity, before the date of banishment, to become Christians by means of the baptismal ceremony, and, in their extremity, many availed themselves of this privilege. The same religious motive prompted the expulsion of Jews from France and England and other countries.

Occasionally popes of vision and true understanding interceded in this persecution. Gregory I, Clement XI, Martin V, Clement XIII, Paul III, Pius IV, Sixtus V, Pius XI and Benedict XIV, each made such an intercession in his day. Pope Pius XI, in one of the historic statements of modern times, declared: "It is impossible for Christians to be anti-Semitic. Spiritually we are all Semites."

Various lay rulers also displayed humane instincts in their treatment of the Jews, notably Louis X of France, Philip V, Louis XVI and Frederick William III. In general, the Jews were considered the property of the King. They were barred from the ordinary vocations of life. By necessity they were made the moneylenders and tax collectors of the realm, and whenever the rulers needed money they would confiscate whatever their Jews possessed.

After the Reformation the Jews found some relief from the bitter persecution which they had suffered since the first Crusade. Finally, during the eighteenth and the nineteenth centuries, they were "emancipated." The light of liberty and enlightenment had pierced through this dark night in human history. The morning hour of reason and understanding seemed to be dawning. America, with her Declaration of Independence and her Constitution, declaring all men equal and guaranteeing the inalienable rights of free man, was looked up to throughout the world as the guiding star for suffering humanity.

But many countries enforced their oppressive measures until recent years. Thus the May Laws of Russia continued in full force until the provisional government was established in 1917. Kerensky held the portfolio of Minister of Justice in the first provisional government which officially assumed control of the administration in March of 1917. He became Minister of War on May 5. On July 25 he be-

72

came Prime Minister of the second provisional government.

The Jews really believed that the day of universal brotherhood was at hand. They felt confident that they would not be molested in their religious beliefs, and that their citizenship in the lands in which they lived would now assure them the rights, duties, and privileges of all other citizens. They prayed that the day had arrived when each man would be judged by his own work, and by his own merits or demerits; that the derelictions or shortcomings of an individual who happened to be a member of a minority group would not be charged against his entire group; and that justice would prevail everywhere. It was not to be so.

The erstwhile religious hatred turned into a *racial* hatred, and a new campaign against the Jew began. This new warfare was not the result of bigotry and superstition, but was conceived in fraud and deceit. Evil men realized that the public mind could be poisoned against the Jew through fictitious charges, disguised subtly and ingeniously, so as to be the more palatable to unsuspecting people; for the public was regarded as far too stupid to detect the fraud. This racial crusade continues to this day. It has deluded and poisoned many honest minds and has done great injury.

It is beyond the scope of the present study to record all the fraudulent and pernicious accusations leveled against the Jews in modern times, but a few of the important ones must be mentioned.

A Black Night in World Civilization

In ORDER to overthrow the republic of Germany Hitler and his gang captured the mind of the frustrated people by the old trick of holding the Jew responsible for all of the nation's ills and failings. He made a practical application of anti-Semitism. Everything held in disfavor he labeled Jewish: "Jewish Bolshevism," "Jewish Communism," "Jewish international banker," "Jewish profiteer," "Jewish warmonger," "Jewish Versailles Treaty," "Jewish Dawes Plan," "Jewish Young Plan," "Jewish Constitution of the German republic," "Jewish democracies," and "Judeo-Christianity." The device of false labeling was of great importance in the success of his deceptions. The same pattern has been, and is, used by organized anti-Semitism in this country.

After Hitler had gained power, he also labeled Christianity as Jewish. "Jewish Christianity" was a favorite objective for the attack of Nazi theorists. But when the Nazis had triumphed they carried out their threat against German Jewry.

German Jewry had consisted of 550,000 persons, including men, women, and children. The total population of Germany was 65,000,000. Helpless, this small part of the German population, less than one per cent of the whole, was subjected to savagery unprecedented among civilized nations. All their temples and houses of worship were destroyed, all their possessions were confiscated. They were herded into concentration camps, where they were subjected to corporal and bestial punishment and were cruelly murdered by the thousands. Those unable to emigrate were practically exterminated. No cruelty in the world's history ever equaled this persecution.

The neighboring nations stood by. They heard the cries

of agony. They sympathized and expressed sorrow, but that was all. France, Poland, Norway, Czechoslovakia, Belgium, Holland, Denmark, Russia and England united could have stopped this crime against civilization and humanity. International law justifies intervention. In self-interest, however, each of the nations avoided the enmity of Hitler. They failed to understand that the warfare against the Jew was a blind, a spearhead, and they failed to realize that Hitler would be encouraged by their inertia. It confirmed his belief that "humanities," "civilization," "brotherhood of man" and "Christian faith," were dreams and fantasies.

And now these nations have become the victims of this same sadistic power and in the blackout of their national life and peace they may sigh, "If only we had known!"

Nazi anti-Semitism was the deceptive device to gain power which was in turn to be used for the most devouring aggression in history. All the tragedy inflicted upon the neighboring nations and peoples would never have soiled the pages of modern history, had these victim nations united and intervened in behalf of persecuted Jewry. The tragedy of Jewry was but a rehearsal for Hitler's greater aggressions to come.

Whenever great nations witness with complacency the commission of a great national or international sin which outrages the tenets of humanity and civilization, retribution follows just as surely as the night follows the day.

With these facts of contemporary history written over the skies of the world, no one can honestly entertain the thought that the Jews instigated this world war; that they, and not Hitler and his sadistic gang, lighted the fires which consumed all that was good and noble in the nations neighboring on Nazi Germany.

I warn my fellow citizens that there are in America men and women who would, at the opportune time, use the spearhead of anti-Semitism to gain political power. Some of these rabble rousers and demagogues are well known. Those behind the scene who scheme and play with the pattern made by Hitler are the real traitors to the fundamental principles and traditions of our government.

75

The unscrupulous political tricksters in our midst who raise false issues and indulge in destructive criticism will clear the path for political anti-Semitism, and when the time is ripe—when the masses are frustrated, either through economic depression, political misadventure, spiritual retrogression—or military reverses—this diabolism of the dark past will test whether democracy, the Constitution, this nation, can endure.

Anti-Semites Are Paralogists

FROM whatever point of view we diagnose anti-Semitism, the inevitable conclusion is that it is irrational. In the main, anti-Semitism is a commingling of emotional attitudes, of old superstitions, remnants of religious hysteria, fear complexes, lingering myths, false racialism, egotisms and snobbery. This hodgepodge in the mind fosters and breeds a paranoia which resists all reason and logic. The individual who honestly and intelligently investigates whether or not his anti-Semitic attitude has any factual basis will inevitably thrust this prepossession from his mind.

Anti-Semitism has no more logic or reason behind it than the belief in witchcraft had. No cult has ever indulged in so many paradoxical accusations. The anti-Semite assumes a conclusion and then invents a fictitious premise. He builds fiction upon fiction. The purveyors of anti-Semitism, quote as authority for "factual" statements, others who are like themselves, and many of these purveyors use assumed names. In fact, some have adopted three or more names under which they have written concerning their cult and then *they have quoted what they themselves have written under another name*! In this manner they hope to credit and to fortify their assertions with a semblance of authenticity.

Lloyd George—in an article in the London *Daily Chronicle* in 1942—stated, concerning the charges of the anti-Semites against the Jews:

> If they are rich, they are birds of prey; if they are poor, they are vermin; if they are in favor of war, that is because they want to exploit the bloody feuds of Gentiles to their own profit. If they are anxious for peace, they are either instinctive cowards or traitors. If they give gener-

ously—and there are no more liberal givers than the Jews—they are doing it for some selfish purpose of their own. If they don't give, then what would you expect of a Jew? If labor is opposed by great capital, the greed of the Jew is held responsible. If labor revolts against capital—as it did in Russia—the Jew is blamed for that also.

To these may be added: The Jew is charged with being the international banker and also with being a Communist. He is charged with being a superstitious monotheist and also with being an atheist. He is charged with being clannish, and also with trying to enter social groups and societies from which he is excluded. He is charged with being a materialist and at the same time with having an unfair percentage of teachers in the universities (particularly in pre-Nazi Germany); also that he has a disproportionate number of musicians and other artists; that he is represented in numbers too great in the medical profession and in chemical research; that he is unduly active in social service, and in all other altruistic professions and vocations. But university teaching, music, research, and social work—are these professions or vocations which materialists would seek? He is also charged with an excessive percentage of government employment (although it be through open civil service examinations), and if he refuses to serve the government he is charged with a selfish determination to make more money in other fields.

If he succeeds in business enterprise, he is a profiteer; if he fails in business, he lacks business judgment or is a crook. If he is a loan broker for an insurance company, though he has no personal interest save the usual commission on the loan, he is a Shylock; if he underbids the rate of interest, he is a chiseler. He is damned if he does, and he is damned if he does not.

It is true that similar unfair criticisms are made of non-Jews, but *not against the individual as a member of a group or sect*. When the individual who is criticized happens to be a Jew, he is usually criticized primarily *because he is a Jew*.

The conscious, or unconscious, dislike of the Jew is quite naturally responsible for the suspicion, or the inclination to believe, that the Jew's character, his behavior, or his ethics are inferior. Consequently, the misdeeds or the idiosyncrasies of any one Jew are regarded as characteristically "Jewish."

If it were feasible to make an accurate inventory of all the good qualities of the Jew and of the non-Jew and also of all the bad qualities of the Jew and of the non-Jew—or of the percentage of individuals who are good and bad in either group—the Jew would not suffer by the comparison. As a matter of fact, by all the rules, the Jew should be better than the others, for his moral and ethical teachings and his commandments precede by centuries the concept of these by the non-Jewish group.

In morals, ethics and behavior all groups have their good and their bad. Were it practical to have the total of each group and to separate the sheep from the goats, the good from the bad, the percentage would be about even for each racial or religious division. The Russian-Jewish philosopher, Ahad Ha-'Am, very properly asked:

Who has ever weighed the Jew against the non-Jew of the same class—the Jewish tradesman against the non-Jewish tradesman; the persecuted Jew against the persecuted non-Jew; the starved Jew against the starved non-Jew, etc.?

To this may be added, as far as our country is concerned: Who has weighed the merits and the demerits of the immigrant Jew against the immigrant non-Jew; the Polish, or Russian, or Balkan, or German Jew against the Polish, or Russian, or Balkan, or German non-Jew? Who has weighed the Jewish industrialist against the non-Jewish industrialist, or the Jewish union laborite against the non-Jewish trade unionist? Who has weighed the Jewish moneylender against the non-Jewish moneylender? To judge correctly each of the many subdivisions which constitute our society, every stratum would have to be appraised. Who has ever compared the qualities of Judges Cardozo, Brandeis, Alschuler and many other eminent judges with the qualities of the non-Jewish judges on the same bench, and likewise who has ever compared the poor Jew with the poor non-Jew, or the well-to-do Jew with the well-to-do non-Jew? Who has compared the liberally educated Jew with the liberally educated non-Jew? Who has compared the Jewish tailor or shoemaker with the non-Jewish tailor or shoemaker?

The Myth That the Jew Is Rich

THE myth that Jews are rich is widely believed. No one has ever produced facts or statistics to warrant it. Yet this myth has been, and is, a vital, contributing factor in the growth of anti-Semitism. Any minority group presumed to have a disproportionate share of wealth creates envy. From the premise that the Jew possesses great wealth stem these accusations and slogans: "The Jewish international bankers," "Jewish usurers," "As rich as a Jew."

This belief is readily accepted because the general public knows of a few Jews who are apparently prosperous. People know the Jewish merchant; possibly the largest store in town is owned by a Jew. But the general public does not know the great mass of Jews. To the uninformed, any one single prosperous Jew in the community typifies every Jew. In rural communities it is frequently observed: "One never sees a Jewish beggar." An old story reflects that state of mind. A villager boasts to a stranger that there isn't a single Jew in the village, and the stranger retorts, "That is the reason it has remained a village."

For every well-to-do Jew there are at least a thousand poor Jews. The families of the Rockefellers, Fords, Morgans, Harknesses, Mellons, Vanderbilts, Whitneys and Du Ponts possess in the aggregate more wealth than all the combined resources of all the Jewish bankers and industrialists of this country, and perhaps of the world.

Count Heinrich Coudenhove-Kalergi states:[1]

With very insignificant exceptions the leading German industrial magnates in the after-war period were non-Jews, and, above all, their prominent representative Hugo Stinnes. Had Stinnes been a Jew, all the anti-Semites in

[1] *Anti-Semitism Throughout the Ages*, p. 236.

the world would have availed themselves of this circumstance and made the Jews responsible for the prolongation of the war and the inflation. Had Ivar Kreuger been a Jew, all the anti-Semites would have shouted after his fall: "Such are the Jews." Since, however, he was not a Jew, but a Swede, nobody dreams of making the Swedish nation responsible for the case Kreuger. Had, however, Morgan been a Jew, a whole literature would undoubtedly have existed today trying to prove that his banking house was the center of a Jewish world-conspiracy and of Jewish plans for world dominion.

The wealthiest and largest industries in this country are oil, automobile, steel, industrial chemicals, railroads, insurance and public utilities, in none of which the Jews have any appreciable financial or managerial interests.

The Temporary National Economic Committee, of which United States Senator Joseph C. O'Mahoney was chairman, reported concerning the stockholdings in two hundred of the largest American industrial corporations the fact that thirteen families, including Ford, Du Pont, Rockefeller, Mellon, McCormick, Hartford, Harkness, Duke, Pew, Pitcairn, Clark, Reynolds, and Kress, held as of December 31, 1937, a total of $2,700,574,000 of stock. It was further explained that this holding was only a part of the wealth of these families. Not a single Jewish family was included in this list.[2]

The *Survey Graphic* of February, 1939, published the result of a survey which is of considerable interest. It stated that:

A quarter of the union carpenters of New York City are Jews; a fifth of the electrical workers; nearly half the painters and paper hangers; half the plasterers; nearly half the plumbers and steam fitters; more than half the sheet metal workers. These are the union figures. The proportion of Jews among the non-union workers is greater. * * * * The point is that the unhealthy concentration in commercial pursuits forced upon the Jew by

[2] Investigation of Concentration of Economic Power, Temporary National Economic Committee, 1940. Monograph No. 29, p. 116.

the Old World anti-Semitism, itself operating to intensify anti-Semitism, is gradually breaking up here. People still say, to be sure, "You never see a Jewish artisan or farmer." Parrots will go on saying it.

That more than half of the sheet metal workers and nearly half of the plumbers and steam fitters of New York City are Jews will undoubtedly surprise everyone who has never investigated the facts regarding Jewish handicrafts.

To relate a personal experience may not be amiss. I was raised in a rural city of the Midwest, which had a population of about thirty-five thousand. There were about eight Jewish merchants in the community and some smaller shopkeepers. A Jewish professional man had never established himself there. After graduating from the university, I began to practice my profession as a lawyer in my native city. My family had long been established there and was well known. When the public announcement was made that I had opened an office for the practice of law, our neighbors seemed surprised. They had never known of a Jewish lawyer. I know personally that, with the exception of those who had been intimate with my family, I had a general distrust to overcome, but, after a few years, I am quite certain that I came to be regarded as worthy of trust.

One day a prominent citizen called at my office to retain me to "sit" in a lawsuit. He explained that his lawyer was a Catholic and that he had considerable misgivings and mistrust of all Catholics. He desired that I should "sit" in the case to watch his lawyer. I knew his lawyer intimately. He was a man of the highest moral and professional ethics, and was considered by the Bar as one of its leaders. I assured my visitor that he had no reason to fear and that he was perfectly safe in entrusting the entire case to his lawyer, and that this lawyer needed no one to watch him. Of course, I refused to be retained for such a purpose.

The general public knows little of the great mass of Jews in the lower economic strata. These people live in tenement dwellings in the congested districts of the great cities. Though poor, they are recompensed by the solace of their religious faith and family life. Here live the needleworkers, cigar makers, shoemakers, peddlers, laborers and small shopkeepers. These comprise the great majority in American Jewry.

Jewish influence in the industrial and economic spheres has been greatly overestimated. The prominence of Jews in certain businesses or industries gives a false impression as to the importance of the Jew in the general economic structure of the nation.

For example, the prominence of the Jew in the motion-picture industry is often referred to by those who have an exaggerated idea of Jewish influence in business. That certain Jews were pioneers in this industry and helped to make it first among its competitors throughout the world is completely disregarded.

It is of interest to note that only two out of nineteen directors of Radio-Keith-Orpheum Pictures, Inc. are Jews; that only four out of nineteen directors of United Artists Corporation are Jews; that only two out of thirteen directors of Universal Pictures, Inc. are Jews; that nine out of twenty-one directors of Warner Brothers are Jews; that five out of fifteen directors of Paramount Pictures, Inc. and one out of eighteen directors of Twentieth Century Fox are Jews. Metro-Goldwyn-Mayer, Inc. and Columbia Pictures have a slight majority of Jews in the directorate. These are the figures of 1937 and probably have not changed materially since.

It has also been charged frequently that the Jews control the radio industry. This, too, was a new field, one which demanded pioneering and vision. The Board of Directors of several radio networks contain Jews and non-Jews in the following proportion:

National Broadcasting Company, one Jew out of thirteen; Columbia Broadcasting Company, eight Jews out of thirteen; Mutual Broadcasting Company, one Jew out of nine.

The executives of radio networks number the following: National Broadcasting Company, one Jew out of twenty; Columbia Broadcasting Company, six Jews out of sixteen;

Mutual Broadcasting Company, one Jew out of eight; Blue Network, no Jew out of four.

It is frequently stated that the Jews control the American press. Outside of the New York *Times*, with its great prestige and its high rank among the newspapers of the land, the interest of the Jews in newspapers is very small. There are four Jewish chains of newspapers; the total circulation in the four respective groups are 489,870; 391,209; 289,126; and 198,610. These figures are, indeed, quite insignificant when compared to the Hearst papers' total circulation of 5,500,000; Patterson-McCormick's daily circulation of 2,-332,156; and Scripps-Howard's daily circulation of 1,794,-617. The total circulation of newspapers supposedly controlled by Jews, aside from the New York *Times*, is 1,368,815 and the total of the three national chains owned by non-Jews, namely, Hearst, Patterson-McCormick and Scripps-Howard is 9,626,773. The New York *Times* daily circulation in 1942 averaged 455,000; its Sunday circulation was 788,000.

The International Yearbook of *Editor and Publisher* reveals that there are 916 daily newspapers in 544 cities with population over 15,000. Of these only thirty-three are owned by Jews. Thus Jews own or control only 3½ per cent of the total number of these daily papers.

There is also a general impression that the Jews are predominant on the New York Stock Exchange. A survey made in 1941 revealed that of the thirty-three members of the Board of Governors of the New York Stock Exchange, only four were Jews. Of the eleven officers none were Jewish. The New York Quotation Company had no Jews among its fifteen directors and none among its eight officers. The New York Exchange Building Company had no Jews among its nine officers and only one Jew among its five directors.

Many people have also surmised that the Jews control the banking institutions of this country. Of the 362 directors and trustees of various banks belonging to the New York Clearing House Association listed in Poor's Financial Records of 1940, there are only twelve Jewish directors of banks, or 3.31 per cent Jews. These figures are of particular importance when it is considered that New York contains

85

the largest Jewish population of any city in this country and that more than 35 per cent of the total population of New York City is Jewish. The following are the largest banks in New York City and of the country and have no Jew upon their boards of directors: the Bank of New York; Central Hanover Bank and Trust Company; Chase National Bank of the City of New York; Chemical Bank and Trust Company; Continental Banking and Trust Company of New York; Corn Exchange Bank and Trust Company; Federal Reserve Bank of New York; First National Bank of the City of New York; Guaranty Trust Company of New York; Irving Trust Company; and Title Guaranty and Trust Company.

There are a number of Jewish houses in the investment banking field such as Kuhn, Loeb and Company; Speyer and Company; J. & W. Seligman and Company; and Lehman Brothers. But statistics show that between the years 1925 and 1929 the foreign loans made by banks of this country aggregated $10,207,600,000. J. P. Morgan and Co., financed $1,514,000,000 and all other non-Jewish bankers floated a total of $7,360,500,000. All the Jewish bankers combined floated a total of $1,133,100,000. Thus, the entire group of Jewish bankers negotiated during this period only about 10 per cent of the foreign loans.

The foreign loans that were outstanding on March 1, 1935 were largely made by non-Jewish concerns.[3] These loans are held in the following percentages: J. P. Morgan, 19.8 per cent; National City Company, 11.71 per cent; Chase, Harris, Forbes, 8.45 per cent; Guaranty Company, 6.88 per cent; Bancamerika-Blair, 6.18 per cent; and Lee, Higginson Company, 4.23 per cent. All of these were above the highest of the Jewish houses, namely, Kuhn, Loeb and Company with 2.88 per cent. Dillon Read, which has some Jewish interests, had 11.44 per cent. In these supposedly Jewish concerns it is further noted that they do not contain Jews exclusively. Thus in Kuhn, Loeb and Company the following non-Jews are members: Elisha Walker, George W. Bovenizer, and William Wiseman; and in J. &. W. Seligman

[3] *Fortune*, February, 1936.

86

Company there are Frederick Strauss, Earl Bailie and Francis Randolph. The investment house of Lehman Brothers has the following non-Jewish members: John M. Hancock, Joseph K. Thomas, John Randolph Fell and others. Until his recent death, Thomas Hitchcock was also a member of the firm.

The charge that the Jews control international banking or, as is frequently stated, that the international bankers are Jews is another myth clearly disproven by the facts.

Some of the outstanding Jewish characteristics also contribute to the general misapprehension that the Jews are rich. The Jew is very frugal, but as soon as his economic condition permits he provides his family with the very best that he can afford. If a member of his family falls sick, he seeks the best available medical attention and hospitalization. He is intent upon giving his children a liberal education, which is one reason for the trite criticism that the Jews attend the universities far beyond their proper proportion. A father and mother will sacrifice every comfort and will economize severely so that the son may have the advantage of a liberal education. If he has acquired enough to supply the reasonable wants of his family, the Jewish parent seeks for them the benefits of the outdoor life during the heat of summer, or relief from the cold during the winter months. That is why we see Jews in large numbers at resorts. Also, when industry and sobriety enable him to provide a better home for his family, he does so, and leaves the congested tenement district for more wholesome surroundings. Frequently these desires are considered evidence of Jewish wealth. I believe it is a fair statement that in no other group do those usually termed "the immigrant classes" spend their limited means to such advantage, socially and culturally.

Unfortunately, there are some Jews who become conspicuous by the use of ornamental jewelry or loud dress. These individuals are criticized as much by the cultured Jew as by the non-Jew. Doubtless some non-Jews transgress equally in matters of dress and appearance, but if the offender happens to be a Jew, he is especially subject to censure. This has given rise to the comment that the Jews are ostentatious when, in fact, no more Jews err in this respect than do non-Jews. It is again an instance where the conduct of a few individuals who happen to be Jews is assumed to be characteristic of the conduct of an entire people.

Many years ago, Dr. Lyman Abbott, then editor of the *Outlook* and one of the great minds in America, wrote a complimentary article entitled "The Debt Christianity Owes to the Jew." Some correspondence ensued thereafter between Dr. Abbott and myself. He expressed the thought that Jewish ostentation in public places, such as resorts, injured him greatly. In reply I suggested that now and then some American Jew did transgress good taste in what is generally termed "ostentation." I inquired whether those he referred to were not of the immigrant group who had, perhaps, come from the Balkans, Poland, Italy, or similar lands and had carried with them in this regard the manners of the people amidst whom they had lived, and that in this respect they were no different from the non-Jewish immigrants from the same countries. Dr. Abbott admitted graciously that he had not studied this phase of the subject sufficiently to warrant his original criticism.

The Jew's liberal support of charities is conceded almost universally. Philanthropic demands upon the Jew have been for many, many years quite abnormal. He has had to supply the funds to feed and to clothe hungry, naked persecuted Jews in other parts of the world. He has had to maintain his eleemosynary institutions in this country and, in addition, he has felt it his duty to contribute to the public charities of his own community. But the Jew does not complain about this. His earliest lessons taught him that to give and to give liberally is a blessing, not a hardship. Even among the poorest there is some little sum set aside for charity. I have never known a Jew who fitted the stereotype of the miser.

A few Jews may be termed rich, but this does not make "the Jews" rich. A few Communists may have been born Jews, but this does not make all Jews Communists. These accusations are without foundation or substance and are

88

pure generalizations intended to propagate hate and antipathy.

The charge that the Jew is a Communist and, at the same time, that he is a capitalist is one of the many anti-Semitic paradoxes. The anti-Semite, when speaking to the capitalist class, abuses the Jew as a Communist. A Communist is, basically, one who is opposed to capitalism. When the anti-Semite speaks to those in the lower strata of economic life, he brands the Jew as a capitalist. If the Jew is a capitalist, self-interest would compel him to oppose Communism; and if he were a Communist, he would necessarily be against the capitalist. Lack of logic never disturbs the anti-Semite.

It may seem to some that it was unnecessary to answer each accusation, and to some it may appear that doing so is apologetic. But one who is falsely accused may with propriety show the falsity of each charge, since the effect is to pyramid falsehood upon falsehood so that no reasonable man can possibly give credence to such charges.

The statement that the Jews are in the moving picture industry in disproportionate number, or disproportionately engaged in merchandising or in the medical profession, will not affect a reasonable person. Jews may be fitted best in the vocations in which they appear disproportionately. The same may be said of the Italians, who are disproportionately represented in the operatic field, of the French in the finer restaurant field, of the Irish in the legal profession.

Although some accusations seem immaterial in the appraisal of the merits of the Jew as an American citizen, they do, however, bear upon the problem and the facts are shown in the interest of truth.

Some Conventional Libels

ONE libel, referred to in the previous section, is that the Jew instigated this war. This is pure Nazi propaganda. Daily and incessantly the short wave German radio has hurled this accusation through the ether. It was rather interesting that in June, 1943, this accusation was suddenly turned about, and the charge was made over the German radio that the Catholic hierarchy had instigated this war. On June 13, 1943, the Pope denounced the charge as without the slightest foundation.

Every intelligent person knows that the present war was initiated by German aggression. Germany claimed that she had not been defeated in World War I and availed herself of the intervening period to rearm more intensively than any nation had ever rearmed in the history of the world. She constantly repudiated the Versailles Treaty. She launched political, and then military, warfare against her neighbors, successively attacking one nation after another. After each aggressive act the other nations sought to end the aggression by further appeasement of the aggressor. But Germany's promises to desist were violated as speedily as they were made.

First, she demanded the Sudeten area of Czechoslovakia; after her demands were met and she received the Sudeten area she seized the entire country and enslaved its population.

She next insisted that she must have the Polish Corridor. Despite her ten-year peace pact with Poland, she proceeded to conquer and to ravage the entire country, enslaving the Polish people. Thus the area of warfare was constantly extended until other nations, convinced that Germany's promises and treaties could not be relied upon, were compelled to accept the challenge and enter this devastating conflict to halt the conquerors once and for all.

How then can anyone charge the Jews with having instigated this war? On the contrary, German responsibility for this crime against the world is indisputable.

For one kindness of fate the Jews must be ever grateful in this dark hour of human misery, and that is that Hitler, Goering, Goebbels and Rosenberg are not Jews and did not stem from any Jewish parentage. Has any mind the power to imagine the effect upon the Jews of the world had it been otherwise? Even the bitterest anti-Semites have not yet claimed that the work of the Nazis was a "Jewish conspiracy."

The Nazis claimed that the Germans of Jewish faith possessed or controlled the wealth of Germany. Statistics of the pre-World War II period, immediately prior to Hitler's regime, show that of the 550,000 Jews in Germany, 115,000 were wage earners. Of this number, 30,000 were unemployed. Of the 170,000 persons in the Jewish community of Berlin, 40,000 were on relief.

Yet there was no accusation too degrading for the Nazis to use. Their hatred mounted to the pitch of insanity. Not satisfied with the destruction of Jewry itself, the Nazis decreed that everything which had emanated from the Jewish mind must also be destroyed. The great songs of Heinrich Heine were so embedded in the German heart that they could not be eradicated; but the Nazis forbade the mention of the author. The greatest efforts of world-renowned literary men were banned. The monuments erected by the German people to honor some of its great Jews of the past were demolished.

The Nazis, however, do not always carry their doctrines to their logical conclusions. In medicine, for example, the Nazis dared not ban the accomplishments of the Jews they hate. A Christian doctor writes ironically in a Riga paper:

A Nazi who gets syphilis must not allow himself to be cured with salvarsan, as this was discovered by the Jew Ehrlich. In fact, the very diagnosis of his disease is to be rejected, for the Wassermann reaction is also the work of a Jew. If the patient is suspected of having gonorrhea, he must not have the bacilli investigated, for it was Jewish physicians, Neisser and others, who discovered the gonococci. If he suffers from cardiac debility he must abstain from using the classical remedy digitalis, as that derives from the work of Ludwig Traube. If he has toothache he must refuse injections of cocaine, for this was a discovery of the Jew, Carl Koller. Typhus cannot be treated, as to do so one would have to resort to the methods of the Jews Vidal and Weil. If your patient suffers from diabetes he must avoid insulin, which is an indirect result of the researches of the Jew Minkowsky. If he has headache he must abstain from using pyramidon and anti-pyrin, as Spiro and Filehene were Jews. If he suffers from convulsions, he is incurable, as the remedy, chloral hydrate, was discovered by the Jew Oscar Liebreich. Similar conditions apply to psychic ailments; psychoanalysis is the work of the Jew Freud. Furthermore he must abstain from profiting by the results of medical research carried out by Politzer, Barany and Otto Warburg, the dermatologists Jadassohn, Bruno Bloch and Unna, the neurologists Mendel, Oppenheim, Kronecker, Benedikt, the lung specialist Fraenkel, the surgeon Israel, the anatomist Henle, etc.

The irony is no less in other branches of science and cultural life from which the Nazis excluded the Jews.

As I write this chapter I am in receipt of the transcript of an address by Dr. A. G. Hooper, senior lecturer at the University of Witwatersrand, Johannesburg, South Africa. It is so pertinent to our discussion that I must quote the following:

A second method—one of which we grow tired, but one the importance of which we should not underestimate —is to make the Jews the scapegoat for all that is alleged to be wrong in the Union.

Hitler has obligingly supplied us with the clue to the use of anti-Semitic propaganda. In Rauschning's book, *Hitler Speaks*, Hitler is quoted as saying: "Anti-Semitic propaganda in all countries is an almost indispensable medium for the extension of our political campaign," and in *Mein Kampf*, he said: "The intelligent leader must be in a position to insist that his various opponents belong to the same category." Hence, everything of which they disapprove becomes Jewish. "The Jew Rosenfelt, the Jew Smuts, the Jew-Lovers Churchill and Eden, Stalin and the Jews." About the only anti-Axis leader to whom they have not attributed Jewish connections, as far as I know, is Chiang Kai-shek; quite an oversight on their part.

They dislike our democratic system because it permits the expression of opposition opinion, but they give as the reason of their dislike that democracy is a "Jewish fraud." Every act of aggression by Hitler was preceded by a campaign against "the Jewish war-mongers who seek to encircle the Reich."

In this process of labelling as Jewish all they dislike the Nazis have no hesitation in making accusations against the Jews that are obviously incompatible one with another. For example, recently they alleged (1) that "the Jews are a cowardly race who, not wishing to shed their own blood, prefer to have their battles fought by others"; and then (2) alleged that "American airmen who deliberately bomb and machine gun Italian women and children, when shot down, turn out to be Jews." So the Jews are pacifists and internationalists as well as plotters of war, communists as well as international bankers, the founders of capitalism as well as the chief rebels against capitalism. Obviously these contradictory tendencies cannot characterize Jews as a *group*; it is true that individual members of the group are all these things. But then it is equally true that individual members of any other group are all these things.

The fact of the matter is that in origin anti-Semitism has darn little to do with the Jews at all. The Nazis merely took advantage of the general discontent in most countries to further their own political aims. They made people aware of their dissatisfaction with existing conditions, and then directed that vague dissatisfaction against one specific object: the Jews. In South Africa, as elsewhere, anti-Semitic propaganda was directed to the economically depressed in town and country; and ignorance, hardship and misfortune were deliberately exploited for the Nazis' political ends.

Hatred for something, it does not matter what, unifies one's followers, and makes them forget their other troubles. The Nazis' propaganda might have been anti-Catholic, anti-Japanese, even anti-Afrikaans, and would have been if any of these antis would have suited their purpose as well. But it happened that anti-Semitism, for them, had several advantages. Before Nazi movements could be started in other countries, an atmosphere had to be created in those countries favourable to their growth. The Jews were international, and attacks against them provided an entry into almost every country; the Jews therefore could be represented as responsible not only for local troubles, but for the world's troubles. *Indeed, the fact that the Nazis have chosen so widespread a group to attack is the best evidence of how widespread their own aims of domination are.* It scarcely matters whether the charges of the anti-Semites are true or false; the charges are made in the attempt to destroy our democratic way of living, and anti-Semitism should be resisted for that reason alone.

In other words anti-Semitism is introduced by the Nazis into all countries which they wish to control, including therefore South Africa. It is part of their plan to divide and weaken us, to create political division among the democracies and weaken their resistance to the ideology of Nazism. And one of the most dangerous things about Nazism is that it often poses as a patriotic movement to preserve a Christian country from aliens.

And recent anti-Jewish propaganda from Zeesen confirms these views, and shows that it still aims at breaking the unity of purpose of Germany's enemies, but that it now aims also at diverting attention from Germany's responsibility for the war and at putting that responsibility on the Jews, and it perhaps reflects a growing sadism developed from a sense of guilt and coming defeat.

Anti-Semites in the United States, since Pearl Harbor, have used a trick accusation falsely to impute war guilt: the charge that scrap iron was exported in abnormally large

94

quantities before Pearl Harbor to Japan, and that this was done by Jews. The facts are:

First, that among *large* scrap-iron dealers there are many non-Jews.

Second, that all shipments of scrap were known to the government and were approved; for at that time our government wished to give Japan no cause for complaint, hoping against hope that armed conflict with the Japanese could still be avoided.

Third, there is no reason to point particularly to scrap iron since all other necessary products were also exported to Japan, including airplanes and parts, oil and petroleum products, copper, lead, and machinery, in which industries the Jews played no part, or a very negligible one. Government statistics show that scrap iron ranked *fifth* in the total value of such export items.

Fourth, according to the Institute of Scrap Iron and Steel, the amount of iron sent to Japan in a seven-year period prior to Pearl Harbor, if retained at home and consumed by American mills, would have been sufficient for no more than a *two months' supply.*

Fifth, in accordance with the *Foreign Policy Bulletin* of February 7, 1941, issued by the Foreign Policy Association, Inc., during the first ten months of 1940 total American exports to Japan increased $12,000,000 over the same period in 1939, but exports in scrap iron fell by nearly $10,000,000 and shipments of steel rose $12,000,000; and the export of petroleum and copper showed increase. Despite this increase, Tokio complained of economic pressure from the United States. The total amount of petroleum and oil products shipped during that period far exceeded in volume and in value the scrap iron exported. There can be, therefore, no justifiable complaint against the Jews in this field and certainly no warrant for a generalization against "the Jews."

Merely to illustrate a point, let us recall that on May 4, 1886, the entire country was shocked by what has become known as the "Haymarket Riot" in Chicago, when a number of policemen were killed by the explosion of bombs manufactured and utilized for this occasion by a group of anarchists. The leaders of the anarchistic "cell" were arrested. They were tried and found guilty. All of those convicted were German. Those who escaped the death penalty and were sentenced to the penitentiary were later pardoned by Governor John Peter Altgeld, a splendid man, also a German-American. Of course, German-Americans could not be and were not charged with this terrible crime because the great majority of the German-Americans were entirely opposed to anarchism and certainly did not approve of the acts of these conspirators. Had these anarchists been Jews and had Governor Altgeld been a Jew, it would have been a great triumph for the hate-mongers and a tragic episode for all American Jewry.

It is not difficult to create hate against any minority group. A few unscrupulous people can invent accusations against any group, basing their libels upon fictions, half-truths, unreasonable conjectures, and even upon absurd superstitions.

Canards and Hoaxes

ANTI-SEMITIC propagandists label all men whom they dislike as Jews. In nearly every instance those so labeled are antagonists of the frauds promoted by the hate-mongers. As authority for their canards the propagandists usually cite the publications of their fellow propagandists; it is not unusual that the compliments are returned, each citing the other as an authority. For deception and fraud are no barriers to the anti-Semites. It does not even deter them that their deceptions, frauds and misstatements are easily detected.

A few specimens of these canards and hoaxes must be recorded:

Pope Pius IX was a Jew.[1]

Pope Pius XI is a Jew whose real name is Lippmann.[2]

President Roosevelt and the Roosevelt family are Jews. Their original name was Rosenfeld.[3]

Rexford Tugwell is a Jew.[4]

Wallis Simpson is a Jewess.[5]

President Wilson's second wife was a Jewess. Her father adopted the name of Bolling after arriving in America.[6]

Newton B. Baker, former Secretary of War, was a Jew. His former name was Becker.[7]

[1] Lazare, *Anti-Semitism*, p. 320.

[2] Cited from *Völkischer Beobachter*, in *Universal Jewish Encyclopedia*, Vol. 3, p. 7.

[3] William Fiske, *Americans Awake! Your Country Is at Stake*, p. 13. Also Pelley, *Dupes of Judah*, p. 51.

[4] *Liberation*, March 31, 1934, p. 2.

[5] *Ibid.*, February, 1937, p. 13.

[6] *The Hidden Hand*, published by the Judaic Publishing Co. (Anti-Semitic), London, S. E.; cited in *The Jewish Peril and the Hidden Hand*, by Elias Newman.

[7] *Ibid.*, p. 41.

President Wilson's great-grandfather came from Poland and was a Jew.[8]

Bainbridge Colby, former Secretary of State, changed his name from Colinsky. He was a Jew, born in St. Louis, Missouri.[9]

Former Secretary of the Navy Daniels was a Jew on his mother's side.[10]

Frances Perkins is a Jewess whose original name was Matilda Wutski.[11]

Prime Minister Churchill is part Jew.[12]

King Haakon is a Jew. His real name is Cohen.[13]

The Queen of Holland is half Jewish.[14]

President Benes of Czechoslovakia is a Jew.[15]

Alexander Kerensky is a Jew.[16]

Cordell Hull is a Jew.[17]

William Randolph Hearst is a Jew, a descendant of certain Hertzogs on his father's side who were prominent Jews.[18]

J. P. Morgan was a Jew, his real name being Morganstern.[19]

Sinclair Lewis (Levy) is a Jew.[20]

Bismarck was a half Jew.[21]

Nikolai Lenin was a Jew.[22]

[8] *The Hidden Hand*, published by the Judaic Publishing Co. (Anti-Semitic), London, S. E.; cited in *The Jewish Peril and the Hidden Hand*, by Elias Newman.

[9] *Ibid.*, p. 42.

[10] *Ibid.*, p. 42.

[11] *One Million Silver Shirts By 1939*, Pelley Publishers.

[12] George E. Deatherage, *Knights of White Camelia*, December, 1936.

[13] Reprint of article in *Evening Standard* of London, cited in *La Voz Israelita*, April 5, 1941.

[14] *Ibid.*

[15] *Ibid.*

[16] Andrew Fabius, *The Rothschild Money Trust*, p. 17.

[17] *What Every Congressman Should Know*, Pelley Publishers, p. 11.

[18] *Liberation*, December 9, 1933, p. 3.

[19] Andrew Fabius, *The Rothschild Money Trust*, p. 28.

[20] *The Broom*, March 20, 1939, p. 1; also *Liberation*, December 7, 1938, p. 10.

[21] *Liberation*, December 9, 1933, p. 3.

[22] *Hidden Empire*, Pelley Publishers, p. 6.

Leon Henderson is a Jew.[23]

Mussolini is a half Jew.[24]

Anthony Eden, brother-in-law of Litvinoff-Finklestein, through their marriages to sisters, Jewesses.[25]

Masaryk is a half Jew.[26]

Alexander Hamilton was a Jew, the West Indian Jew.[27]

Thomas Mann is a Jew.[28]

Heywood Broun was a Jew.[29]

De Valera is an American-born Portuguese Jew.[30]

In the above instances one source is mentioned for each lie quoted. But these same canards were carried in many other anti-Semitic publications. They are part of the stock in trade of the merchants of hate.

The labeling of these prominent figures as Jews would unquestionably be complimentary to the Jews, but that was not the intention of the propagandists, who desired to injure these individuals by ascribing Jewish origin, or connections, to them.

General Eisenhower has also been labeled a Jew. When he was in Africa some newspaper reporters asked him whether he had heard the news that the Eisenhower family were "typical Jews." He laughed heartily and replied that it reminded him of an incident which had occurred to his brother Milton. He said that some time ago Milton was approached by a gushing dowager. The conversation ran like this:

"What a wonderful family you Eisenhowers are! One brother died at Bataan; one brother is in charge of our army in Europe; and you are doing an important job here—a great family. What a pity it is that you are Jews!"

"No, madam, what a pity it is that we are not!"

[23] *The Broom*, August 4, 1941, p. 2.
[24] *The New Liberation*, June, 1937, p. 5.
[25] *Liberation*, April 14, 1938.
[26] *Ibid.*, August 7, 1938, p. 4.
[27] *Ibid.*, February 21, 1939, p. 2.
[28] *Ibid.*, August 7, 1940, p. 4.
[29] *Ibid.*, May 7, 1939, p. 5.
[30] *Ibid.*, July 21, 1939, p. 4.

Among other hoaxes may be cited the charge that the Jews were responsible for the Versailles Treaty;[31] that the Jews were responsible for the creation of the League of Nations and for the Bank of International Settlements;[32] that the Jews were responsible for the past and present wars;[33] that the Jews financed the Russian Revolution;[34] that the Jews own approximately one half the wealth of America;[35] that with the exception of one or two, the New York banks are owned by Jews;[36] that 70 per cent of the steel and munitions industries are owned by Jews;[37] that 80 per cent of the metropolitan press is owned by Jews;[38] that the Jews acquired the *Literary Digest,* junked it, and created instead *Time* and *Life*;[39] that Jews acquired the *Saturday Evening Post*;[40] that Lincoln, McKinley and Harding were murdered by Jews;[41] that the Chicago *Daily News* is owned by Jews[42]; that Benjamin Franklin opposed the admission of Jews into America at the Constitutional Convention[43]; that 62 per cent of all the value of real estate, industries, resources and finances in the United States is owned or controlled by Jews[44]; that Jews are migrating to the United States at the rate of 17,000 per week, and they now comprise nearly one sixth of our population[45]; that Marshall Field & Co. is Jewish owned[46]; that the Jews are reputed to own 100 per cent of the metropolitan newspapers in both

[31] *The Rothschild Money Trust,* by Andrew Fabius, p. 9.
[32] *Ibid.,* p. 9.
[33] *Ibid.,* p. 9.
[34] *Ibid.,* p. 10.
[35] *Ibid.,* p. 37.
[36] *Ibid.,* p. 37.
[37] *Ibid.,* p. 37.
[38] *Ibid.,* p. 37.
[39] Andrew Fabius, *The Rothschild Money Trust,* p. 47.
[40] *Ibid.,* p. 47.
[41] *Ibid.,* p. 56.
[42] *Ibid.,* p. 113.
[43] *Ibid.,* p. 92.
[44] A. J. Christiansen, *Dangerous Forces Are Seizing America,* p. 10.
[45] *Ibid.,* p. 2.
[46] *The Press,* February 23, 1941.

England and France, and likewise 100 per cent of news and advertising agencies in those two countries.[47]

One of the outstandingly reckless instances of purveying of libels was *Social Justice*, the publication sponsored by The Reverend Charles E. Coughlin of the Shrine of the Little Flower, Royal Oak, Michigan. As late as 1938 the spurious "Protocols of the Elders of Zion" was published *with a note by the editor* that the authenticity of the same had been disputed! The fact that the "Protocols" was a literary forgery created by the Black Hundreds of Russia to promote anti-Semitism in Russia had been well established and was widely known. Nevertheless, this periodical reprinted the forgery with the evident purpose of promoting anti-Semitism in this country. (A discussion of the fraudulent character of the "Protocols of the Elders of Zion" appears on page 39.) To give authentic guise to the "Protocols," *Social Justice* printed in its issue of October 3, 1938, page 11, an article entitled "The Truth about the Protocols," allegedly written by one Ben Marcin, a fictitious name, purposely chosen because of its Jewish flavor. In this article was included the following material calculated to arouse anti-Semitic feelings in the reader:

In 1901 Rabbi Rudolph Fleischman of the Polish city of Schocken, now called Skoki, stated:
"The Protocols really did exist and they were no forgery. Moreover, they were positively of Jewish origin."
In 1906 Rabbi Grunfeld of the Polish city of Swarzedz gave the following characteristically Jewish answer:
"My dear questioner, you are too curious and want to know too much. We are not permitted to talk about these things and not allowed to say anything, and you are not supposed to know anything about the Protocols. For God's sake be careful, or you will be putting your life in danger."
In 1924 Dr. Ehrenpreis, at one time Chief Rabbi of Sweden, later banished from Soviet Russia (who became disgusted with the cruelty of the Jews and joined the Greek Orthodox Church) said:

[47] Andrew Fabius, *The Rothschild Money Trust*, p. 46.

"Long have I been well acquainted with the contents of the Protocols, indeed, for many years before they were ever published in the Christian press. The Protocols of the Elders of Zion were, in point of fact, not the original Protocols at all, but a compressed extract of the same! Of the 70 Elders of Zion in the matter of the origin and of the existence of the original Protocols, there are only 10 men in the entire world who know."

These statements, supposedly made by these rabbis, were featured in this issue of *Social Justice* in heavy type in box form on the front page of the publication!

An inquiry was immediately made of Dr. Marcus Ehrenpreis concerning the authenticity of the above statements. On November 4, 1938, a cablegram was received in Chicago from this rabbi from Stockholm. The message read:

DENY ARTICLE. NEVER VISITED RUSSIA. NEVER JOINED ORTHODOX CHURCH. STILL SINCE 1914 RABBI STOCKHOLM. STATEMENT CONCERNING PROTOCOLS PURE INVENTION.

EHRENPREIS.

Every rabbinical and other religious source in America likely to have any record was searched for evidence of the existence of the two other rabbis. The efforts were fruitless. Inquiries were also made in Poland concerning the other two rabbis mentioned, Fleischman and Grunfeld. On December 16, 1938, the following letter arrived from a rabbi of Wilno:

In reply to your letter dated October 7, 1938, I beg to inform you that I know no Rabbi Rudolph Fleischman of Skoki, and likewise no Rabbi Grunfeld of Swarzedz, and I did not know them in the past.

Then I took information from the Central Bureau of the Agudath Harabbanim (Union of Rabbis) in Warsaw. To them also the two above mentioned names are fully unknown, either for the present time or for the past.

As a matter of fact, there never was a Rabbi Rudolph Fleischman of the city of Skoki or any other city, and there never was a Rabbi Grunfeld of Swarzedz, Poland, or any other city. All three alleged utterances by the said three rabbis are purest fiction.

Prominent Catholic church dignitaries have repeatedly cautioned that Father Coughlin and his paper, *Social Justice*, are *not* the expression of the Catholic church, and many of them have publicly denounced the actions of Father Coughlin and of his publication, *Social Justice*.

Many of the anti-Semitic attacks were copies from the *Trans-Ocean News Service*, a Nazi propaganda agency, from which articles were reprinted almost verbatim in *Social Justice*. At the time that these and similar attacks were made upon the Jews, *Social Justice* had a circulation of over one million. This publication was suspended April 20, 1942.

Father Coughlin brought suit against the Detroit *Free Press*, charging that the *Free Press* had libeled him. The damage claimed was $1,000,000. This case was entitled "Charles E. Coughlin vs. the Detroit *Free Press*, in Circuit Court of the County of Wayne, State of Michigan." The number of the case was 211,525. The declaration consists of ten pages, with three counts, charging the defendant with specific acts of libel in its publication, the Detroit *Free Press*. The defendant's answer to the declaration consisted of 67 legal-sized typewritten pages, denying that the plaintiff was libeled and setting forth in 116 statements the facts justifying the alleged libels. The plaintiff replied to the defendant's answer and denied the allegations. The case was then voluntarily dismissed by the plaintiff, Charles E. Coughlin.

Anti-Semitic propagandists of America are apt students of Hitler's theory of propaganda. In his book, *Mein Kampf*, Hitler stated that the people "Will more easily fall victims to a great lie than to a small one." These propagandists believe that the public is so stupid it will believe what it sees in print, and that the truth, even if given later on, will never catch up to the lie.

The public is prone to believe that men do not publish untrue statements for fear of heavy penalties under the law. But the public does not realize that many of these propagandists would welcome prosecution because they could capitalize upon the notoriety they would achieve through such court actions. These propagandists would fight any action against them, relying upon their constitutional guarantees of freedom of speech and of the press, and upon the theory that group libel is not actionable.

As Curtiss MacDougall has said, "Human events and thoughts seem to have been determined as much by what is untrue as by what is true, and it is important to dip deep into the well of human credulity and find what is at the bottom."[48] He also adds, "When a hoax achieves the longevity to qualify for classification as either myth or legend, hope of stopping it almost may be abandoned."[49]

It may be said safely that no people or sect in the history of the world has been the victim of so much obdurate, continued, violent and inexhaustible false propaganda as has been the Jew.

In the art of propaganda there is no more cunning device than what we earlier termed "labeling"—that is, ascribing that which is generally unpopular to persons or things whose discrediting is sought. Hitler labeled Bolshevism as Jewish. It served his purpose until he entered into the Stalin-Hitler pact. Then the tag "Jewish" had to be removed. It would not do for Hitler to be party to an agreement to protect a "Jewish Bolshevik" government, or for a "Jewish Bolshevik" government to protect the Nazi government. The entire Nazi hate propaganda against Bolshevism was stopped. Bolshevism ceased to be Jewish, and Russian Communism was no longer inimical to Nazism and, therefore, of course, it could no longer be Jewish. Immediately thereafter, the Nazis affixed the label to the democracies. The theme song became the "Jewish democracies," the "Jewish Allied governments," the "Jewish Christianity," the "Jewish war," "Jewish capitalism." Label legerdemain is a great propaganda art.

[48] MacDougall, *Hoaxes*, p. 7.
[49] MacDougall, *Hoaxes*, p. 293.

When Hitler breached his agreement with Stalin and, in violation of the mutual nonaggression pact, invaded Russian territory and began the Russian-German war, then, of course, the erstwhile labeling of the Russian government had to be restored.

Abba Hillel Silver has pointed out that Prince Bismarck, during his reign, identified all liberal movements of his day as Jewish; that the Dominicans sought to discredit Humanism and the new learning in the pre-Reformation by labeling them as Jewish. He also states, "The guiding principle is the same—inodiate a cause by attaching to it an unattractive label. It is very serviceable to pin an existing historic prejudice on your opponent."[50]

[50] Abba Hillel Silver, *The World Crisis and Jewish Survival*, Richard R. Smith, New York, 1941, p. 162.

Character Assassination

THE prolonged effort to assassinate the character of the Jews affords one of the most convincing evidences of the spiritual strength and stamina of this people. The unrelenting campaign, waged for hundreds of years against their morale and character would have destroyed and annihilated any group unfortified by great faith and lofty ideals. A Christian savant has said that if the Jews had been guilty of one hundredth part of the accusations leveled against them, they could not have survived.

A people of impure motive and without a peerless philosophy of life could not have survived these centuries of adversity and persecution. If the Jew had been guilty of even a few of those bitter accusations, he could not have preserved the purity of his home nor have retained the filial affection of his children. Nor could he have produced such outstanding world masters in music, poetry, drama and science as well as the finest leaders in the field of philanthropy.

Neither could the Jew, after suffering to the limits of human endurance, turn to his God in the dark quiet of the night with the prayer, "Lord, Thou hast been our refuge in all generations." To have survived the inhuman sufferings he has endured for centuries and still to have maintained his dignity and his faith in his God required the stuff and the strength which sustained the martyrs of all the faiths in the past ages.

When his present maligners were yet savages, the Jew was already learning these supreme lessons of ethics and morals —"Who shall ascend unto the hill of the Lord? He that hath clean hands and a pure heart."

No people were ever enjoined to a higher concept of

moral duty than the Jews by the command, "You must swear to your own hurt and change not."

It is commonplace for the active anti-Semite to ackowledge that the Jewish individuals whom he happens to know personally are excellent citizens but also to claim that these individuals do not typify the Jewish people, but are "exceptions." The false stereotype of the Jew, which he has in his mind, does not harmonize with the individual Jews whom he happens to know; therefore these individuals become "exceptions." To him only the false stereotype of the Jew delineates the character and the soul of the Jewish people he hates.

Conversely, while the Jew holds his own people in the highest esteem, he has a bitter feeling toward any individual Jews who may, by their behavior, degrade his honor. For the Jew is ever zealous that the honor and the integrity of his people be not degraded or defiled; that is one of his noblest desires. It is almost a universal truth that Jewish individuals guard their good reputation earnestly; Jews who are careless on this score are very rare. The Jew is similarly careful, not only of his individual good name, but also of the good reputation of his people. I know of no other sect or cultural group which stresses the importance of the group reputation as the Jew does. Of course, there may be a very good reason for this caution. In nearly every country he is treated as a minority; he has no group power; and he believes that the false accusations against him can be met effectively only by the most exemplary conduct of his entire group. This also accounts for the bitter attitude of the Jew against any fellow Jew who, by his behavior or conduct, degrades the honor of his people.

Effect of Frustration

Anti-Semitism is not rational. It is an emotional attitude, with roots buried deep in ancient superstition and bigotry. Not founded on reason, it does not lend itself readily to the remedy of reason. It makes no impression on the anti-Semite to argue as Shakespeare did:

> Hath not a Jew eyes?
> Hath not a Jew hands, organs, dimensions, senses, affections, passions?

The scientific treatment is to uproot the source of this emotional attitude. The combating of anti-Semitism has two objectives—first, to restrain it, within bounds, and to prevent it from contaminating that part of the public which is not yet infected; and second, to eradicate it as a social problem and to drive this insidious hallucination from the mind. The latter is a slow, although not insuperable, process.

Anti-Semitism is a mental condition. Like all other mental disorders, it must be treated patiently and scientifically. Haphazard attempts at correction are of no value. Abuse will not help, but may, instead, aggravate it. To ignore anti-Semitism in the hope that it will wear itself out is as unsound as to permit any insanity to persist without restraint or treatment.

Science has demonstrated that it is natural for man, upon every frustration, to indulge in some compensating aggression. This weakness of the individual man is likewise present in the mass mind. However, the aggression of the mass mind is usually more violent than that of the individual, and is directed against an object which is weak and disliked. This is the process which creates the "scapegoat." That is why anti-Semitism is more virulent during every economic depression, after every defeat in war, even during war agitation, and during any great catastrophe such as the plague known as the Black Death.

There are two methods of treating aggression. First, to create a hatred or dislike of another group, which affects, directly or indirectly, the interests and welfare of the frustrated group. This practice would not only be unmoral and base but would afford no solution of the social problem. The unjust aggression would not be cured, but would merely be diverted from one group to another. Second, properly to correct the aggression requires re-education upon the fundamental errors responsible for that attitude.

Many experiments in re-education have been made with satisfactory results. Often there is little difficulty in re-educating individuals since many influenced by the erroneous concepts responsible for anti-Semitism are honest but deluded persons. Of course, this excludes the professional anti-Semite, who plies his trade either for profit or for power. *The greatest difficulty is the lack of opportunity to reach those most in need of re-education*. That is why the educational process is slow.

The minister of a large and influential church in an eastern city observed the placard of a candidate for Congress posted on the side of his garage. The candidate happened to be a Jew. The following Sunday this minister delivered, from his pulpit, a violent harangue against the Jews. The accusations were many, among them the allegation that they drive their automobiles recklessly! As far as this minister knew, the bill poster himself may have been a member of his church and the candidate completely unaware where his placards had been posted. . . . This was a clear case of frustration with its usual aggression. Later, through the efforts of friends, the minister was re-educated on this matter. He candidly admitted his error and tried to undo the mischief for which he had been responsible from his own pulpit.

A professor of science in a large university discovered that examination questions had been taken from his desk. A young Jewish lad was responsible for the prank, and he was punished for his misbehavior. Later, the professor found that two other sets of questions were missing. He accused the same youth, who, however, denied the second charge. The professor was profoundly disturbed and agitated. He referred to it in the classroom during his lectures and charged baldly that "the Jews" were thieves! It required several efforts to re-educate the educator. The professor was finally impressed that in moral philosophy it is improper to reason from the particular to the universal; that the particular may be an exception to the rule. Also, that if the boy who was responsible for this prank had happened to be a New England Yankee, the educator would not have indicted all Yankees as thieves. The professor finally saw his error and, later, volunteered to devote his efforts to the re-education of others. . . . These two cases are typical of many similar incidents.

An experiment in the re-education of small groups was attempted in a parlor meeting where twenty-two persons were present. These were urged to ask questions about the Jew. Their questions clearly revealed the insidious effect of anti-Semitic propaganda. But every question was answered carefully with full facts and data. At the close of the meeting, those present agreed that such meetings were extremely valuable and that the misconceptions of this particular group had been clarified through the parlor experiment.

In Germany, the frustration of the German people provided a fertile soil for the poisonous seed of anti-Semitism. That frustration, and the anti-Semitism which followed, were used to bring about the defeat of the republic and to bring the Nazis to power in Germany. It is doubtful if Hitler could have ever risen to power in Germany had he not so cunningly unleashed the terrors of anti-Semitism and played so maliciously upon this frustration of the German people.

If the biographers of Hitler can be relied upon, his anti-Semitism is typical of an aggression which is the result of an early frustration. To the committee of the Akademie der Bildenden Künste in Vienna he had submitted a drawing which he desired to have exhibited in the Akademie. The committee rejected that drawing as lacking in merit. The chairman of the committee happened to be a Jew. This incident started Hitler on the career which made him the outstanding anti-Semite of all history. It may be that had the Akademie der Bildenden Künste permitted the exhibition of his drawing, the history of the world might have been spared some of its bloodiest and most shameful pages.

Yet anti-Semitism seems to require no actual contact with Jews. One man had an unfortunate business experience. No Jew was in any manner connected with it. Yet he became a crusader of hate against the Jews. . . . A woman disappointed in her professional career, in which no Jew was concerned, made a practice of having tea at her home for the purpose of expounding the supposed derelictions of the Jew. Such cases are displaced aggressions.

The malicious propaganda of hate against the Jew for the past several years has had its effect. If this propaganda of hate had been directed against the Catholics, or against foreigners, or against Masonry, or against any other group, that group would have suffered similarly as the object of aggression.

The Jew is, and has been, the most readily available object of mass antagonism. He was made its special object by the Church during the Middle Ages, when he was the victim of the superstition, bigotry and legends of the period. True, the terror of religious persecution might have been avoided by baptism, and many accepted this escape. But the vast majority of Jews remained loyal to their faith and convictions. While religious persecution has become obsolete, the effects of it continue to this day.

A peculiar mental reaction is that men generate an intense hatred for the victims of their own wrongs. It is a defense mechanism behind which guilt seeks shelter. To forgive those whom we wrong is the rarest of all virtues. Usually the perpetrator of a wrong seeks to justify his action by unjustified accusations against his victim. Slanders, libels, scurrilous attacks, malicious and sordid inventions are employed for the purpose of creating revulsion against the victim. Experienced lawyers in criminal cases use the technique of picturing the victim of the crime as an unsavory character, a derelict, a criminal, a liability to society, thereby seeking to lessen and to minimize the guilt of their client, and also to divert the attention of the jury from the real issue on trial, the guilt of the defendant. This technique is, alas, frequently successful.

The long and bitter persecution of the Jew is a striking example. Whether the persecution was by the governments of Spain, of Russia, or of any other government, the process was the same. No government ever forgave the Jew for the wrong it did to him. The wrongs inflicted only intensified the hatred of the victim. Every effort to analyze the case of the persecution was resisted.

History is rich in examples of men who generated hate against the victims of their wrongs. The most recent is Hitler, who annihilated German Jewry. His victims are either dead, or are in concentration, or slave labor, camps. His sin will not permit the *corpus delicti* of his wrongs to remain dead and buried. The campaign of vilification goes on. Even the immense burden of the war does not divert him from his hate campaign, although now that hate is not confined to the Jews. His other victims, the Poles, the French, the Norwegians, the Czechs, and the Dutch must also be hated. When Hitler and his conspirators cease to hate the victims of their own wrong, they will collapse.

No one can appreciate the antagonism and dislike of the Jew today unless he is conversant with the treatment accorded to him prior to his emancipation and from the date of the first Crusade. The period of religious fanaticism, superstition, and bigotry is responsible for the false stereotype of the Jew.

John Morley said: "I want to know what men did in the Thirteenth Century, not out of antiquarian curiosity, but because the Thirteenth Century is at the root of what men think and do in the Nineteenth. It is the present that we seek to understand and to explain."

The dislike of the Jew is caused largely by the fact that the mind of the present is nourished by the teachings of the past. If these teachings of the past are wholesome, then they contribute to the development of a better mankind. If, however, these teachings are tainted, then development of the mind is retarded and the advance of civilization is slowed down or even halted.

As long as this dislike of the Jew continues, he will be the object of aggression. To correct this dislike, whether conscious or unconscious, is the task of those who have an abiding faith that there is a solution for every social problem.

Nazi Propaganda in America

THERE was no organized anti-Semitism in this country prior to the first World War. Various individuals did cherish some prejudice against Jews, but it manifested itself principally in social discrimination, which could be classified as "class snobbishness." In his article in the Jewish Encyclopedia (1901), Professor Gotthard Deutsch stated that there was no anti-Semitic movement in the United States. In the Encyclopædia Britannica (1910), Lucian Wolf took the same viewpoint.

After the first World War the Ku Klux Klan was organized and Catholics, Jews and Negroes became the targets of its calumnies. But the Klan was short-lived and soon succumbed through its own infamy. Isolated individuals also tried to inject anti-Semitism into the American scene. The only prominent person to engage in that task was Henry Ford, who was deluded on that score, and later recanted for the wrong he had done. Various minor figures also made attempts to create hatred against the Jews, but these were notoriety seekers, professional agitators, or mental derelicts suffering from frustrations. In Germany, the Nazi party, in order to gain a hold upon the nations, used the Jew as a scapegoat for all the ills suffered by the frustrated German people. This technique seemed to fit the situation admirably.

William Dudley Pelley, now serving a Federal penitentiary sentence (to be followed by another penitentiary sentence passed by the state court of North Carolina), copied his procedure from the Nazis and organized the "Silver Shirts." His ambition was to become a Fuehrer and to create a political anti-Semitic party in this country. In 1933, the Nazi party of Germany gained control of the government and immediately began a propaganda cam-

114

paign against the Jews in the United States! No propaganda effort in the history of the world ever approached this one in its magnitude, cost and villainy. Millions of dollars were expended by the Nazi government *in this country* for this purpose. Ships were loaded with books, pamphlets, brochures, and other printed matter to be distributed by the propaganda machine which had been created here. Short-wave radio broadcasts were beamed at this country constantly, carrying the foulest and most scurrilous attacks against the Jews. Under the direction of Nazi officials, militant organizations such as the Friends of New Germany, the Friends of Hitler, and the German-American Bund, were formed in the United States. The consulates of Germany were enlarged in this country, and their personnel was increased, all for the purpose of supervising the vast Nazi propaganda effort. An estimate, published in *Editor and Publisher*, placed the total expenditure of the Nazi foreign propaganda at $100,000,000 per year. Upon his arrival in this country, Dr. Gerhardt Westrick of the German Embassy deposited $5,000,000 in a San Francisco bank. In 1940, notwithstanding the fact that there was no business from American sources, the Germany Railway Information Office greatly increased its personnel, for this Railway Information Office devoted its efforts chiefly to propaganda.

During the latter days of the German republic the consul general of New York had a staff of thirty-three; in 1940 it had been augmented to a hundred and sixteen! In Philadelphia the business of the German republic was conducted by *one* acting consul; in 1940 a complete staff, headed by a former ex-Minister and Envoy as its consul, was installed. The personnel of the San Francisco consulate rose from eight to twenty-eight. All of the other German consulates in the country more than doubled in staff members in 1940. That year the employees of the German Library of Information were increased from four to thirty-three. The staff of the German Steamship Lines in this country was increased, although there was no travel from this country to Germany. The German Library of Information sent weekly news magazines, numbering over 174,000 copies, to newspapers and to publicists. The German Railroad Information Service continuously flooded the United States with its propaganda poison. The German consulates directed their attention principally to propaganda among the unemployed and, particularly, among ex-service men.

The *World Service*, published in Erfurt, Germany, was issued in six languages, and was afterward increased to eleven language editions. At its masthead was the subtitle: "International Correspondence for Enlightenment on the Jewish question." Each copy stated: "The reproduction of this bulletin is permitted and desired." On February 21, 1941, there were circulating in this country, 115 German language newspaper publications, 90 per cent of which were pro-Nazi. The Postmaster General, in reply to an inquiry from Senator Kenneth McKellar, chairman of the Senate Committee on Post Offices, stated that since December 23, 1940, postmasters at ports of entry had been directed to treat as non-mailable more than fifteen tons of mail emanating from Germany. This step was taken not because of the subversive content, not because it was poison fed to the mind of the American public, but solely because the agencies forwarding the same had not registered as propaganda agents under the law. The communication further stated that as soon as the forwarding agents had complied with the Foreign Agents Registration Act, this mail would be distributed. It is rather curious that we would handle such mail, in such volume, at immense expense to this country, even without reimbursement. If we had sent by mail to Germany exact copies of our Declaration of Independence and the Constitution of the United States, neither would have been distributed by the German post office because these documents contain principles in direct conflict with Nazi doctrines. But packages containing more than fifty printed propaganda books and brochures, inimical to our American democratic principles, were sent freely from Germany to individuals in this country.

A letter accompanying one transmittal from the *World Service*, American Section, stated:

From a mutual friend we hear that you are interested in our fight against the hostile forces of world Jewry. We therefore take this opportunity of sending you a copy of the *World Service,* together with pamphlets and leaflets. There is no charge; our request is merely that you use the material as propaganda in our mutual fight.

One of the leaflets enclosed read:

You can help save America, yourself and your family from the folly of other nations by making the truth known to your friends and neighbors. Ask them to subscribe or contribute to the support of this paper. Inform yourself and inform others. Do not depend upon rumors or daily (controlled) press. Get the facts and decide for yourself. Then join a fighting organization in your area to become active in spreading the truth. The books noted below can be secured through your organization. The publications and organizations listed below are fighting the battle with all they have—help them.

At meetings of various German societies postcards addressed to the Centralstelle für Erforschung-Kriegursachen, Berlin, were distributed to all present. Those present were requested to answer the inquiries on the postcards. Addresses were solicited of those to whom sample copies and prospectuses of the organization could be forwarded.

Questionnaires were distributed at these meetings, and all were requested to reply and to send the same to Ernst Venekohl, Berlin. The names of those who desired reading matter from the old fatherland were requested; also information as to the occupation, full address, year of immigration, from what town, etc. Requests were also made for lists of German-speaking organizations with which the individual was affiliated and he was asked whether the German language was spoken in his home; also whether the German language was taught in the public schools in his city and whether there were any German language schools in his city; and in the event that no German-teaching school existed, could one be established, and who would take charge of the same? The names and addresses of persons of

German descent who would be willing to receive German reading matter were also sought.

Many American universities received a number of students from Germany. These students were not sent to learn the American ways but for the purpose of furthering Nazi propaganda. An address by Mr. Goebbels to a group of German students who were to be sent to America, appeared in the *Newsweek* of September 6, 1937. Goebbels apprised the students of the purpose for which they were being sent to America; he urged them to make known "the true spirit of the new Germany." He gave them a lecture on methods of propaganda.

The report of the Congressional committee known as the "McCormick Committee" investigating foreign activities, gave an accurate account of the German propaganda efforts in this country, as a result of which Congress enacted a law compelling all foreign propagandists to register as such in the office of the Secretary of State. This law did not stop the propaganda. It made no effort to stop the propaganda. It merely required the registration of propaganda agents, but even this law was generally disobeyed and many of these propagandists have since been convicted for their failure to comply.

Pertinent questions we may ask are: "Why was Nazi Germany interested in the internal affairs of our country? Was this poison of hatred scattered over the American nation purely to 'save' America from the Jew? Was it prompted by nothing more than altruistic impulse? Was it for fear that America would be weakened and ruined unless it went anti-Semitic? Was its purpose to make America stronger, more prosperous, and more united? Why was a foreign power so intensely interested in the internal affairs of America?"

Our country is a republic, a representative democracy, with a strong constitution. The Nazis are enemies of every government which is not dictatorial or authoritarian. Christianity and the democracies are anathema to the Nazis, who believe that the citizens exist to serve the state and not that the state exists to serve its citizens. The Nazis believe that personal liberty weakens government and that a government "for supermen" must control the lives, the thoughts and the beliefs of its citizens. The abnormal interest which Nazi Germany took in the internal affairs of our country was for no other purpose than to weaken and, ultimately, to destroy our form of government, its institutions, its philosophy, its faith in liberty, justice and humanity.

For the several years before Pearl Harbor, this Nazi propaganda had its effect in the United States. It could not be otherwise. Millions of dollars were spent and hundreds of men were engaged to spread the propaganda. Counter-propaganda is of little effect. In his scholarly work, *Behemoth*, Franz Neumann stated that democracy can never completely divorce propaganda from truth because there are competing propaganda machines and they must ultimately prove their value by actual performance in the social life of a nation. He pointed out that the propaganda of Germany did *not* concern itself with truth. He also said:[1]

> National Socialist propaganda cannot be beaten by a democratic super-propaganda but only by a superior democratic policy that eliminates the soft spots.

A very important point was stressed by Mr. Neumann in the statement:

> What National Socialism has done and is doing with its propaganda is to take advantage of the soft spots in the social body. That is the technique it has developed to the fullest. Such soft spots are visible in any social organism. There is class struggle from above and from below; there are religious and racial antagonisms, clashing economic interests, competing political groups—all fertile grounds for a skilled propaganda machine.

Of course, one soft spot is always the historic scapegoat, the Jew. As Hitler has stated:

[1] Franz Neumann, *Behemoth*, Oxford University Press, New York, 1942, p. 438.

The task of propaganda is not to weigh the rights of each side, but to emphasize exclusively the one that is to take the place of the other by the medium of propaganda. Propaganda does not have to state the truth objectively, not so far as it is favorable to the others; nor to place the truth before the masses with doctrinary candor, but must serve its own interest uninterruptedly.

Dr. Donald S. Strong has said:[2]

The Nazis' rise to power in Germany had the immediate effect of starting anti-Semitic groups in the United States. The more widely it is accepted throughout the world, the more readily Fascist ideology circulates in the United States. Moreover, the growth in prosperity and in international prestige of the Fascist countries will enhance the attractiveness of their ideology and will increase its acceptability in the United States.

The same author stated that the one hundred and twenty-one anti-Semitic organizations which have appeared in the United States in recent years are products of the depression, the repercussion to Hitler's rise to power, the slight growth of revolutionary sentiment and the belief that the New Deal is Communistic.

In 1940, the eleven outstanding anti-Semitic organizations were the German-American Bund, Silver Shirts, National Union for Social Justice, Defenders of the Christian Faith, Edmondson Economic Service, American Vigilant Intelligence Federation, Industrial Defense Association, James True Associates, American Christian Defenders, Order of '76, and Paul Reveres.[3]

It is ironical that Gerald Winrod, the head of the Defenders of the Christian Faith, and Father Coughlin, the leader of the National Union for Social Justice and the Christian Front, disseminated the same anti-Semitic libels and yet were antagonistic toward each other, for Winrod is also anti-Catholic. The following is an example of Winrod's tirade against Catholicism:

[2] *Organized Anti-Semitism in America*, published by the American Council on Public Affairs of Washington, D. C.
[3] Dr. Donald S. Strong, *Organized Anti-Semitism in America*, p. 16.

The rapidly developing cooperation of Catholics and Jews in gaining control of the American government was illustrated when Al Smith and Jim Farley (Catholics) united their efforts recently in supporting Governor Lehman (Jew) for reelection in New York.

It seems strangely paradoxical that the Roman Catholic Church should be leading the fight against the filthy Jewish motion picture industry. Rome has never been particularly famous for moral reform efforts. Prohibition has no greater foe than the Roman church.

Mr. Pius, of Vatican City, can simply never resist throwing slurs at Protestants. Speaking recently before the Catholic Press Exposition . . . he denounced Protestantism and referred to Catholicism as "the only guardian of true and genuine Christianity." In the same breath he voiced approval of Mussolini's Ethiopian massacre.

The final destruction of the Greek Orthodox and Roman Catholic Churches in the end-time of this age is anticipated in Revelation 17:16.

Another outstanding peculiarity of anti-Semitic organizations is that, in their propaganda, they are very friendly to Japan! James True bemoans the "diabolical unfairness of our press in handling news of the Sino-Japanese conflict," and used this allegation as proof that the American press was Jew-controlled!

In general, anti-Semitic propaganda by native Americans was first inspired by the gigantic Nazi propaganda machine, and these "native" hate-mongers have ever since copied both the material and the techniques of the Germans.

With zealous care our democracy protects the physical health of its citizenry, at every port of entry, from foreign infections and diseases. In like manner, it protects our animal and plant life from foreign blights. But no ingenuity has ever been devised to protect the mind of the public from the poisonous propaganda inspired by religious and racial hatred. The guarantees of free speech and free press have been so abused that one questions whether the Bill of Rights guarantees freedom of speech and press for the utterance and dissemination of poisonous libels.

Many Americans contended sincerely that our country was immune from attack and from invasion by the Axis. They believed that our correct foreign policy was absolute isolation. That such a doctrine was, and is, fallacious is apparent. Its fatal error was that it did not demand that our isolation be respected by the Axis. Students of public affairs recognize that in warfare, propaganda in foreign lands is of vital importance and is, indeed, of vast aid in the strategy of war.

Our isolation was flouted by the Nazi government from the day the Nazi party gained control in Germany, for the Nazis immediately invaded America with their poisonous propaganda. The attendant purpose was to divide American unity and to weaken and ultimately to destroy our democracy. This is no exaggerated statement. Who can fail to see what would have happened in this country had this immense propaganda machine continued to function in America and had its destructive force not been halted by the villainous attack upon Pearl Harbor?

If the German government had really wanted to respect the isolation of our country, it would have announced a policy of noninterference in our internal affairs and would have solicited a similar policy of noninterference in its own internal affairs. Instead, however, it believed that the American public was naïve and continued its destructive propaganda here, directing the attention of the American public to the soft spots in our social make-up and structure, hoping thereby to divert American public attention from the real objective of Nazi warfare.

The repetitious chant uttered in every German gathering was, TODAY GERMANY, TOMORROW THE WORLD. Its slogans were, WORLD CONQUEST, OUR SUPER-NATION, OUR MASTERY OVER BELIEFS AND FAITHS, and A THOUSAND YEARS OF NAZI RULE.

The attack on Pearl Harbor, while carried out by the Japanese, was, of course, the physical attack of the Axis upon America. It awakened many dreamers to the reality of this world conflict. It demonstrated, even to the politically blind, that one-sided isolation can amount to suicide.

This much is certain: Americans did not know, and many have not yet learned, that our country can be invaded by destructive forces though there be no physical attack from without. Insidious propaganda which creates class conflict and which divides our unity, militant organizations which stir up internal strife and sabotage American democracy would, if permitted to continue, have eventually destroyed our government as completely as would a victorious attack. A physical attack from without would never destroy the spirit of American democracy. A sinister attack *from within* is the only force which can destroy our country. The German republic was not destroyed by any attack from without. It was annihilated by the Nazi forces *within* Germany.

The weakness of our national philosophy is that it does not restrain the misuse of those liberties which it so generously grants to all. Even those guilty of these misuses confess that, were they successful, they would deny these same liberties to others. Under our system any group of citizens may advocate a change of our fundamental laws whether that change would be in accordance with the doctrines of the Nazis, of the Communists, or of the Falangists, although any one of these doctrines, if established here, would destroy our government, its Constitution, and its basic philosophy. To deprive our citizens of the privilege of advocating change would negate the very rights which our government guarantees. Therefore, our government and our constitutional rights can be preserved only by an honest and intelligent public opinion, alive to the pitfalls in the propaganda of hatred.

Anti-Semitism Versus American Unity

MOST of the lies published by anti-Semites in this country are inspired by Nazis to sabotage American unity and to break the spirit of our democracy.

The propaganda to create hate enters our country free —there is no embargo. It is not mere coincidence that almost every hate-monger is also anti-English, anti-American, anti-Roosevelt, and anti-Russian, and is also an isolationist and against our war strategy. Every one of them favors appeasement with Hitler. Of course, this does not mean that everyone politically opposed to Roosevelt, or that every isolationist, is an antagonist of the Jew. There are many opponents of Roosevelt and his political and economic theories and many isolationists who feel no hostility toward the Jew; indeed, many are Jews. There are also many Roosevelt opponents who resent the importation of this hatred into our country. The anti-Semite, however, always tries to ally himself with some national cause, seeking thereby to increase his strength and to cloak himself with respectability. Many sincerely interested in an honest cause have been unable to rid themselves of the unsavory elements which have infiltrated into their organizations. Neither Republicans nor Democrats can keep anti-Semites out of their ranks. They can, however, denounce the anti-Semitic hatred and see to it that anti-Semites are not among their candidates for office.

Tolerance of intolerance is the greatest weakness of American democracy. Intolerance is in itself a negation of tolerance. Carried to its logical conclusion, every form of intolerance against any group or sect would destroy the very democracy which permits such intolerance.

Effect of Political Anti-Semitism

IT IS no coincidence that those governments which have subscribed to the principles of anti-Semitism and have practiced it did not prosper long or survive. Some students of history have maintained that the Jews were necessary to the prosperity of those nations or to the stability of their governments. To this theory I cannot subscribe. It may be true that the Jews, by examples of diligence and sobriety, promoted and advanced the welfare of the people among whom they dwelt, but it is not sound to maintain that the Jews are necessary to the prosperity and stability of any land.

For, underlying the decline of governments and nations which have practiced anti-Semitism, we find evidence of the decadence of those peoples; otherwise they would not have indulged the anti-Semitic cults. Furthermore, anti-Semitic governments and peoples have generally been destructive in nature, and not constructive. They have suffered from the obsession that the Jews were responsible for their suffering and maladministration. Such governments and peoples were the victims of insane delusions which prevented them from straight thinking. They were, therefore, unable properly to correct or set aright their ills or misfortunes.

History affords numerous examples. The earliest on record was of that Pharaoh of Egypt described in Exodus. One of the most tragic examples is provided by Ferdinand and Isabella of Spain, in whose reign occurred the expulsion of the Jews in 1492. The decline of that nation began in the following century.

As wicked a rule as any was that of the Russian government under the Romanoffs. The persecution of the Jews was part of a cunning effort to divert the unrest of the people, who chafed under the despotic rule of the Czar. Time and again the peasants were told that the Jews were the cause of their troubles. But the truth could not be forever concealed. When the masses of plain people finally awakened to the fact that they were exploited by a ruthless, conscienceless, despotic clique, operated solely in the interests of the reactionaries, their wrath—with one mighty blast—destroyed the ruling class of one of the largest powers of the Western world. The Jews, as pointed out earlier, played but a very minor role in this upheaval.

The most modern example, and one to which we are witnesses, is that of the Nazi regime in Germany. Because of their defeat in the World War the German people were undoubtedly frustrated. Hitler and his coterie believed that in this state of mind the German people could easily be misled into the notion that the Jews were responsible for their misfortunes. Thereupon, Germans were told that the Jews had instigated World War I and that they were responsible for the iniquities of the Versailles Treaty. They were told that the German republic was governed by Jewish influence and that the Jews were betraying the German nation.

A frustrated people is always willing and anxious to fasten the guilt upon someone, or upon some group, as their scapegoat. Every frustration must have its compensating aggression; here the Jew was made the victim. Little did the depressed Germans analyze their plight. They ignored the fact that there were only 550,000 Jews in all Germany, and that in the war the Jews had suffered casualties in proportion to their numbers, as much as their fellow citizens had. That many Jews had been decorated with the highest honors for outstanding heroism was not considered. Indeed, the repressive laws bore upon these heroes of the Army with the same cruelty and rigor as it did upon other German Jews.

The story of this tragic persecution is too well known today to need repetition here. But it does lend itself to the same analysis as did the previous instance of persecuting nations. The attention of the German people and their government was diverted from the real cause of their suffering to the scapegoat. Consequently, they felt no need to attend to the real causes. Their insane delusion that the Jews were responsible for everything rendered them incapable of discovering and setting aright the imbalances in their situation.

After the property of the Jews had been confiscated, after the Jewish man power had been thrown into concentration camps, after the Jewish houses of worship had been destroyed, after repressive laws forbade the Jew every vocation, there was nothing left that could be done to the hapless Jews of Germany except to exterminate them. That, too, was undertaken. But it was soon evident that the extermination of the Jews was not enough to correct or to relieve the ills of the German people. To continue its existence, the Nazi government had to invent new enterprises to satisfy the minds they had so deluded. Step by step the Nazi Juggernaut moved upon the adjoining countries. Austria, Czechoslovakia, Poland, Denmark, Norway, Belgium, the Netherlands, France, the Balkans, and Greece —these were the moves which marked Germany's first acts in the tragedy of World War II.

The original aggression of the Nazis was against a small group, 550,000 Jews. But this was not enough to satisfy the insane delusions of the Nazi party. This comparatively small aggression was insufficient compensation for the frustration. Greater aggression and ever greater conquests were necessary. The surrounding nations stood by, expressing sympathy for the helpless German-Jewish population, but they did nothing to halt the cruelty. Had the nations at that time availed themselves of their rights under international law to prevent, by force if necessary, the perpetration of such grievous wrongs against a minority people and against the laws of civilization, the subsequent bloody pages of history might never have been written. For it has been a concept of international law that no government may, in the treatment of any one of its minority groups, violate the principles of civilization.

And now, on the night of this bloody carnage, Hitler,

Rosenberg, Goering and Goebbels are flooding the air waves of the world with their propaganda that the Jews are the instigators of *this* war. Strange to say, even such vile, contemptible propaganda finds receptive minds in our country. Did the Jews attack Czechoslovakia? Did the Jews murder Greece? Did the Jews invade Holland? Did Jews have anything to do with the invasion of Norway, of Denmark, of Belgium, and of France? Did the Jews prompt Japan to attack Pearl Harbor? Did the Jews rob innocent women and children of their last morsels of bread in the countries of Europe overrun by the Nazi? *Were not the Jews, in every vanquished country, the first victims of the cruel Nazi hordes?*

When the final chapter of the Nazi regime is written, it will be reported, as was reported of the persecutions of Pharaoh, of Ferdinand and Isabella of Spain, and of the Czar of Russia, that anti-Semitism marked the beginning of its downfall—not because of the extermination of the 550,000 German Jews, but because the minds and the hearts of the Nazis, suffering from the insane delusion that the Jews were responsible for their frustration, rendered them incompetent to mend their real misfortunes.

PART IV

CUTTING THE NOXIOUS WEEDS

Jews in the Americas

THOSE who have not studied early American history may think that the Jew is a newcomer to these shores. Few are aware of his participation in the pioneering and development of our country.

One of the most interesting dramas in history is that of the discovery of America. The story is one filled with adventure, success, and tragedy. Perhaps it surpasses any fiction woven by man's imagination. The cosmology accepted by the Christian world maintained that the earth was flat and rested upon immense pillars. Had any Christian been so audacious as to contend that the earth was round and that it revolved about the sun, he would have been condemned for blasphemy. But science had made little progress; many parts of the Eastern world were as yet unknown to Europeans. The greatest travelers of that period were Jews, who journeyed more from necessity than inclination, since Jewish importers and exporters conveyed the commodities of one region to another in the then known world.

It is of more than passing interest that, long before the voyages of Columbus, Jewish savants had maintained that the earth was round. In the Zohar, compiled by Moses de Leon two centuries before Columbus, is the following statement: "In the book of Rabbi Hamuna the Elder it is further explained that the earth revolves like a ball and that its inhabitants differ in appearance according to climatic conditions. These revolutions bring it about that when it is day on one-half of the globe, night reigns on the other half and that when it is light for one part of the earth's inhabitants, for the other part it is dark." Even in the Palestinian Talmud (A.Z. 42C) the express statement is made that "the world is round." In an earlier period Greek astronomers and geographers had also claimed that the earth was round.

Jucefe Faquin, a Jew of Barcelona,—according to the records of Jaime III, last king of Mallorca,—in 1334, "has navigated the whole then known world." Jafuda (Jehidah) Cresques, the son of Abraham Cresques of Palma in Mallorca, was known as the "Map Jew." A map prepared by him, and presented by the King of Aragon to the King of France, is still preserved in the National Library of Paris. Cresques was a teacher of navigation to the Portuguese and a maker of nautical instruments as well as of maps. Another Jewish navigator was Joseph Vecinho, who was regarded in Portugal as the greatest authority in nautical matters.

Columbus came to Spain when Ferdinand and Isabella, aided by the Inquisition during the last war with the Moors, were reaping a rich harvest from the confiscated wealth of the Marranos (converted Jews). Abraham Ben Samuel Zacuto, a Spanish Jew, who was a famous astronomer and mathematician and had been a professor at the University of Salamanca, met Columbus soon after the latter's arrival in Spain. Zacuto encouraged Columbus and provided him with almanacs and with astronomical tables which were to be of great help on the famous voyages. Zacuto also made a favorable report to Ferdinand and Isabella concerning Columbus and, through his recommendation, Columbus entered the royal service. Columbus also met Abraham Senior and Don Isaac Abravanel, who gave him financial assistance. Luis de Santangel, another Jew, interceded for him with Queen Isabella, and the only problem which remained was the financing of the expedition. Though several members of his family had perished in the Inquisition, Santangel agreed to provide the necessary funds. The transfer of the money was made by Santangel to the Bishop of Avila, who afterwards became the Archbishop of Granada.

The records of this transaction are preserved in the *Archivo General de India* at Seville, Spain. The amount involved was 17,000 florins.

Every Jew who refused to become a Christian was exiled from Spain. The decree of expulsion was issued in the same month that Columbus was commissioned to undertake the voyage he fondly thought would be to India. A remarkable coincidence was that the actual expulsion took place on the second day of August, 1492, which, according to the Jewish calendar, was the exact date of the destruction of the first Temple of Jerusalem in 586 B. C. E., and also of the destruction of the second Temple in the year 70 C. E. Columbus sailed on the third day of August, the day following the actual expulsion. The vessels, crowded with the expelled Jews overwhelmed by misery and anxiety, sighted the three craft of Columbus, which were sailing toward the unknown seas. No one could have dreamed that the captain of the little fleet would discover a new world, one that was to become the refuge and the home of the persecuted and the oppressed of all mankind.

The exact number of men accompanying Columbus is not known, but it was not less than ninety nor more than a hundred and twenty, and among these men were a number of Jews, who had, of course, been baptized into the Christian faith. Among those best known was Luis de Torres, who was employed as an interpreter. Others aboard were Alfonso de Calle, Rodrigo Sanchez of Segovia, the physician Maestro Bernal, and the surgeon Marco.

Land was sighted on the twelfth of October, 1492. Luis de Torres was sent ashore to speak to the native inhabitants, and thus became the first white man actually to land in America. The shores reached, however, were not those of India but of an island in the West Indies. The inhabitants were strange men with copper-red skins. De Torres' ability to converse in many languages availed him little, but the signs he made were partially understood.

De Torres was so impressed with the new land that he finally made it his permanent home and settled in Cuba for the remainder of his life. Therefore, a Jew was among the first, if not *the* first, permanent white settlers in America. In a letter to a Jewish convert in Spain, he described a bird in this new world as "Tukke," the name of a bird mentioned in the Bible (I Kings 10:22) and commonly thought to be a peacock. It was from this name, "Tukke," that the strange bird afterwards became known in the English language as "turkey."

Columbus sent his first report of his discovery to Luis de Santangel and to Gabriel Sanchez, two Jews. It was dated February 15, 1493, and was written on his return voyage.

Columbus' second voyage was ordered by Ferdinand on March 23, 1493. The King and Queen had decreed that all jewels, metals, monies, clothing and other objects of value taken from the Jews when they were expelled should be confiscated by the royal treasury; likewise, all indebtedness due and owing to Jews was to be paid into the royal treasury. It was from these funds that the second voyage of Columbus was financed. Another decree was that 10,000 maravedis be paid from this money to Columbus, for the King had promised that sum as a reward to the one who first sighted land. A sailor by the name of Lepe was really the first to sight and to cry, "Land!"[1] But he did not receive the reward. As a result, Lepe refused to go on Columbus' second voyage. He settled in Africa and there again espoused his old faith. Whether that faith was Judaism or Islamism is not recorded.

Some historians have claimed that Columbus was a descendant of Jews. Various evidence is offered, among which is the fact that those who most encouraged Columbus and who were really responsible for the favorable consideration of his enterprise by Ferdinand and Isabella were Jews; that his first report of the discovery was to two Jews; that he made a small bequest to a Jew in his last will; that his name was not Columbus, but Colón. All of these and other matters mentioned by these historians are not sufficiently con-

[1] *History of the Jews in America*, by Peter Wiernik, The Jewish Press Publishing Company, 1912, p. 16.

clusive to establish the fact that Columbus was a Jew or a descendant of Jews.[2]

Among the first Jewish immigrants to the new world were children who had been torn from their parents at the time of the expulsion. In the very early days many Marranos also sought refuge here. But South America, where they arrived, was claimed by Spain and Portugal, and the infamous Inquisition soon followed the refugees. The Jews in the Spanish and the Portuguese settlements of South America were persecuted with the same ferocity they had known in Spain and Portugal. By royal permit, Juan Sanchez, a converted Jew, whose father had been burned at the stake, was the first to obtain permission (1502) to take five loaded vessels of wheat, barley, horses and other wares to Haiti and Santo Domingo.

On May 7, 1516, the Inquisitor General of Spain, Cardinal Jiménez de Cisneros, appointed Fray Juan Quevedo, Bishop of Cuba, his delegate, and authorized him to select the officials to hunt down and to exterminate the Marranos. Encouraged by Cardinal Hadrian, the Dutch Grand Inquisitor of Aragon, who later became pope, Emperor Charles V, by edict of May 25, 1520, ordained Alfonso Manso, Bishop of Porto Rico, and Pedro de Cordova, Vice Provincial of the Dominicans, as Inquisitors for the Indies. One of the first victims of the Inquisition was Diego Caballera of Barrameda, whose parents had been condemned by the same tribunal in Spain.

The persecution of the Marranos and of others in the American islands and in South America make a tragic chapter in the early history of the Western Hemisphere. Even the virgin soil of the new world had to be desecrated by the fanaticism of Spain and Portugal.

[2] This question may never be definitely decided, although Arthur Brisbane, the great American journalist who had studied the question thoroughly, maintained that Columbus was a Jew. Salvador de Madariaga, author of *Columbus*, Macmillan, 1940, held similar views. Samuel Eliot Morison, author of *Admiral of the Ocean Sea*, Little, Brown, 1942, denied that Columbus was other than "a Genoese-born Catholic Christian, steadfast in his faith and proud of his native city."

133

By conquest Holland possessed Brazil. The Dutch encouraged immigration and there was soon a large settlement of Jews at Recife. One of the very earliest settlers was Efram Sueiro. In 1642, six hundred Spanish-Portuguese Jews, who had migrated to Amsterdam, embarked for Brazil. Among them were many men of education, and the Jewish community in Brazil became a vital force in that country in the pioneer days. But the Portuguese contested Holland's right to Brazil. There followed bloody battles, in which the Jews took a prominent part. On January 23, 1654, a large part of the settled portion of Brazil was ceded to the Portuguese, on condition, however, that a general amnesty should be granted. The Jews were promised fair and equal treatment. However, the new Portuguese governor ordered them to quit Brazil at once, and sixteen vessels were placed at their disposal to carry them and their property wherever they chose to go. These vessels drifted to various lands. Some returned to Amsterdam, Holland, but one vessel finally reached New Amsterdam, now New York.

The island of St. Thomas, then under Danish rule, had a Jewish governor named Gabriel Milan for four years, from 1684 to 1688.

The first settlement of Jews in North America took place in 1654. Prior to this time there were individual Jewish settlers who most likely came from the West Indies. A group settlement, however, was made in 1654 in New Amsterdam, now New York. (This occurred thirty-four years after the Pilgrims landed in Plymouth.)

Jacob Barsimson was the first Jewish settler in New Amsterdam, arriving from Holland on the "Pereboom" on August 22, 1654. About a month later, twenty-three refugees from Recife arrived on the vessel "St. Charles." These were given the privilege of settling, on the condition that they support their own poor. The most prominent of these immigrants was Asser Levy. In July, 1655, Abraham d'Lucena applied for permission to establish a Jewish burying ground; that privilege was granted on July 14, 1656. This cemetery is on Oliver Street and New Bowery in what is now New

York. In 1682 Jacob Barsimson and Asser Levy petitioned to be allowed to stand guard like other burghers. The petition was denied by the Governor and the council, but the matter did not rest there. For these men insisted upon equal rights, and on April 21, 1657, the Governor and his council, under direction from the home government in Holland, granted the privilege. To Holland must, therefore, be given credit for the first emancipation of the Jew.

In 1664 New Amsterdam was captured by the British. The charter of liberties and privileges adopted by the colonial legislature in 1683 declared, "No one should be molested, punished or disquieted or called in question for his religious opinion, who professed faith in God by Jesus Christ," which, of course, meant that the Jews were excluded from this religious freedom. A petition by the Jews to the Governor in 1686 for liberty to exercise their religion was denied. At about the same time instructions came from James, Duke of York, to whom New York was granted by his royal brother, which read in part: " . . . to permit all persons of whatever religion soever, quietly to inhabit within the government, and to give no disturbance or disquiet whatsoever for or by reason of their differing in matters of religion." The first synagogue in North America was situated on the south side of present Beaver Street, between Broadway and Broad Street, in New York.

The next important settlement was in Newport, Rhode Island. Under Roger Williams Rhode Island pioneered in religious liberty in the new world, and here the oldest Jewish congregation in North America was established. Newport was founded in 1638; by 1658, fifteen Jewish families had arrived from Holland, had made Newport their permanent home, and had founded a congregation. This Jewish settlement was increased steadily by newcomers. Among the prominent members of the Jewish community were Jacob Rodriques Ravera and Aaron Lopez. Ezra Stiles wrote concerning Aaron Lopez, ". . . that for honor and extent of commerce he was probably surpassed by no merchant in America." Into America Ravera introduced the manufacture of sperm oil, a skill he had brought from Portugal. That industry and candlemaking provided the principal commercial enterprises of the Jews of Newport.

Considering the influence of the Old Testament in colonial days, it may be said, at least symbolically, that the Declaration of Independence and the Constitution of the United States were written by the light of the candles made by the Jews of Newport.

Fourteen years after Lopez had settled in Newport, he had a hundred and fifty vessels engaged in trade with the West Indies alone. He also carried on an extensive trade with Europe and as far as Africa, and induced more than forty Jewish families to settle at Newport. Other Jews settled in New Haven and also in Hartford, where the town records mention the residence of several Jews in 1659.

The first Jew to reside permanently in Philadelphia was Jonas Aaron. A considerable number settled prior to the middle of the eighteenth century; among them were Joseph Marks and Samson Levy, both of whom became prominent in the life of the city. Isaac Miranda arrived in 1710 but was later converted to the Christian faith. In 1738, Nathan Levy applied for a plot for a Jewish burial ground; permission was granted September 25, 1740. This site was located at Spruce Street near Ninth Street.

In 1730 Jews were residing in Lancaster, Pennsylvania, before the town was organized. Joseph Simon was the best known Jewish resident. Myer Hart and Michael Hart were among the eleven original families who founded Easton, Pennsylvania, about 1750.

The colony of Maryland, established in 1634, also numbered Jews among its early inhabitants. In January of 1656 the physician, Jacob Lumbrozo, arrived. He had a large professional practice and became a landowner. Despite the religious intolerance of the colony, he was granted letters of denization on September 10, 1663. Maryland was one of the last to remove the civil disability of its Jewish citizens.

Dr. Samuel Nunez escaped the clutches of the Inquisition of Lisbon and arrived in 1733 at the then newly founded colony of Georgia. While Georgia was not liberal in its treatment of Jews, General James Edward Oglethorpe, the Governor, was a liberal-minded man and not unfriendly. Arriving on the second vessel to reach the colony from England in July, 1733, forty Jewish immigrants settled at Savannah. The Governor publicly bade them welcome.

The first male white child born in the colony of Georgia was Isaac Minis, born in 1743. Abraham d'Lyon introduced the culture of grapes into Georgia in 1737, and other Jewish settlers engaged in the cultivation and the manufacture of silk, the knowledge of which they brought with them from Portugal. Joseph Ottolenghi became the superintendent of the extensive silk industry of the colony, and was elected a member of the General Assembly, where he served from 1761 to 1765. Jews also settled early in the Carolinas and in the other colonies.

Judah Monis lived at Cambridge, Massachusetts, and became baptized, but throughout his entire life he observed the Jewish Sabbath. From 1722 to 1759 he was instructor in Hebrew at Harvard University and wrote the first Hebrew grammar printed in America. Another early Jewish settler in Massachusetts was Solomon Franco, who lived there in 1649. But the religious intolerance of the Puritans did not make Massachusetts a hospitable place. When Joseph Frazon died in Boston in 1704, there was no plot for his burial and the body had to be sent to Newport.

The steady influx of Jews from South America, the West Indies, Holland, England and Germany continued. At the time of the Revolution, the American Jewish fathers were firmly established. They had their houses of worship, their cemeteries, and they participated in the affairs of the colonies.

The Old Testament exerted a singular influence upon the spirit of the pioneers. The great public issue before the outbreak of the Revolution was the authenticity of the divine right of kings. To refute this theory of the rights of the king, the colonials referred to the Old Testament. The historian Lecky said that the early Protestant defenders of civil liberty derived their political principles from the Old Testament. Reverend Jonathan Mayhew, a vital force at this time, delivered a sermon, in Boston in 1766, which was thereafter known as "the morning gun of the Revolution." He said: "God gave Israel a king in His anger because they had not sense and virtue enough to like a free commonwealth and to have Himself for their King—where the spirit of the Lord is, there is liberty—and if any miserable people on the continent or isle of Europe be driven in their extremity to seek a safe retreat from slavery in some far distant clime—oh, let them find one in America."

The Reverend Samuel Langdon, president of Harvard College, delivered a sermon in May, 1775, using a text from Isaiah: "And I will restore thy judges as at first." He said, "The Jewish government, according to the original Constitution which was divinely established if considered only in a civil view, was a perfect republic. And let them who cry up the divine right of kings consider that the form of government which had a proper claim to a divine establishment was so far from including the idea of a king, that it was a high crime for Israel to ask to be in this respect like other nations, and when they were thus gratified, it was rather as a just punishment for their folly."

Reverend Ezra Stiles, president of Yale College, delivered a sermon in May, 1783, at Hartford, in which he pointed out that from the Hebrew theocracy to his day the high mark of popular government had been reached in America, where it had been transplanted by divine hands in fulfillment of the Biblical prophecy from the days of Moses to Washington. He referred to the American nation as "God's American Israel," and to Washington as "the American Joshua." Other Christian preachers were similarly inspired in their sermons.

The committee to prepare the design for the seal of the United States, which was appointed on the day that the Declaration of Independence was adopted, consisted of Benjamin Franklin, John Adams and Thomas Jefferson. This committee proposed one seal depicting Pharaoh sitting in an open chariot, a crown upon his head and a sword in his hand, passing through the dividing waters of the Red Sea in pursuit of the Israelites, with rays from the pillar of fire beaming on Moses, who was represented as standing on the shore extending his hands over the sea, and causing it to overwhelm Pharaoh.

In the armed conflict under General George Washington the Jews took an active part. Four Jews received the rank of lieutenant colonel; three became majors; and many achieved the rank of captain.

David S. Franks served as aide-de-camp to General Lincoln and was sent to Europe by Robert Morris with dispatches to John Jay in Madrid and to Benjamin Franklin in Paris. On January 15, 1784, Congress resolved that a triplicate of the definitive treaty be sent to the Minister Plenipotentiary by Lieutenant Colonel David S. Franks, and he again sailed for Europe. The following year he was appointed vice-consul at Marseilles, and was later selected to serve in a confidential capacity concerning the treaty of peace and commerce with Morocco. On January 28, 1789, he was granted four hundred acres of land in recognition of his services during the Revolutionary War.

Isaac Franks, who was born in New York, enlisted in Colonel Lesher's regiment of New York volunteers at the age of seventeen. He was captured by the enemy but escaped three months later. He was appointed to the Quartermaster Department and was made forage master at West Point. In 1781 he was appointed by Congress as ensign in the Seventh Massachusetts Regiment. It was in his house at Germantown that President Washington resided during the prevalence of yellow fever in 1793.

Solomon Bush was deputy adjutant general of the state militia of Pennsylvania. He was dangerously wounded in the fight to take Philadelphia. Captured by the English, he was afterwards released on parole. In 1779 he was promoted to the rank of lieutenant colonel. He was pensioned in 1785.

Colonel Isaacs of North Carolina was wounded and taken prisoner at Camden on August 16, 1780; he was later exchanged. Lewis Bush was a first lieutenant in the Sixth Pennsylvania Battalion and was made a captain on January 24, 1776. He was later transferred to Colonel Thomas Hartley's Continental Regiment, where he was commissioned a major. He took part in the Battle of Brandywine, and was wounded and died four days later. Benjamin Nones served as a volunteer in Captain Berdier's regiment under Count Pulaski during the siege of Savannah, and received a certificate for gallant conduct on the field of battle. He became a major. Jacob de Leon and Jacob de la Motta were captains and served under Baron De Kalb. Noah Abraham was a captain in the Cumberland County Militia of Pennsylvania. Aaron Benjamin became regimental adjutant. Manuel Mordecai Noah served under General Francis Marion. Isaac Israel was a captain in the Eighth Virginia Regiment. Nathaniel Levy of Baltimore fought under Lafayette. Abraham Pinto served in Company X, Seventh Regiment, of Connecticut. William Pinto was a volunteer. Throughout the war Solomon Pinto served as an officer in the Connecticut Army; he was wounded in the battle to take New Haven. Mordecai Sheftal was chairman of the Revolutionary Parochial Committee of Savannah. Appointed commissary general to the troops of Georgia, he received a grant of land as a reward for his services.

Major Benjamin Nones and Colonel Isaac Franks also served on General Washington's staff. Phillip Moses Russell was a surgeon at Valley Forge, and upon his retirement in 1780 he received a letter of commendation from General Washington.

Among the prominent Jews who assisted in the financing of the war were Mordecai Sheftal, Manuel Mordecai Noah, Benjamin Levy, Hyman Levy, Samuel Lyons, Isaac Moses and Benjamin Jacobs. Perhaps the most outstanding of those who rendered services in this regard was Haym Salomon. He cooperated with Robert Morris, the financier of the American Revolution. Aaron Levy of Philadelphia was a partner in various business enterprises with Robert Morris.[3]

When Washington was elected to the Presidency of the new republic, several of the Jewish congregations presented him with letters of salutation and encouragement. Washington's replies to these express his great humanity and his appreciation of the Jewish contribution to the building of the republic. To the Hebrew congregation of the City of Savannah, Georgia, he said: "May the same wonder-working

[3] There were no records kept in this regard by the Jewish communities and Simon Wolf searched the original governmental records for the basis of his book, *The American Jew As Patriot, Soldier, Citizen,* which contains the data of the Jewish contribution to the Revolutionary period.

Deity, who long since delivered the Hebrews from their Egyptian oppressors, planted them in a promised land, whose providential agency has lately been conspicuous in establishing these United States as an independent nation, still continue to water them with the dews of heaven and make the inhabitants of every denomination participate in the temporal and spiritual blessings of that people whose God is Jehovah." In reply to the letter from the Hebrew congregation in Newport, he said: "It is now no more that toleration is spoken of as if it were by the indulgence of one class of people that another enjoyed the exercise of their inherent natural rights, for happily, the government of the United States, which gives to bigotry no sanction, to persecution no assistance, requires only that they who live under its protection should demean themselves as good citizens in giving it on all occasion their effectual support."

He closes this letter with: "May the children of the stock of Abraham who dwell in this land continue to merit and enjoy the good will of other inhabitants—while everyone shall sit in safety under his own vine and fig tree and there shall be none to make him afraid."

To the congregations of the cities of Philadelphia, New York, Charleston and Richmond, he said: "The liberality of sentiment toward each other, which marks every political and religious denomination of men in this country, stands unparalleled in the history of nations." He closed his letter with: "May the same temporal and eternal blessings which you implore for me rest upon your congregation."

The propaganda of hate against the Jew and the pronouncements of super-patriotic and pseudo-patriotic hatemongers have explicitly charged that the Jew was a foreigner. They have insinuated that all Jews are immigrants. It is undoubtedly true that the test of a good American is not whether he is native born or a descendant of the first or second generation of immigrants; nor is descent from the Revolutionary fathers any test of true Americanism. Yet the pride with which any group of citizens claims participation in the building and development of this country, of its government, and of its institutions is certainly pardonable.

The simple fact is that only two groups in America are not immigrants or descendants of immigrants. These two are the Indian and the Negro—the Indians because they are the aborigines of this continent, the Negro because he did not come to this country as an immigrant but was forced into this country as a slave. The great majority of Americans consists of men and women who either sought a haven of refuge from religious or political persecution in Europe, or descend from men and women who did. By the labors of its loyal citizens, whether native born or naturalized, this nation has grown strong and prosperous. It need fear no foe in all the world except the saboteurs of true Americanism concealed in our own midst. As long as the American people obey the dictates of Washington and Jefferson, we need not fear for the stability and strength of our government and our nation.

Two pronouncements should ever be kept before the American public. First, that of Washington: "Happily the government of the United States, which gives to bigotry no sanction, to persecution no assistance, requires only that they who live under its protection should demean themselves as good citizens in giving it on all occasions their effectual support." Second, that of Thomas Jefferson in a historic letter to Manuel Mordecai Noah written on May 28, 1818, in reference to the sufferings of the Jewish people in the past. Jefferson said, "Your sect by its sufferings has furnished a remarkable proof of the universal spirit of religious intolerance inherent in every sect, disclaimed by all when feeble and practiced by all when in power. Our laws have applied the only antidote to this vice, protecting our religious, as well as our civil rights by putting all on an equal footing. *But more remains to be done, for although we are freed by the law, we are not so in practice; public opinion erects itself into an inquisition, and exercises its offices with as much fanaticism as fans the flames of an auto-da-fe.*"

The hate-mongers and the propagandists who strive to sway public opinion would, if successful, wreck and destroy this great citadel of human freedom.

Immigration Since 1933

DURING the past two years propagandists have repeatedly offered the public ludicrous figures on recent immigration. Their purpose was to arouse the American public to the presumed danger, from such immigration, to our economic and political welfare. They claimed again and again that during the past ten years 7,000,000 Jews had entered this country! The absurdity of such a claim is at once apparent, since the total Jewish population of this country is only 4,771,000. The Jewish population of the entire North American continent including the West Indies, is approximately 5,000,000. The total Jewish population of the world prior to the Nazi catastrophe was no more than 15,757,000.

What are the facts?

From 1890 to 1907 immigration of Jews to this country was but 12 per cent of all those who entered the land.

Between 1908 and 1924 the Jews numbered but 10 per cent of the new immigration.

Between 1925 and 1934 the Jews were but $4\frac{1}{2}$ per cent of the total.

The immigration of Jews in each of these periods had materially decreased.

The total number of immigrants from all countries, including all nationalities and all sects, was, in 1939, only 82,998; in 1940 the total immigrants numbered 70,756; in 1941 they numbered no more than 51,776; in 1942 only 28,781 had entered. Since Hitler came to power the *total* refugees of all faiths immigrating to this country have numbered but 250,000.

The total annual immigration permitted from quota countries alone under the Act of Congress is 153,774.

While the total immigration of all nationalities and sects in 1942 was 28,781, the immigration from Canada was over

10,000 and from Latin America some 5,000. The total number of immigrants from all European countries both free and occupied was 11,153.

So another anti-Semitic fiction is exploded. What a pity that the public cannot be saved from such deceit and fraud!

If there is any ground for complaint, it is that in this greatest crisis in centuries America has failed in her historic hospitality to the peoples of persecuted nations.

In 1942 we permitted only 11,153 immigrants from free and occupied European countries to enter this country. In not a single year of the past four years have the quotas of permitted immigration been utilized.

If ever there were need for a haven of refuge for persecuted humanity, it was during these four years. Thousands were at the emigration ports pleading to be saved, but the sacred message which America had carved upon the Statue of Liberty in New York Harbor, a sonnet written by the Jewish poetess, Emma Lazarus, was blacked out:

> Give me your tired, your poor,
> Your huddled masses yearning to breathe free,
> The wretched refuse of your teeming shore.
> Send these, the homeless, tempest-tost to me,
> I lift my lamp beside the golden door!

Yet America has been greatly enriched by the refugees who escaped from Nazi persecution; not by property or gold, but by a value too great to be weighed by standards of wealth. The intellectual aristocrats of the world, both Christian and Jewish, are now in America and have been, or are now in the process of becoming, citizens of this country.

The list is long and honorable: Fritz Haber, Albert Einstein, Thomas Mann, Sigrid Undset, Maurice Maeterlinck, James Franck, Victor Franz Hess, Otto Loewi, Otto Meyerhoff—all Nobel prize winners; also Enrico Fermi, great Italian physicist. Kurt Goldstein, who, after the first World War, directed the German hospital for brain injuries, is now at Tufts College in Massachusetts, where his great talents will aid American injured. The famous physicians,

Siegfried Thannhauser, Otto H. Warburg and Robert Mayer, are on the faculty of the University of Minnesota. Max Bergmann is now a member of the Rockefeller Institute for Medical Research. Walter Fuchs is on the staff of the Mineral Industry Experiment Station of Pennsylvania State College. Richard Goldschmidt is on the faculty of the University of California. Max Rheinstein, formerly of the University of Berlin, is on the faculty of the University of Chicago. Kasimir Farjans, formerly of the University of Munich, is on the faculty of the University of Michigan. D. C. Ernst Berl is research professor at Carnegie Institute of Technology. Dr. Bela Schick, who discovered the famous Schick Diphtheria Test, is at Mount Sinai Hospital in New York. Rudolph Schindler, the inventor of the gastroscope, is continuing his great work here.

The New School for Social Research and its University in Exile, located in New York, has the following refugees, Christian and Jewish, upon its faculty: Max Ascoli, Marcel Barzin, Hans Staudinger, Gerhard Colm, Julius Hirsch, Richard Schueller, Max Wertheimer, Henri Gregoire, André Spira, Fernando de los Rios, and Adolph Lowe.

Hans Kelsen is on the faculty at Harvard. Arthur Nussbaum is on the faculty at Columbia. Boris Nikolayevsky and Hans von Hentig are serving the government in Washington. Erwin Panowsky is on the faculty at Princeton. Paul Tillich is on the faculty of the Union Theological Seminary in New York. Karl August Wittfogel is on the faculty at Columbia.

Among the great painters, Christian and Jewish, we have George Grosz, Lionel Feininger, Eugen Spiro, Fernand Leger, Marc Chagall, Amadee Ozenfant, André Masson, Yves Tanguy; the sculptor Jacques Lipschitz, and many other renowned artists.

Among the world-renowned writers we have these refugees, Christian and Jewish: André Maurois, Jules Romains, Antoine de St. Exupéry, Henri Bernstein, Julien Green, Franz Werfel, Lion Feuchtwanger, Eric Remarque, Bert Brecht, Ferdinand Bruckner, Bruno Frank, Leonhard Frank, and Emil Ludwig.

Among symphonic and operatic conductors, Christian and Jewish, we have Arturo Toscanini, Bruno Walter, Otto Klemperer, Fritz Stiedry, and Fritz Busch; and among the composers Igor Stravinsky, Darius Milhaud, Paul Hindemuth, Arnold Schönberg, Erich Wolfgang Korngold, Bela Bartok and Jaromir Weinberger. Outstanding artists in music, drama and other fields have enriched the cultural, spiritual and artistic life of America.

Hereafter European students will come to the universities of America to sit at the feet of scholars whom Nazi-Fascist intolerance forced to seek a home where thought and expression were not regimented, and where free intellects could enjoy the freedom they need to create in the arts and the sciences.*

Refugees who were industrialists in Europe have founded factories, which, although comparatively small in size, yet helped to employ American labor in the pre-Pearl Harbor period and, since the war, to further the victory effort. They have contributed creative wealth to our land.

By not filling its entire immigration quotas during the past four years America missed a great opportunity. We would have been greatly enriched and, at the same time, we could have kept faith with our historic role exemplified by that Statue of Liberty which lifts her lamp "beside the golden door" for the persecuted and the oppressed.

[1] For a more complete list of emigrees, I would refer to the *American Mercury*, Vol. LVII, No. 235, and "A Survey of Alien Specialized Personnel," issued by the National Refugee Service, Inc.

The Jew's Contribution to Civilization

I FIND this subject, the Jew's contribution to civilization, the most difficult of all to treat, not for want of material, for that is abundant, but because I fear that my purpose may be misunderstood.

Some may say: The Jew is bragging again about his great men and their accomplishments. Others may say: These men are great, and their achievements are great, but not because they happen to be Jews. To the last expression I cheerfully give my approval, because these men are great world figures and they accomplished great things in spite of the handicap that they were Jews.

The number of Jews who have made notable contributions to civilization is unusually large, but I believe that there is a logical reason for that situation. The Jews of European countries were severely restricted as to vocations. Military careers were closed to them, as, of course, were careers in the Church. Civil service opportunities in government were rarely afforded; political and diplomatic vocations were beyond hope; university posts were barred, except to those who would be baptized. Consequently, the young Jew with ambition and intellectual promise was sorely tried to find avenues through which he might express his talents. Any young man with mentality equal to that of the Jew could enter the military, or embark upon a government career, or seek a position in the Church, but the young Jew had to carve out his own career, and he had to make it "the hard way." He could receive recognition only if he succeeded in something unusual, or in some venture which had not been tried before. So well was this condition appreciated that Jewish fathers always admonished their young that they must be of pure gold "in order to be taken for silver."

Such severe pressure—and no inherently superior mentality or ingenuity, in my opinion,—accounts for the high percentage of the great among men of Jewish parentage or descent.

The Nobel prizes are awarded each year to the world's most distinguished benefactors. The officials who award these coveted distinctions are all non-Jews. Up to 1940 the record shows that the Jews were only three quarters of one per cent of the population of the Western world; they are now far less. But the Jews who have received the Nobel prize number more than one tenth of all the Nobel prize recipients, or to be exact, 10.145 per cent. The total number of Nobel prize winners is 207 and 21 are Jews.

Before the Nazi regime the German Jew constituted less than 1 per cent of the German population. But one third of the 43 Nobel prizes awarded to Germans went to German Jews. All living Nobel laureates became forced exiles from Germany when the Nazi party came into power.

The Jewish Nobel prize winners, from all countries, are Tobias Michael Carel Asser for peace work, Adolph von Baeyer for chemistry, Robert Barany for medicine, Niels Bohr for physics, Henri Bergson for literature, Paul Ehrlich for medicine, Albert Einstein for physics, James Franck for physics, Alfred H. Fried for peace work, Paul Heyse for literature, Fritz Haber for chemistry, Gustav Hertz for physics, Gabriel Lippman for physics, Karl Landsteiner for medicine, Otto Loewi for medicine, Otto Meyerhoff for medicine, Albert Michelson for physics, Otto Wallach for chemistry, Otto H. Warburg for medicine, Richard Willstater for chemistry, and Elie Metchnikoff for medicine. Were we to add men of remote Jewish ancestry, the list would be materially increased.

Mankind is, as a general rule, lacking in gratitude. We daily employ the great discoveries achieved after years of bitter toil, but we give little or no thought to our benefactors. We daily accept conveniences, such as electric power, radio waves, air travel, automobiles, steam-propelled engines, and medical remedies without thought of the discoverers or inventors. We enjoy these benefactions every hour of the day as though they had been known and used for ages. Only when we are suddenly deprived of them do we realize how important they have become in our lives.

Men of every enlightened nation and sect have contributed to the discoveries and inventions now in daily use. It is my purpose to treat of only those discoveries and inventions to the credit of men of the Jewish fold. I do so because the public knows so little of the contributions which the Jew has made in these important fields. With rare exception, works on this subject fail to mention the religious group to which the inventor or discoverer belonged. In fact, it frequently happens that the inventor, though a German Jew, is classified merely as a German.

The telephone is a wonderfully useful device; today we can hardly see how we could ever get along without it. The gramophone and the radio, which have added so much to entertainment as well as to education, are also of inestimable value, thanks to Emile Berliner, a German Jewish immigrant, who arrived penniless at Ellis Island in 1870. Washing bottles for a living, he attended night classes at the Cooper Union Institute in New York. Later he became a dry goods clerk and a salesman for a clothing concern. He studied physics and electrodynamics under Dr. Constantine Fahlburg of New York City. His own bedroom was his workshop. The landlady was kind enough to remove her wash from the lines so he could demonstrate his invention. He used a small drum, a sewing needle and a guitar string to demonstrate that sound could be transported by this device. The microphone and the transmitter owe their origin to this discovery, and that transmitter was of basic importance to the telephone. The original Berliner "microphone" transmitter, loaned by the American Bell Telephone Company, is now in the Smithsonian Institution in Washington. It is said that politicians who had come to Washington for the Rutherford B. Hayes inauguration attended a demonstration of Emile Berliner's invention in the back yard of a Washington rooming house. I have taken the following from the Universal Jewish Encyclopedia:[1]

> Berliner invented the loose contact telephone transmitter, or microphone, and patented it in 1877 as a telephone receiver, thus making the Bell telephone a practical instrument. The Bell Telephone Company soon bought the right to the Berliner transmitter, and he was engaged for three years as chief instrument inspector. The original Berliner microphone, precursor of the modern radio microphone, now occupies a place of honor in the Smithsonian Institution in Washington. He continued making improvements in telephony, and was the first to use an induction coil in connection with transmitters. In 1887 he invented the gramophone or disc phonograph, later popularly known as the Victor Talking Machine. It utilized a groove of even depth and varying direction, a flat disc instead of a cylinder, and a record which not only vibrates but also propels the reproducing stylus. For this invention he was awarded the John Scott Medal and the Elliot Cresson Gold Medal by the Franklin Institute of Philadelphia, which also awarded him the Franklin Medal in 1929 for his work in perfecting the microphone. Likewise Berliner invented and perfected the present method of duplicating disc records, and in 1925 invented the acoustic tile for securing better acoustics in auditoriums.

Wireless telegraphy was so dramatic that it stunned the imagination of men everywhere. The world had become familiar with the telegraph by which sound was made to travel along a wire. But to telegraph without wire connections, to make sound travel *through the air* from one instrument to another located at a great distance, was more than intriguing. To send messages from one ship to another at a distance was astonishing. Marconi is credited with the invention of wireless telegraphy and with radio transmission. It was, however, the experimentation of Heinrich Hertz, who verified that electromagnetic waves could be transmitted through space which made possible

[1] Vol. 2, p. 220.

Marconi's invention. All radio engineers are familiar with what are called the "Hertzian waves."

Every great and useful invention has, so to speak, an ancestor. The fundamental discovery is often lost sight of when incorporated in the finished product.

The cosmic rays, which play such an important part in the power of the world, the measurement of the velocity of light, by which planetary distance can be determined, and many other erstwhile secrets, were made available to man by the invention of the interferometer by Albert E. Michelson, the first American Nobel prize laureate. It is claimed that Einstein's theory of relativity helped to prove certain phases of Michelson's invention.

Few inventions exceed the automobile in usefulness. The inventor of the horseless carriage must have had an extraordinary imagination. In 1864 Siegfried Marcus built the first automobile; in 1875 he made an improved product, the first benzene-driven vehicle to run. This motorcar is in the possession of the Vienna Automobile Club. Its patents were registered in Germany in 1882, four years before any automobile was built in that country. The City Council of Mecklenburg affixed a tablet to the birthplace of the inventor.

It is interesting to note that in 1854, prior even to this invention, an electrically driven automobile was constructed and driven through the streets of Darmstadt by M. Davidsohn. More important, in 1854, shortly before petroleum was first refined and utilized in America, Abraham Schriner, a Galician Jew, discovered a similar refining process, but he died in poverty before his efforts were commercialized.

The only Jew connected with the invention of the steam locomotive in the pioneer days was Joseph Simon of Lancaster, Pennsylvania.[2] In a joint workshop with his partner, William Henry, he made the first steamboat experiment. However, it was not successful. But under their tutelage

[2] Jews were settled in Lancaster, Pennsylvania, as early as 1730 before the town and county were organized and Joseph Simon was among the first arrivals. Wiernecke, *History of the Jews in the United States*, p. 76.

Robert Fulton developed his ingenious idea for the construction of the first successful steamboat in 1807.

Aviation is a modern science. Yet, flying must have been one of the earliest dreams of man. Angels depicted in human form always had wings and the cherubim in the churches were always pictured with wings. Through wonderful ingenuity the dreams of early man have come true. We now fly, and distance has been annihilated. In this science, too, the Jew made an important contribution.

In 1890 David Schwarz, a German Jew, devised a rigid airship with a gas container made of metal. He offered his invention to the Austrian War Ministry, which could not accept it because of its lack of funds. In 1892 Schwarz went to Russia and constructed an airship in St. Petersburg. Defects in the materials used made it only partly successful. But thereafter, the German government invited him to make a trial flight. He had now arrived at the realization of his great ambition. He was confident that with the German government's assistance, proper materials could be procured, and his dream would be realized. Upon receiving the official telegram of invitation, his joy affected him so that he collapsed and expired on the street.

However, his years of effort were not in vain. His widow continued his work, and under her direction a new airship was constructed. At the trial of this ship Count Zeppelin was present, and seeing the merits of the invention he purchased the patents from the widow. The "Zeppelin" soon became world renowned. By coincidence, the chief construction engineer of the Zeppelin Works was also a Jew, Karl Arnstein, who in 1924 piloted the first Zeppelin across the ocean to America.

To the development of the airplane, Emile Berliner made another contribution, for he invented a stabilizing device. Theodore von Karman is acknowledged as one of the pioneers in the mathematics of aviation. Henry Deutsch de la Menothe founded the Aero-Technical Institute of St. Cyr.

The name of Philipp Reis, a German Jew, though unknown to the general public, will always be respected by physicists. He was very poor, but at the early age of twenty he copied the general structure of the ear and made an electrified eardrum. In 1864 he demonstrated his invention before a conference of physicists in Giessen. The telephone was the child of this invention. He had neither the means nor the ingenuity to commercialize his device. Alexander Graham Bell and Edison improved upon it and made it of commercial value. The standard works of reference record Reis as the inventor of the telephone. In 1878 a monument was erected to his memory by German physicists at Friederichsdorf, Germany, inscribed with the epitaph, *Der Erfinder des Telephones* "Inventor of the Telephone."[3]

There is, perhaps, no science which lends itself less to profit and acquisition than astronomy. Yet Jews have always been votaries of this interesting study. Before the sixteenth century there were 252 Jewish astronomers in Europe.[4] Abraham Zacuto, an astronomer of great fame, contributed to Columbus' knowledge on the epic voyage, for the vessels of Columbus' little fleet were equipped with Zacuto's astronomical tables and instruments. When Jews were expelled from Spain in 1492, Zacuto went to Portugal and was there appointed astronomer royal and historiographer. When the Jewish persecutions reached Portugal, in 1497, he took flight to North Africa. There he prepared the "Astronomical Tables" and also wrote *Sepher Juhasin,* a classic in Jewish literature.

Joseph Vecinho, a pupil of Zacuto, translated the "Astronomical Tables" into Latin and Spanish; they were published by a Jewish printer, Samuel d'Ortas, and were twice reprinted in Italy. Vecinho was also physician-in-ordinary to John II of Portugal. He was forced to baptism under the name Diego Mendes Vecinho and became famous for his scientific work at the Portuguese court. However, he

[3] Prof. Philip Lenard (Nobel laureate and a non-Jew) states that the telephone was invented by a Frankfort teacher of physics, Philipp Reis, in 1860.

[4] Cecil Roth, *The Jewish Contribution to Civilisation*, Macmillan & Company, Ltd., London, 1938, p. 189.

remained a Jew in faith, and his descendants in the next century were professing Jews in Italy.

The famous Alfonsine Tables, which were basic to astronomy, were the works of Judah ben Moses Cohen and Isaacs ben Sid of Toledo, Spain. These tables were re-published many times and were studied by both Kepler and Galileo. Another astronomical table was made by Joseph ibn Wakkar of Toledo, Spain; another by Emanuel ben Jacob, also known as Bonfils de Tarascon, which was translated from Hebrew into Latin, was used by scholars during the Renaissance.

One of the outstanding personages in this field of science was Sir William Herschel, who was of Jewish parentage. It was he who discovered the planet Uranus, two billion miles away. Benjamin Franklin said of his achievements, "I hardly know which to admire most, the wonderful discoveries made by Herschel, or the indefatigable ingenuity by which he was able to make them."

Benjamin Gompertz won distinction for his tables showing phases of the fixed stars. In the middle of the nineteenth century the asteroids between Mars and Jupiter were discovered by Herman Goldschmidt. The two-part telescope in common use was the work of Maurice Loewy. The Eclipse Expedition to Siam in 1875 was headed by the scientist Sir Arthur Schuster. The use of photography in astronomy was first introduced by Max Wolf of Heidelberg. Among other pre-eminent astronomers was Wilhelm Beer, brother of the composer Meyerbeer.

In the majestic field of philosophy the Jew has furnished an outstanding intellect in every age.

Philo, the Grecian Jew, was the most important figure after Biblical times. His philosophy was of great help to the structure of patristic Christianity.

Moses Maimonides, who was the greatest Jewish philosopher of the Middle Ages, wrote *Guide for the Perplexed* in 1190 and influenced generations with his defense of Judaism. Isaac Israeli wrote *On the Elements* and *On*

154

Definitions, which were both founded on Aristotle, and were later used by medieval Christian students.

Baruch Spinoza was the greatest of all Jewish philosophers for the world at large. Every student of philosophy is acquainted with his *Ethics.* His influence has been apparent since post-Kantian speculation and down to modern times.

Albert Einstein, formerly of Germany, now of America, is so towering an intellect in our own century that students of every land where the intellect is still free acclaim him a master mind. In 1922 he was awarded the Nobel prize. He is best known, of course, as the "father" of the theory of relativity.

Cecil Roth says of modern Jewish philosophers:[5]

> Bergson, it has been said, has rediscovered time, and it is as the rediscoverer of time that he will probably be remembered. And so Einstein, among his many fruitful ideas, rediscovered space, and Freud rediscovered dreams. Each of these men started, as it were, anew. They looked on all problems with new eyes. They brought to the tired discussions of centuries the freshness of approach of a child and their results, too, are elementary, elementary in the profound sense that they reach deep, offering a foundation for a whole world view. These Jews, and innumerable lesser ones with them, are among the master builders of the modern intellectual world, and it is not for us to "claim" or "reject" them as "Jewish" or "unJewish"; they are men. If the fruitful doctrines of creative evolution and dialectical materialism are due to Jews; if the Jew, Herman Cohen, founded a new and fruitful school of Kantian criticism, or if the Jew Meyerson indicated new paths in the interpretation of science; or if the Jew Durkheim stimulated new ideas in the study of human society, or the Jew Wurms established the International Sociological Institute, or the Jew Husserl initiated a new movement in logic and metaphysics, these are contributions freely given to civilization as a whole, and, in civilized times, as freely received.

[5] *The Jewish Contribution To Civilisation,* Macmillan & Company, Ltd., London, 1938, p. 165.

Medicine and hygiene were favorite studies of Jews from their early days. Superstition in Europe made the advance of these sciences most difficult. To lighten the burden of mankind from pain and suffering was considered a sacrilege by less enlightened church authorities. Yet the services of Jewish physicians were employed by many lay rulers and also by high ecclesiastics. It would lengthen this treatise unduly to give a history of the Jewish contribution to medicine. The subject is so fascinating that we forego it with deep regret.[6] My purpose is to direct attention to a few Jews whose discoveries are connected with modern medicine.

Ferdinand Cohn, pioneer in bacteriology, made possible the discovery of his pupil, Robert Koch, regarding the tubercle bacillus. The discoveries of Pasteur were also founded on the work of Cohn.

Dr. Lydia Rabinowitsch-Kempner, bacteriologist, was assistant professor of bacteriology at Women's Medical College, Philadelphia. In 1898 she was attached to the Robert Koch Institute, Berlin, served there as Koch's associate in many of his important researches, and made discoveries of her own concerning pasteurized and raw milk and the parasitic protozoa and trypanosoma. Upon her return to Germany after a series of lectures at the University of Pennsylvania in 1896, she founded the Institute of Bacteriology. Subsequently she collaborated with Professor Orth in the Pathological Institute of Berlin University. She was the first woman to receive the rank of professor in Prussia (1912).

Elie Metchnikoff was outstanding in his work on infectious diseases and was the author of the theory of phagocytosis.

Working under Pasteur, Waldemar Haffkine discovered the method of inoculation against cholera and thereby reduced the mortality from this malady over eighty per cent.

[6] I recommend Cecil Roth's book, *The Jewish Contribution To Civilization*, and the list of authorities cited by him for more detailed information.

In recognition of his work, the Bacteriological Laboratory at Bombay was renamed the Haffkine Institute.

Alex Besredka, working at the Pasteur Institute, invented a serum against typhus.

Paul Ehrlich gave the world salvarsan, also known as 606, the cure for syphilis. Thousands upon thousands of children, as well as adults, have been saved (by Ehrlich's discovery) from the ravages of this dread disease.

August von Wassermann developed the Wassermann test, which was employed in the diagnosis of syphilitic disease. In 1927 Reuben L. Kahn found a new method for diagnosis, which has since replaced the Wassermann test.

Albert Neisser discovered the organism of gonorrhea. Jacob Henle, said to be the greatest microscopic anatomist gave the world the result of his studies of the cellular structure of the skin and of the tissue lining of the intestines.

Julius Cohnheim, professor at the University of Kiel, discovered that inflammation is the passage of white blood cells through the walls of the blood vessels, the same being the origin of pus. Many claim that his discovery revolutionized pathology.

Moritz Schiff's work on the nervous system and glands was an outstanding achievement. Benedikt Stilling was a pioneer in certain difficult operations—notably abdominal operations—and was an authority on the nervous system. Bernard Zondek is known for his discovery of the rabbit test for pregnancy.

Simon Flexner of the Rockefeller Institute developed the serum against meningitis. Henry S. Gimbel of Johns Hopkins Hospital evolved the treatment for inflammation of the brain.

Bela Schick discovered a test for immunity to diphtheria, which is now known as the Schick test.

Herman Nahin invented the "Nahin knot" used in tying internal arteries.

Alfred Einhorn introduced novocain. Julius Ritter discovered the whooping cough bacillus. Joseph Goldberger of the United States Public Health Service discovered the importance of Vitamins B and G in pellagra.

There is no science which is of greater importance in our time than chemistry. The number of Jews who have engaged in research work in this field is impressive. We must content ourselves with the mention of a few outstanding figures.

Adolf Frank made a study of the consumption of potash by plant life. The consequence was the creation of the great potash industry with its by-products of bromide, ammonia and the various chlorides.

Frank, and his co-worker, Nicodem Caro, perfected a method of obtaining nitrogen from the air, and Fritz Haber continued these researches until he discovered a method for producing ammonia from nitrogen in the air, thus making available an unlimited supply of fertilizer for the soil. These particular discoveries were, unfortunately, largely responsible for Germany's staying power in the first World War. Haber was granted the Nobel prize in 1919 for his accomplishment, but he became an exile from Germany when the Nazis came to power.

Victor Meyer, whose apparatus for the determination of vapor densities is now used, discovered in impure benzene the sulphur compound thiophene. His discoveries, which made practical the development of various industrial chemicals, were of great importance.

Heinrich Caro discovered aniline red, induline and eosin, and was the co-discoverer of phosgene dyestuffs. He revolutionized the industry, and these discoveries incidentally gave great aid to the field of medicine.

Richard Willstater was another chemist who was responsible for the dominating position of Germany in the dye industry. Since the Nazi regime, this industry has found new homes in other lands, and America has profited considerably from the Jewish immigrants who were Germany's chemists. Henceforth we shall be independent of Germany for our dyes.

Adolph von Baeyer was a half Jew. He discovered eosin, used in medicine, and made other medical discoveries which have been a blessing to mankind.

Ludwig Mond revolutionized the chemical industry in

England. He is credited with the process for the recovery of ammonia soda, and also with the process for extracting nickel from its ores.

Jacques Loeb was a pioneer in the Rockefeller Institute and rendered outstanding service in colloid science, and also in physiological research.

Herbert Freundlich, considered the foremost authority on colloids, became an exile from Germany, and joined the faculty of the University of London. Kasimir Farjans, director of the Physical Chemical Institute at Munich before the Hitler regime, is one of the best known physical chemists. Friederich Adolph Paneth was, prior to the Nazi regime, a foremost figure at the University of Berlin where he did outstanding work on radioactivity.

In literature, the Jew has made no mean contribution. The Old Testament, as well as the New Testament, was written by Jews. In modern times, one of the outstanding writers was Isaac D'Israeli, who, in the very infancy of modern English literature, became a noted author. His son, Benjamin D'Israeli, later as Lord Beaconsfield, one of Queen Victoria's Prime Ministers, was also an author of ability, and his literary efforts are enjoyed to this day.

Francis Cohen, who later adopted his wife's name, Palgrave—and her religion—was an important figure in English literature, and was the founder of a dynasty of famous men.

Bret Harte, the American author, was the grandson of Bernard Hart, a London Jew who migrated to America.

Israel Zangwill was a genius in English letters. Leonard Merrick was a short story writer of first rank.

Among the American authors, those who have enriched our literature are Fannie Hurst, Bret Harte, Ludwig Lewisohn, Edna Ferber, Waldo Frank, John Cournos, George Jean Nathan, Robert Nathan, Octavus Roy Cohen, Ben Hecht, Lillian Hellman, Louis Untermeyer and Konrad Bercovici.

Michel de Montaigne, the great French essayist, was the son of a Jewish mother whose name was Antoinette de

Louppes or Lopez. She belonged to a Jewish Spanish or Portuguese family which had suffered under the Inquisition. Anatole France, whose writings bear similarity to Montaigne's, was also a descendant of Jewish stock.[7]

One song known and beloved throughout the English-speaking world is "Home, Sweet Home," written by John Howard Payne, who was the son of Sarah Isaacs, and the immediate descendant of a baptized Jew.

Moses Mendelssohn was the author of "Phaedon" and was known as the "German Socrates." His literary efforts, as well as his philosophy, made a deep impression upon Germany in his time.

Heinrich Heine, the great romantic poet, composed many of the songs which the Germans love to sing, among them "The Lorelei." The Nazis sing his songs but are forbidden to mention Heine's name as their author.

Ludwig Börne occupies a most important part in the history of German literature. Berthold Auerbach was the author of many famous works of fiction in German. Paul Heyse, a Nobel prize winner for literature in 1910, was a half Jew.

Among other great German Jewish littérateurs are Jacob Wassermann, Franz Kafka, Stefan Zweig, Arnold Zweig, Lion Feuchtwanger, Emil Ludwig, Ernst Toller, Alfred Neumann, Franz Werfel, Max Brod, Ernst Lissauer, Ludwig Fulda, Walter Heymann, and Arthur Schnitzler.

Max Nordau was a great French author. His greatest work was *Regeneration*. D'Ennery was co-author of the famous drama, *The Two Orphans*.

Henri Bernstein was a leading Parisian dramatist. Henri de Rothschild wrote under the pen name of André Pascal.

Marcel Proust, the French novelist, author of the great *Remembrance of Things Past,* was the son of a Jewish mother. Georg Brandes of the University of Copenhagen was a prominent literary critic; his brother Eduard Brandes was a distinguished playwright. Henrik Hertz is a famous Danish poet.

[7] Cecil Roth, *The Jewish Contribution to Civilisation*, p. 99.

Sweden produced several Jewish littérateurs of fame, among them Ludwig Oscar Josephson, Sophie Elkan and Oskar Ivar Levertin.

Among the modern Dutch authors are Herman Heijermans, the novelist, and Isaak Costa, the poet.

Rumania's greatest poet is Ronetti Roman, a Jew, who is the author of *New Lamps for Old*.

Italy, with a population of only 48,000 Jews, produced many outstanding Jewish men of letters, among them Salamone Fiorentino, Giuseppe Revere and Guido da Verona.

To music and art the Jews have contributed so much that it would require an entire volume to give an adequate account of their contributions. I must content myself with the mention of a few distinguished artists and musicians.

Rosa Bonheur, the painter, was the first woman to receive the Grand Cross of the Legion of Honour (1894).

Jacques Offenbach's compositions numbered more than one hundred; one of the best known was "The Tales of Hoffman." He was the son of a synagogue cantor at Cologne.

Giacomo Meyerbeer was a great composer of operas. Felix Mendelssohn may be said to be present at weddings all over the world because of his beloved "Wedding March."

Ignaz Mocheles was renowned in pianoforte, and his brother Joachim is in the foremost rank of violin artists.

Elie Halévy is among the first rank in French music, and his opera "La Juive" is performed during every opera season.

Walter Damrosch, the venerable American conductor and composer, rendered invaluable service to American music.

Among the present well-known musical artists, the following are outstanding: in violin, Federico Consolo, Joseph Joachim, Ferdinand David, Mischa Elman, Jascha Heifetz, Fritz Kreisler, Efrem Zimbalist, Leopold Auer, Toscha Seidel, Yehudi Menuhin, Joseph Szigeti, Bronislau Hubermann and Adolph Pollitzer; in piano, Isidor Achron, Anton Rubinstein, Nicholas Rubinstein, Myra Hess, Ossip Gabrilowitch, Moritz Moszkowski, Moriz Rosenthal, Harold

Samuel, Joseph L. Lkevinne, Vladimir Horowitz, Solomon, Mark Hambourg, Artur Schnabel, and Artur Rubinstein.

Two foremost figures of the stage were Rachel, "the Queen of Tragedy," a Jewess, and Sarah Bernhardt, a half Jewess. Among the great living Jewish actresses are Alla Nazimova and Elisabeth Bergner.

Outstanding among the actors of the world are: upon the English stage, Isaac Isaacs; in Holland, Louis Bouwmeester; in Austria, Ludwig Barnay; in Germany, von Sonnenthal, Emanuel Reicher, Rudolf Schildkraut, Fritz Kortner and Max Pallenberg; in the United States, Paul Muni, David Warfield, Helena Modjeska, Joseph Schildkraut, and Edward G. Robinson.

In operatic roles, those outstanding are Giuditta Pasta, Pauline Lucca, Rosa Raisa, Lilli Lehmann, Julius Lieban, Joseph Schwarz, Alexander Kipnis, Hermann Jadlowker and Richard Tauber.

Among conductors of orchestras and operas may be mentioned Walter Damrosch, Hermann Levi, Bruno Walter, Otto Klemperer, Ossip Gabrilowitch, Ferdinand Hiller, Leo Blech, Pierre Monteux and Alfred Hertz.[8]

The charges that the Jew is a middleman, and that he is a materialist, are disproven by the large number of Jews engaged in altruistic vocations and professions. It is difficult to understand how a materialist could take so prominent a part in the arts and the sciences. The world of art and science is surely for visionaries and dreamers, and not for the materialists.

Mr. Joseph Jacobs makes the statement that "the claim of the Jews to a 'place in the sun' in modern life must be based upon their capacity for contributing valuable elements to that life."[9] To this end I have endeavored to show, although quite sketchily, some of the contributions which the Jews have made in modern times. Many Christian min-

[8] See Appendix for a roll call of Jews pre-eminent in other fields of science and art.

[9] Joseph Jacobs, *Jewish Contributions to Civilization*, the Jewish Publication Society of America, 1919, p. 44.

isters have written favorably on the debt which Christianity owes the Jews. But contributions made in the Biblical epoch are not enough. Every cultural group has a continuous duty toward mankind. No cultural group may rest entirely upon the laurels it won in the past.

The eternal query to each cultural group must be: What contribution are you making to help establish the world as a happier, better, cleaner, healthier and more peaceful abode for humankind?

The names selected as contributors to civilization are from *The Jewish Contribution to Civilization*, by Cecil Roth, the Jewish Encyclopedia, and *Ezekiel Through Einstein* by Francis J. Oppenheimer.

Credits and Debits in Behavior

WHEN we start to judge the merits and demerits of any group, other than our own, it is natural, because of egotism and group loyalty, to magnify the demerits and to minimize, or ignore, the merits.

But to appraise fairly, we must have a standard of judgment. We may take the best of our own group as the standard and say that all groups that do not measure up to that standard fall below the 100 per cent mark. That is clearly not fair, for we have not made a judicious appraisal of the whole, but have selected the best, or the outstanding figures of our group. None who pride themselves on their unbiased minds will subscribe to such techniques. Fair men and women do not hesitate to admit the demerits of their own group. They can conclude that not all Methodists are true Christians, that not all masters in the slave era were kind and considerate, that not all industrialists have been fair and reasonable to their employees, if such conclusions are warranted.

If we were to judge a group of nationals from the Balkans, we might point out that they are very conspicuous in their dress and demonstrative in their behavior; that they are clannish and, where foregathered, likely to be boisterous; that they are foreigners and have made no contribution to the establishment of the government whose blessings they now enjoy. Such an indictment is all that is necessary to incite group hatred. For we have said nothing about their merits.

It is, therefore, hazardous to appraise the merits or the faults of any group. The admonition, "Judge not, that ye be not judged" is indeed pertinent.

But the mass mind constantly passes judgment on the Jews *as a group*. At one time a particular criticism is invoked, at another time an entirely different criticism is pronounced, although the second stricture may negate the first.

A taxpayer may have his income tax return scrutinized and examined by an official of the Treasury Department, who happens to be a Jew. The examiner is thorough and proficient. The taxpayer is annoyed and peeved by the investigation and relieves his pent-up aggravation by the accusation that the official is "a Jew." The taxpayer then criticizes the Treasury Department on the ground that it has too many Jews in its service. (As a matter of fact, the percentage of government employees who are Jews is less than the ratio of Jew to non-Jew in this country.) The merit and ability of these public servants are not the cause of complaint but only the fact that they happen to be Jews.

In the club car of a train a certain individual talks too loudly and he is conspicuous by his demeanor. Immediately other passengers will say, "That's the Jew." In another car a group, perhaps having imbibed too many highballs, become boisterous to the discomfort of all others. They are not Jews; therefore, no criticism is expressed.

Numerous other examples could be related. The subconscious dislike, or hate attitude, will come to the surface on the least provocation. Why should there be so sharp, and even violent, a reaction? Largely because of the effect of the teachings of childhood regarding the Jew, feelings which afterward condition the mind to anti-Semitic tendencies.

As observed earlier, the Jew is criticized as a capitalist and when that statement has served its purpose, he is condemned as a socialist, or as a Communist. He is calumniated as a warmonger and when that has served its purpose, he is vilified as a pacifist; this occurred in Germany during the first World War. He is criticized as a materialist and, when that charge has been overworked, he is criticized for having an undue proportion of his coreligionists engaged in the sciences and in the arts, in music, in social work, and in education, none of which vocations lend themselves to the profit motive.

The fact is that no one can and no one has, with certainty, weighed the merits against the demerits of the Jew, or of any other people *as a group*.

In general, these credits are conceded to the Jew: He is frugal; he is held in regard for his sobriety; he observes his family obligations and duties; his filial respect and affections are noteworthy; he is charitable; he is law-abiding; he has a passion for knowledge and education; he has marked sympathy for the unfortunate; he is loyal to the religious faith of his fathers; he is a fervent advocate of peace whenever peace is feasible; his ratio of criminality in heinous crimes such as murder, burglary, assault with deadly weapon, rape, etc. is very low.

His debits, charged against him by the general public, are: he is clannish; he is ostentatious; he is keen in business; he is overreaching; he is likely to push himself into places where he is not wanted; he lacks culture; he is disproportionately engaged in government employment; he is a hard competitor; he is guilty of commercial crimes.

The last criticism requires comment. The ratio of commercial crimes committed by Jews *is* somewhat in excess of the ratio of heinous crimes, but as the percentage of Jews in commerce is much greater than his percentage in the total of the general population, this charge is not justified.[1] Statistics of prisoners in the New York penal institutions from 1940-1942 show that the percentage of Jews to the total prisoner population is 2.02 per cent; whereas, the percentage of Jewish population in New York State is 17.24 per cent. Statistics available in seven states, which compose 80 per cent of the Jewish population in this country, show that the percentage of Jewish prisoners is 2.09 per cent, whereas, the percentage of population of Jews in these seven states is 7.56 per cent.

The other debits or criticisms, alluded to before, have been treated and explained in other parts of this book. But even assuming that the charges against the Jew were true, a comparison of the credits and the debits with a similar list of credits and debits for any other groups—not the *individual* best or the *individual* worst of each group— would prove the Jew not wanting in merits.

[1] The statistics are given in Appendix.

Seeing Our Shortcomings in Others

When we point to the shortcomings and derelictions of other groups it is usually a reflection of our own shortcomings and derelictions. When the pulpiteer denounces "the atheistic Jew" he knows that there are also atheistic Catholics and atheistic Protestants. He is, however, certain that his accusation against the atheistic Jew will find a receptive audience even among the atheistic Christians. But should he condemn the atheistic Christian, the same atheists would probably not listen to him.

When the business integrity of the Jew is attacked the challenge will find immediate approval, although the business integrity of the Christian is not one whit better or on a higher plane. The public pays little attention to any attack upon the integrity of businessmen at large, but should the Jewish businessman be the object of an attack it will find no more enthusiastic audience anywhere than among the non-Jewish businessmen who are derelict in their conduct. The public never considers itself *in pari delicto*.

Other Mass Hatreds

THERE have been other hatreds leveled against other religious sects. A study of anti-Semitism is incomplete without an understanding of the hatred for these other groups. In these it will become apparent that the prime basis for the hatred was either religious or theological difference, and that to justify and to effectuate that hatred, bitter accusations, scurrilous attacks and base fictions were employed, similar to those in current use against the Jew. The pattern is identical. There is only one accusation used against the Jew which is not also used in the mass hatreds of other religious minority sects. That is the charge of deicide, which has, necessarily, the special religious prejudice behind it.

Why has it always been necessary to invent base accusations against the objects of religious antagonism? One reason is the feeling that religious intolerance must be camouflaged. Another reason is the desire to maintain that those who differ from the religion and theology of the majority are unworthy, unmoral, wicked and sinful; for what other reason can explain the rejection of the faith and theology held by the majority?

If anti-Semitism were stripped of every one of its by-products and had to rely only on its basic accusation, namely the Jews' denial of the Christian faith, it could not hope to survive long in the modern world. Religious intolerance is incompatible with present enlightenment.

Since the accusations against the Jew are of the same pattern and mold as the accusations hurled against other sects we must review briefly the persecutions of several of these minority groups or sects.

The Huguenots of the sixteenth and seventeenth centuries suffered bitter persecution, chiefly because their doctrines dissented from the faith of the established Church. To arouse a mass hatred against them their opponents portrayed the Huguenots as a group possessed of devilish design, of frightful wickedness, and capable of the most traitorous behavior. The religious and theological differences alone were not enough to arouse the masses against the Huguenots. Consequently, hateful accusations were made and espoused both by the Church and by the State of that day. The Huguenots were alleged to have incited revolution, sedition and treason. They were also accused of having entered into secret conspiracy against both the Church and the State. The individual Huguenots were charged indiscriminately with lewdness, with scandalous behavior, with usury, and even with devouring little children at their nocturnal meetings!

The campaign against this religious minority resulted in bloody riots and finally terminated in the historic Massacre of St. Bartholomew's Day in 1572. The Huguenots emigrated from France. To elude their persecutors they came to the Western Hemisphere and settled, in 1555, in Brazil and, in 1562, in Florida. Those who settled in Florida were decimated in 1565 by attacks of the Spaniards. Mass emigration of these people to North America started early in the seventeenth century and continued steadily. They founded settlements in Virginia in 1610. Others came to New Amsterdam in 1623, to Delaware in 1660, to Boston in 1662. History now regards the Huguenots as largely an honest and forthright people, who made valuable contributions to their new homeland through their industry, diligence, and high character.

The Friends, or Quakers, are a religious sect which also endured the fires of persecution. The popular name of this sect, the Quakers, is an indication of the derision with which they were once regarded. The Quakers were persecuted both by the Church and by the State. They were charged with disloyalty, vagrancy, Sabbath-breaking, blasphemy, heresy, public indecency, and witchcraft. They were also criticized as sly, untrustworthy, untruthful, avaricious, and money-mad. They were specifically charged with incendiarism and with causing pestilence!

One of the early writers said of them that they followed their concern in pursuit of riches "with a step as steady as time and with an appetite as keen as death." A specific charge, and one generally believed, was that they were guilty of setting fire to the city of London and also that they were responsible for the great pestilence.

They sought refuge in America, but opposition awaited them there. Virginia ordained that the captain of a vessel was subject to a penalty of one hundred pounds for each Quaker whom he had brought into the colony. Every Quaker who entered was imprisoned without bail until some responsible person would give security that the Quaker would leave the jurisdiction of the colony. Connecticut termed the Quakers "the cursed sect."

In 1678 the legislature of Massachusetts proclaimed that "when the Quakers first arrived, they were insolent and contemptuous toward authority." They were charged with transgressing Puritan laws and some were even put to death for imaginary or for trivial causes.

In Virginia the Church of England was established under the rule of the Bishop of London. Under the law all persons were prohibited from housing, or from permitting, Quaker assemblies in or near their houses. It was prohibited to publish or to dispose of any books or pamphlets containing the tenets of the Quaker faith.

The principal Quaker settlements were in Pennsylvania, New Jersey, Delaware, and Rhode Island. Since colonial days they have generally enjoyed the esteem and respect of their fellow citizens. They have contributed unselfishly to the welfare of this country.

The Mennonites are a Protestant sect which originated in Switzerland in the sixteenth century. They were persecuted in Austria in 1529; in Russia in 1788, and in Germany in 1867. The charges against them were Communism, immorality, polygamy, and the destruction of civil and social institutions. Specific charges were made of rebellion, of sorcery, and of adultery. The refusal of a Mennonite to bear arms led to mob action, and the Mennonites left Germany, or what was then Prussia, for Russia. From Russia they migrated to the United States. The greatest influx into the United States took place between 1873 and 1880. The Mennonites also established colonies in Canada, in Mexico, and in Paraguay. After settling in this country, the Mennonites clung to the German language, and were "notably clannish." During the first World War the churches of the Mennonites in Illinois and in Oklahoma were burned and the members of the church were roughly treated. But as a general rule, the members of this sect were law-abiding, industrious, and frugal, and engaged chiefly in agricultural pursuits.

The Mormon sect, or the Church of Jesus Christ of the Latter Day Saints, was founded by Joseph Smith in 1830 in Palmyra, New York. They first settled in Missouri but were driven out of that territory in 1838. They then settled in Illinois and founded a colony at Nauvoo which was often raided and was regarded as a menace by other settlers. The Mormons were not only charged with polygamy, they were also accused of being a political group whose actions were inimical to the general welfare. In 1846 the Mormons were driven out of Illinois and, under the leadership of Brigham Young, started the long overland trek to Utah. At the time the Mormons entered there were no white settlers in the Utah Territory. Today a large majority of the citizens of Utah are Mormons. Polygamy has been renounced and abandoned, and the industrious Mormons enjoy peace and the fruits of their considerable industry and diligence.

The Anabaptists were charged with Communism and with the teaching of revolutionary doctrines, indecency, immorality and polygamy. The persecutions against this sect reached their height in 1526. From Switzerland, southern Germany and Austria many members of this group fled to America. Others migrated to Holland and northern Germany. It is claimed that the Mennonites in this country are the descendants of the Anabaptists.

The Cathari were a Catholic Christian sect which suffered severe persecution during the twelfth century. The accusations used against them were that they sought to promote Communism and conspired against the State. They were also charged with heresies and with fostering revolt against the Church.

Other minor sects like the Arnoldists, the Humiliati, and the Apostolic Brethren were accused of similar offenses and were also persecuted.

The Shaker sect was founded in 1747 in England. They settled in this country in New Lebanon, New York, in 1777. Here they were persecuted. They were charged with being English spies and were also accused of blasphemy and sedition. Mother Anne, the prophet of the group, was described as a "lewd, debauched, vile" person. The persecution, however, was not by the government but by mobs. The Shakers attempted to settle in Massachusetts and in Connecticut, but were unsuccessful. Among the various crimes of which they were accused were heresy, castrating males, naked dancing at their nightly meetings, promiscuous debauchery, and the murder of their illegitimate children. But the communal projects of the Shakers seemed to be successful and they were industrious in farming as well as in manufacturing. This sect has gradually declined, and few Shaker communities are now in existence.

The Waldenses were a large religious group founded in the Cattanian Alps in the ninth century. When they were ordered to return to the Catholic church, they refused to do so. They were then accused of many crimes and base practices, including the worship of Lucifer in the form of a black cat. They were accused of making cake meal with the blood of infants—the old ritual murder charge. They were accused of fostering revolution. They were charged with Communism, witchcraft, blasphemy, free love, and with vile offenses against morality. After the "Easter Massacre" in 1626 some Waldenses migrated to this country and settled along the Delaware River and at Staten Island. The falsity of the charges against this sect is now generally conceded.

The Puritans were a Protestant sect which suffered persecution in England under both Catholic and Protestant rulers. Under James I the persecution was particularly severe. The Puritans were charged with disturbing the public peace and with disseminating seditious libel. Because of the repressive laws, many Puritans emigrated to Holland in 1593. The group of Puritans living at Leyden emigrated to this country in 1620 and settled in Massachusetts.

In 1666 the king's commissioners investigated the Massachusetts colony and the Puritans were again condemned. They were charged with indulging in the persecution of all other religious beliefs. It was especially pointed out that the Puritans had put to death many Quakers. It was also charged that they had banished Quakers from their colony on the pain of death and had executed them for returning. The report also accused this sect of hypocrisy. English officials continuously accused the Puritans of persecuting Quakers for their religion, although England persecuted the Quakers just as harshly.

The ruling class of England charged the Puritans of the Massachusetts colony with being highly bigoted. It is a common belief that the Puritans were responsible for our Blue Laws and for the belief in witchcraft. However, they invented neither, but merely copied other European sects in these respects.

Samuel Pepys stated in his diary as of September 4, 1668, that he had attended "Bartholomew-Fair," a puppet play that night. He had enjoyed it, but remarked, "Only the business of abusing the Puritans begins to grow stale and of no use, they being the people that, at last, will be found the wisest."

Gustavus Myers said:[1] "Puritans have been represented by the critical as a gloomy, repressive and superstitious breed and as something dismally apart from their fellow humans elsewhere. Throughout English and American literature and comment the reproach "Puritanical" has recurred, and to this day we often see, as applied to literary movements of recent times, the phrase 'the revolt against Puritanism.'" He declared that there never was a distinctive "Puritanism" and that the Puritans borrowed both witchcraft and Blue Laws from England.

The Albigenses, whose cardinal belief was in dualism—a good god and an evil god—settled in the southern part of France in the eleventh century. The Church made every effort to convert the Albigenses. When those efforts failed charges were made that they practiced heresy, licentiousness, and anarchistic and socialistic doctrines. In 1207 a holy war was launched against the Albigenses. This conflict raged for twenty years. These people were prosperous in southern France where they engaged principally in agriculture. Thousands of them were killed in the persecutions and their property was confiscated. The Inquisition was employed to seek out the Albigenses and, at one time, the sect was practically exterminated. Small groups, however, still exist in parts of the Pyrenees.

The Templars, another religious sect, were founded in the twelfth century. They were a militant order whose goal was the defense of the Holy Roman Empire against the Saracens. The order became very powerful and amassed great wealth, which aroused the jealousy of bishops, and the envy of kings. In the fourteenth century, the persecution of the Templars began. They were charged with usury, revolt, immorality, unholy connection with infidels, spitting upon the cross, sodomy, roasting their illegitimate children, sexual perversions, and general lewdness. Under terrible tortures some

[1] *History of Bigotry in the United States,* Random House, Inc., New York, 1943, p. 12.

174

Templars admitted their "guilt." During the persecution of the Templars these charges were used further to inflame the passion of the people, and many of the Templars were cruelly tortured, burned and driven into exile. The last Templar was burned in 1314.

Historians of this period claim that all the charges were groundless and that the Church had never formally pronounced this sect guilty of the crimes charged against it. The property of the Templars was confiscated by the Crown.

Perhaps no religious group has ever encountered more hostility and bitterness in the United States than the Catholic church. On August 9, 1700, the province of New York enacted a law which provided that all Jesuits, priests, and other ecclesiastics ordained by the Pope must leave the province before November 1, 1700. Those who remained after that date and taught Catholic doctrines, or used its rites, or granted absolutions "shall be deemed and accounted an incendiary, a disturber of public peace and safety, and an enemy to the true Christian religion and shall be adjudged to suffer perpetual imprisonment." Other American colonies enacted similar laws.

In the early days of New York the Catholics were charged with a "Popish plot" to destroy the city of New York as well as other cities. This was, in effect, a revival of the old charge that Catholics had plotted the burning of London. They were also charged with conspiring with the French and Indians to revolt against the colonies. Gustavus Myers states[2] that merely because they were of Catholic birth men were suspected of plotting with the French and Indians. The Governor of New Jersey in 1778 declared that the Catholic priesthood had confederated with kings in the past to make an "iniquitous coalition of spiritual and temporal dominion" and to crush liberty.

Many books containing defamatory and scurrilous attacks upon Catholicism were issued. A book written by David Benedict, pastor of the Baptist Church, contained bitter assaults against both the Catholic church and its members.

[2] *History of Bigotry in the United States*, p. 98.

He particularly condemned clerical celibacy as leading to lascivious debaucheries and crimes. He charged that three million lives had been sacrificed by the persecuting papal power and that in the space of thirty or forty years, the Jesuits alone had put to death nine hundred thousand Christians who had left the Catholic church! Martha Butt Sherwood wrote a defamatory book called *The Nun*; another writer produced *Six Months in a Convent*; Maria Monk published *Awful Disclosures*. These volumes and others of similar nature were printed by the thousands. Every one of the gruesome indictments against the monasteries, nuns and priests was believed by the public, although Protestant ministers and other eminent men vouched that the stories and accusations made in these publications were fictitious libels. Committees composed of Protestants were appointed to inspect convents and returned favorable reports to the public.

Samuel F. B. Morse, who conceived the idea of the electrico-magnetic recording telegraph, was one of the most untiring crusaders against Catholicism in this country. He wrote and issued a book entitled *Foreign Conspiracies against the Liberties of the United States*. Numerous editions of this unfair book were published and had great influence against the Catholics.

On May 28, 1854, a preacher by the name of West addressed a mob at the intersection of Grand Street and East Broadway, New York City, and incited a riot. A few days later, as a result of another harangue against the vices of "Romanism," a riot occurred in Brooklyn. In Bath, Maine, on July 6, 1854, a street preacher aroused a crowd by denouncing Jesuits, Catholics and foreigners. A mob rushed to the Old South Church and literally demolished it. In Buffalo, on July 13, 1854, another preacher addressed a large street crowd on Romanism, priestcraft, and papacy. This also resulted in a riot. A similar outbreak had occurred in Lawrence, Massachusetts, on July 11, 1834. One of the most severe disturbances occurred on August 7, 1854, at St. Louis, Missouri. For forty-eight hours the city was the scene of one of the most tragic riots ever to take place in this country. A similar riot occurred on August 6, 1855, in Louisville, Kentucky. During this period Catholic churches were destroyed in Sydney, Ohio, and in Ellsworth, Maine.

It was during the height of this anti-Catholic movement that Abraham Lincoln, on August 24, 1855, denounced this movement in a letter and said at Springfield, Illinois, "How can anyone who abhors the oppression of Negroes be in favor of degrading classes of white people. . . . As a nation we began by declaring that 'all men are created equal.' We now practically read it, 'all men are created equal except Negroes.' When the Know-Nothings obtain control, it will read: 'All men are created equal except Negroes, foreigners and Catholics. . . .'" This statement by Abraham Lincoln was later misused by politicians and propagandists. It was publicized that Abraham Lincoln had said: "All men are created equal except Negroes, foreigners, and Catholics," of course taking this statement out of its context.

The agitation against Catholics and Catholicism continued. Sometimes it was more pronounced than at other times but it was never quite eradicated. In 1883 George P. Gifford of Milwaukee published his book, *Our Republic in Danger—A Clarion Charge to the Rescue.* Gifford purported to give the wicked designs of the Catholic hierarchy against the United States, and accused the Catholic hierarchy of being a separate, political and anti-Republican supergovernment. The appointment of Archbishop Satolli as apostolic delegate to this country in 1892 was the springboard for a new general attack. Foes of Catholicism claimed that he was a "Vice-Pope" or a "Sub-Pope," and declared that to permit the apostolic delegate to remain in the United States would be to create two governments in this country. At a conference at the Union Biblical Seminary at Zenia, Ohio, on November 3, 1893, the Reverend A. W. Drury declared that the goal of the Romanists was to make America a Catholic country. Others also declared that it was the intent of the Pope to rule this nation!

The pitch to which the religious and race hatred rose at this time may be best appreciated by an extract from a letter of Rev. A. W. Drury, which was printed in the *A.P.A. Magazine* in September, 1896.[3]

> . . . The Irish world constitutes a very large part of the papal army in the United States . . . The political dangers of Romanism are greatly increased by the concentration of Romanists in the large cities and in particular parts of the United States. Roman Catholic saloon keepers determine largely the nominations and elections in our cities. The Romish population furnish the kind of material with which the ward politician delights to reckon. The Old World has unloaded upon us its paupers, criminals, illiteracy and Romanism, including its Jesuits and multitudinous orders. Washington, the capital of the nation, is a Rome-dominated city. The departments swarm with Romanists. Protestants and Romanist alike are in the most oppressive ways bled for the support of Romanist institutions.
>
> . . . It is said that priests see to it that Romanist applicants are supplied with examination lists in advance; that the Romanist heads of departments, in advance of reports to their superiors of vacancies to occur, give information to the Romanist bureau; that the visits of Cardinal Gibbons to the White House are followed by the speedy appointments of Romanists as heads of departments. . . . The Roman Catholic Church is the enemy of our public-school system . . . The nine per cent of illiterates in the United States are very largely Roman Catholics.

It was in this period that the charge was made that the Catholics were responsible for the assassination of Abraham Lincoln. In commenting upon a book by two military officers containing this charge, through the columns of *The American Patriot* and like publications the American Protective Association maintained:[4] "No unbiased man, after reading this vivid yet truthful account of the Great Conspiracy, will for a moment doubt the connection of the

[3] As reproduced by Gustavus Myers in his *History of Bigotry in the United States*, p. 225.

[4] Myers, *History of Bigotry in the United States*, p. 229.

Jesuits with this hellish plot of assassination of America's greatest and most beloved President."

Other stories of various supposed plots and of secret meetings of Catholic prelates were publicized widely. Ex-priests added fuel to the fires of hatred by denouncing their erstwhile associates in the priesthood. As a result of these "exposures," riots occurred in 1893 in Keokuk, Iowa, and in Kansas City. A forgery of the encyclical of Pope Leo XIII was circulated. In this fraudulent document the Pope was alleged to have stated: "It will be the duty of the faithful to exterminate all the heretics found within the jurisdiction of the United States."

Thomas E. Watson, a member of Congress from 1891-1893, carried on a campaign of bigotry and blind prejudice unequaled in our history. He charged that the confessional was a place "in which lewd priests sow the minds of girls and married women with lascivious suggestions"; that at the confessional the priest finds out what girls and married women he can seduce; that having uncovered the trail, he would not be human if he did not take advantage of the opportunity! Watson threatened: "Not always will we tolerate the kidnapping of our children by these Romanist priests. Not always will we submit to their polluting the flower of our womanhood." He charged that the Chief Justice of the United States and the Clerk of the Supreme Court were the Pope's chief servants and that Joseph Tumulty, secretary to President Wilson, was Catholic, and that therefore the Pope had ready access to government secrets.

Few scurrilous documents have been so widely circulated as the fictitious Fourth Degree oath of the Knights of Columbus. In this alleged pledge the members were supposed to disown allegiance to any Protestant or liberal ruler, to vow eternal enmity to Protestants or Masons, and to carry on a war, secretly or openly, against all heretics, Protestants and Masons, sparing no one, without regard for age, sex, or circumstance. This forgery was finally investigated and was exposed in 1913 by a special Congressional committee. However, it continued to be circulated. Indeed, it was now cited

179

as authoritative *because* it had been printed in the *Congressional Record*. The hate-mongers conveniently ignored the fact that it had been the Congressional committee which had condemned this document as a forgery. Indeed, this same forgery was used effectively during the Alfred E. Smith presidential campaign in 1928.

The memorable riot of 1844 in Philadelphia, the result of bigotry and the propaganda of hate, was actually a pitched battle.[5] The first skirmish was fought on May third. The real battle began the afternoon of the sixth of May. The first stand was in the building occupied by the Hibernian Hose Company where a general riot developed. To oppose the anti-Catholics a party of Catholics rallied at Germantown Road. They were attacked with stones and guns. Many persons were wounded; one youth of eighteen was killed while holding the American flag. Disorder reigned throughout the night. Houses were set afire and several were demolished. An attack was made on the convent at the corner of Second and Phoenix Streets. The rumor spread that an attack would be made to set fire to St. Michael's Church, and many Catholics armed themselves and patrolled the church, determined to protect it at any cost. But armed anti-Catholics paraded the district and attacked the homes of the Catholics. In terror women and children fled to the woods for the night.

On the seventh of May, Bishop Kenrick issued a statement, posted throughout the city, which called upon the people to restore order. The placards were torn down by the zealots. In the afternoon a mob numbering from two thousand to three thousand held service for the purpose of restoring order. The military forces were under the direction of Brigadier General Hubbel. The Catholic bishop left the rectory and lived in the home of the Reverend Dr. Tyng, a Protestant clergyman. Other priests were housed in the homes of prominent Protestants. The following Sunday no services were held in Philadelphia in any Catholic church.

This battle had lasted for an entire week. Many houses

[5] This account follows *Catholicity in Philadelphia*, by Father Joseph L. J. Kirlin, published by John Jos. McVey, Philadelphia, 1909.

had been destroyed, families had been made homeless, forty lives had been sacrificed, and many more had been seriously wounded.

Quakers and many other Protestants who had tried to avert this tragedy did all in their power thereafter to heal the wounds. The "Battle of Philadelphia" was a terrifying example of what mob violence could do to a minority against whom hatred had been directed by cunning agitators.

The principal accusations charged against the Catholics in this country were that they owed allegiance to the Pope, which conflicted with their allegiance to this country; that they conspired to make this a Catholic country under the domination of the Pope; that the priests of the Church were guilty of lasciviousness; that in the monasteries priests and nuns took part in licentious practices; that the illegitimate children of the priests were killed and buried in the grounds of the monasteries; that arms and ammunition were stored in concealment, principally in basements of churches; that Jesuits, both male "and female," were scattered throughout the country in a grand plot according to a design of the Vatican; that the Knights of Columbus, a Catholic fraternal organization, required each initiate to take an oath of absolute allegiance to the Pope to which all other allegiance was subservient; that the Catholics had a disproportionate number of their faith in public offices, thus endangering the independence of the nation. These wild accusations and many others have been repeatedly answered by Catholics and also by leading Protestants. Nevertheless, the hatred engendered by these canards has not abated.

The Early Christian Persecutions

These persecutions took place during the first three centuries. They started in 64 A. D. during Nero's reign and did not end until Constantine's Edict of Milan in 313 A. D. During the first century, the persecutions under Nero and Domitian were local and were marked by personal cruelties. In the second century the persecution was aided and abetted with laws against Christianity. In the last half of the second century, in the reign of Marcus Aurelius, a systematic attempt to eradicate Christianity began. It continued through the days of Decius, Valerian and Aurelian in the third century.

In every persecution the charges were that Christians were guilty of treason, and that they were secretly conspiring to overthrow the power of Rome. They were accused of sensuousness and immorality, of offenses against the Roman gods, of meeting in secret places at night for bestial practices, of using human blood for ritualistic purposes, and of causing economic disaster.

As the Roman Empire began to totter, the Christians were charged with responsibility for the economic distress. Many sincerely believed that the Roman gods were angered because this oriental cult was allowed to worship their foreign God. The State confiscated the property of the Christians. Many were condemned to death; others were banished or fled. Through their frugality, the Christians had prospered and had accumulated wealth, and Decius gained considerable booty.

The persecution served a threefold purpose: it helped to finance the empire; it distracted the people's attention from the difficult economic conditions; and it temporarily removed the Christians as a political danger.

The persecutions under Valerian in 257 and under Diocletian in 303 were even more cruel. At the end of the third century, of the one hundred million people living under the Roman rule about twelve per cent were Christians. During the persecution, many Christians were tortured, their books were burned, the bishops were executed, and the property of the church was confiscated. Finally, the Edict of Milan was issued under Constantine in the year 313. The oppressive anti-Christian laws were repealed and the Christians were granted equal rights.

Bernard Lazare[6] points out that the Templars, Arians, Manicheans, Cathari, Albigenses, Patarians, Cagots, Gahets,

[6] In his book, *L'Antisemitisme*, p. 170.

Agotacs, Couax, Oiseliers, Capots, Trangots, Gesitans and Coliberts were all hated and all were subject, with slight variations, to the same accusations that were flung at the Jews.

All the Christian dissident groups were persecuted in their day and many of them were exterminated. These sects were, of course, heretical, which provided the basic cause of the antagonism against them. To make the antagonism effective, violent hatred had to be aroused and every vile accusation was pressed into service. Rumors were spread that the hated ones had tails, that on Holy Friday they emitted blood from their navels, and many other ludicrous libels.

An analytical study of the persecutions against minority groups has shown that they all have a common origin, that they are all born of religious intolerance, and that every one of the scurrilous accusations and libels are merely byproducts employed to arouse the hatred of the masses.

The question has been asked, since the persecution of most minority sects has ceased, why does the persecution against the Jew continue? This implies that the Jew himself may be at fault. It is evident, however, that the very inquiry is founded upon lack of information. The Templars, the Cathari, the Waldenses, the Albigenses, the Stedingers, and many of the other groups did not survive the persecutions. The hate campaigns succeeded in annihilating them. Other minority sects, such as the Huguenots, the Puritans, and the Montanists have all been absorbed and do not exist as distinct cultural groups. The Mormons became the dominant majority group of Utah, and majority strength in itself prevents militant antagonism. Perhaps if the Jews had settled in one particular state and had become a large majority group they might have had no militant opposition today.

Concerning the Catholic group and Catholicism, it cannot be truthfully said that the antagonism is a thing of the past. As a matter of fact, the antagonism against the Catholics is, in certain localities, far greater than that against the Jews. Of course, where the Catholics are the majority group, the antagonism is silenced. Whenever they are the minority group they suffer from the old prejudices. The numerical strength of the Catholics in this country, compared to that of the Jews, helps appreciably to retard aggressive antagonism.

Religious persecution shows clearly that those in power regard every faith or belief different from their own as a grim challenge to their authority. In all ages those who had power have used it to preserve that power for themselves. Any threat to that power must be crushed; that is why minority groups regarded as a threat have been persecuted so bitterly. Nearly every great reformer became a martyr; every people who struggled for liberty has been oppressed. In many instances, the oppression and persecution either from the tyrants or the masses has in itself proved the real merit of the victim. This warfare of the ages will persist until society achieves full democracy, in fact as well as in law.

Semites and Aryans

THE term "Semite" is from the proper name "Shem," the eldest son of Noah, who had three sons, Shem, Ham and Japheth. According to the Bible, the Semites are the descendants of Shem. Assuming that the Biblical account is correct, the Semites are descended from Shem, the Hamites from Ham, and the Chinese, Turks, Tartars, Hindus, Germans, Russians and other peoples from Japheth.

Whether that is scientifically accurate or not, all recognized scientists do agree that *there is no Aryan race.* "Aryan" denotes a language group and not a race. Professor Max Müller, recognized as the greatest authority on Aryanism said:[1] "Aryan is a *terminus technicus* describing one of the great language groups extending from India to Europe." Until recently it was generally conceded that the family of man was divided into five races: the Caucasian, the Ethiopian, the Malay, the Mongolian and the Indian. In recent years, pseudo-scientists created the "Aryan" race on the supposition that language identifies races. Recognized scientists, however, have thoroughly disproven the notion that language groups make racial groups. Similarly, the more modern critics of the Bible hold that there is no Semitic race, and that the nations or peoples speaking cognate languages are not distinct races.

The German pseudo-scientists invented the race theory for political convenience; it is not based upon fact. The slogan "blood and soil," which appealed so to the Germans, is regarded by all true scientists as sheer nonsense.

There is no Aryan, or German, blood and there is no Semitic, or Jewish, blood. All human blood is the same, except for medically important differences. There are four types of blood, called O, A, B and AB. Type O can be mixed

[1] See "Aryan" in the Encyclopædia Britannica, 14th ed., Vol. 2, p. 494.

successfully with the other three, but none of these three can be mixed with one another without clumping of the red corpuscles. In every race of men these four blood types may be found. The Germans have all these four types, so do the Jews. Individual Germans may have the O type, the AB type, the A type, or the B type; the same is true of Jews, Russians, Englishmen and other peoples. Transfusions of blood to the injured on far-flung battlefields have certainly demonstrated these facts to the Germans. The blood of a white man transfused to a Negro, even if so much were given that all the original blood of the Negro were replaced, would not affect his color; the reverse is also true.

The color of the skin, whether dark, light or yellow, is determined by two special chemicals, carotene and melanin. Every individual, however light or dark his skin may be, has some of each chemical in his skin; the only exception would be the albino, who lacks all coloring substance, and there are albinos of both the dark and the light types. The chemical process which produces different color of skin was evidently brought about by many centuries of climatic conditions.

Every anthropologist worthy of the name has concluded there is no Aryan race. The "blood and soil" dogma is another myth sired by Nazi arrogance.[2]

[2] *The Races of Mankind*, by Ruth Benedict and Gene Weltfish.

Differences Between Judaism and Christianity[1]

"Six Hundred and Thirteen commandments," reads an old tradition, "were communicated to Moses, three hundred and sixty-five negative precepts, corresponding to the number of solar days (in the year), and two hundred and forty-eight positive commandments, corresponding to the number of members of man's body." From time immemorial the pious Jew was expected to obey these precepts; first, because they were ordained for Israel by God, and second, for thus only could he obey the divine Torah, or teaching. Yet the earliest attempt to compile these injunctions was not made until the eighth century. One of the most widely accepted compilations was that of Maimonides, who flourished in the twelfth century. He searched the Bible for all the six hundred and thirteen laws and grouped them into their two categories, the negative and the positive. These rubrics include moral and ritual proscriptions as well as purely religious dicta, and range from commands about God and prayer to those of holy day and dietary law observances. All of life's activities are thus covered, for the Jewish mode of life is based upon the Torah. God's continuous revelation of His will and its proscriptions were codified into law. Yet Judaism is more than a legal system; it is also a religio-ethical doctrine whereby the Jew lives. The general moral laws are obligatory upon all mankind; they were also adopted by the early Christians. The Jewish observances are a specific responsibility of the Jews.

Since Christianity sprang from the loins of Judaism—Jesus was a Jew, as was St. Paul, and probably all the other Apostles and most of the original converts to the new dispensation—it is to be expected that there should be

[1] This section was written for this book by Rabbi Dr. Felix Levy.

marked resemblance between mother and daughter, as well as striking differences. The following are the chief similarities between Christianity and Judaism:

1. Both faiths accept the Old Testament (the Jewish Bible) and its teachings as authoritative because the book is inspired by God and contains His words.

2. The following doctrines are common to the two faiths: Belief in one God, the Creator, Ruler, Guide and Judge of the universe. Idolatry of all kinds is condemned. While both religions interpret monotheism somewhat differently, Judaism has always regarded Christianity as a daughter or a sister in monotheism.

3. Man is formed in God's image and by that token all men are brothers. To realize this global fraternity becomes man's duty.

4. Both claim to be "the universal religion." The world will some day be filled with the idea of one God. There will be not uniformity of belief but unity of men in recognizing the Father. The Jew frankly recognizes there are many roads which lead to God, and none can claim that his own is absolutely right. No religion, he believes, holds the *only* key to salvation.

5. The period of the universal recognition of God's Fatherhood and of man's brotherhood is called the Messianic era of good will and peace among all men, the Kingdom of God on earth. Both faiths look toward a Messiah. The Christian turns to the past for him; the Jew awaits him in the future.

6. Because God is just and merciful, man who is formed in His image and thus has a divine spark in his soul, must become godlike, i.e., a moral creature, responsible to his Maker for his conduct. The ethical outlooks of both religions, with their doctrines of reward and punishment, are clearly related.

7. Man has something of God in him, his soul. This is indestructible and man is immortal. In their orthodox aspects both religions subscribe to the doctrine of bodily resurrection.

8. In both faiths rites and cults are often alike. The basis

of Christian prayer and of the liturgical portions of the mass is Jewish; the Christians keep the Sabbath, most sects on Sunday; Christian holy days resemble the Jewish holy days, though as with Passover and Pentecost there are wide divergencies.

The main *differences* between the two faiths are:

1. The Jew interprets "Israel" as a people, the Christian as all who accept Jesus, thus making a difference between "Israel in the flesh" and "Israel in the spirit." This "racial exclusiveness" is an historic fact (Israel was pre-empted as the people of God for His service), and does not mean arrogance on the part of the Jew, but rather implies suffering, because he has assumed the greater responsibility. His election does not imply superiority, but only *priority* in the recognition of man's duty to win the world to God. The Jew does not agree with Christianity's claim of having accepted that burden completely, though he does admit that the daughter religion is rendering magnificent service here. The Jews must remain a people with their special Jewish duties and their own moral and religious tasks.

2. The Christian faith has added the New Testament to the Old Testament. According to Christian teaching, the new covenant has abrogated the old. The Jew does not accept the authority of the new dispensation.

3. The New Testament religion is of faith (faith in the crucified Christ whose death makes the Torah or Law unnecessary). The contrast, however, is not completely justified; nor is that of Christianity as "the religion of love" and Judiasm as "the religion of Justice." Both faiths teach love *and* justice, and both again have law as well as doctrine or creed. It is largely a difference of emphasis: Christianity centers around a divine person as God's revelation, Judaism around the Commandments or Torah.

4. Christianity stresses belief or dogma as the only way to salvation. Judaism emphasizes conduct. Again, we must not draw too sharp a division between faith and works in the two religions. Judaism emphasizes deed and Christianity, faith. In Judaism salvation is not denied to the wor-

189

shiper of another religion. Some Christian sects exclude the nonbelievers from redemption.

5. Judaism has no mysteries in the Christian theological sense; for example, no sacraments, no mass.

6. Judaism is vigorously monotheistic and rejects even the division of God's unity into any parts. Christianity divides that unity in the Godhead. The Jew worships the Father alone; Judaism does not accept the divinity of Jesus. Individual Jews may recognize him as a great personality and a powerful force in human history.

7. For the Jew the Messiah, belief in whom the Jew shares with the Christian, has not yet come. The Jew would adduce as proof for this conviction that peace and good will, inevitable at the advent of the Redeemer, have not yet appeared. The Messiah is still "tarrying," says the Jew.

8. According to Judaism the Messiah does not come to save man from original sin—which can only, according to Christian teaching, be washed away by the blood of the sacrifice of the Son of God on the cross—but simply and directly to redeem mankind. There is no evil in man which has been transmitted to successive generations from Adam. Man's soul is not tainted. Judaism has no baptism. The Jew prays every day that the soul, which came to him pure from God, may remain pure. Nothing decently human or even fleshly is objectionable to the Jew; therefore, we have no celibacy or asceticism as the highest form of service of God. All of the bodily pleasures may be made legitimate through sanctification, i.e., using them for God's sake, not by suppressing them.

There is no apostolic succession in Judaism, no hierarchy, and no distinction between priest and people, between layman and cleric. The rabbi has no more power than the "unordained" Jew. Authority in Judaism springs from common consent and respect for knowledge (particularly of the Torah) and not from any power transmitted through the Church and residing in any individual.

Emotion Versus Reason

THERE are minds which have made anti-Semitism their supreme faith, and eagerly believe and absorb every scurrility against the Jew; the evident falsity of a charge is of no consequence. Every statement which fortifies, or coincides with, the anti-Semitic belief is accepted as true. The very fact that a statement is in harmony with their preconceived notions is enough to establish it as true.

Any suggestion that their faith may not be founded on fact is bitterly resented as an unwarranted intrusion.

These minds are affected by an emotional block. When the function of the mind is ruled by emotion, all reason is barred. The possessors of such minds always seek to convert others to their beliefs, and they often become fanatic crusaders for their faith. But they will not tolerate anyone who seeks to rationalize with them or to create any doubt in their minds. Such mentalities are psychopathic cases; their mania is almost incurable.

The majority of persons who, through ignorance, or rather lack of knowledge of the special subject, are inclined to anti-Semitic attitudes are still susceptible to reason. Such individuals, although affected by a false stereotype of the Jew, may still be re-educated by the weight of factual evidence and through the rational process. For an honest person, one who is not completely enslaved by his emotions, will welcome the correction of any false belief or notion. Such a person is willing to examine the facts upon which his belief is founded. He is willing to judge whether the facts support that belief, and he will conscientiously exercise his reason, either to fortify his belief or to discard it. If, after a thorough and efficient review, he concludes that the facts were but erroneous impressions, he will dismiss this attitude from his mind. Indeed, he will experience no chagrin,

191

but will, on the contrary, be happy to have freed his mind from an emotional servitude which might cause suffering to innocent people.

The fictions, superstitions and bigotry of the past still influence the minds of the present. The past has a mortgage upon the present and we must pay mental tribute until this burden is raised. That many individuals of splendid mentality share erroneous conceptions about matters pertaining to the Jew and Judaism, or that they are ignorant of the facts, is not surprising. Few persons, unless their attention is directed toward this subject, through some special incident, have ever taken the time to acquaint themselves with any firsthand knowledge about the Jew or Judaism. There are so many fields that men must study and investigate that few of us can be informed in all of them. Consequently, the anti-Semitic propagandist has a fertile field for his doctrines of hatred and aggression.

For those who know that they are possessed by feelings of antagonism or prejudice, against the Jew, and who have a genuine desire to be fair and just, I suggest the following process:

First, try to discover and isolate the particular fact which is the cause of that prejudice or antagonism. This should not be a generality or a mere conclusion which is, in reality, the *effect* of prejudice, rather than the *cause*.

When this first step has been taken, try to establish whether the alleged fact is a true or a false impression.

Ordinary common sense and reason is all that is required for the third step. If the prejudice proves unworthy, dismiss it from your mind and let it never again affect your attitude or conduct.

A very simple instance will illustrate the suggested procedure: Take the notion that the Jews are not trustworthy in business relations. How do we know whether this accusation is true or not? You may have had an unfortunate experience in a business transaction with a Jewish competitor or associate and may have fallen into the error of reasoning from the particular to the universal. If the same unfortunate business transaction had been with a Scotchman, a Frenchman or an Englishman, would you conclude that all Scotchmen or Frenchmen or Englishmen were untrustworthy? Of course not.

If we have had no personal experiences of this kind, we may fall back upon the weak defense that it is "the general impression among people." Exactly in that manner has the Jew been depicted in the literature of the past. We know, however, that bigotry, superstition and intolerance were the rule and not the exception in the past and that the Jew was the unfortunate victim and the scapegoat for all ills, and that he was persecuted unmercifully by both church and lay rulers. We must appreciate that all the statements made about the Jew in the past are no more factual than all the statements made in the past about the Knights Templar, the Cathari, the Huguenots, the Catholics and the Protestants. No one has ever, through facts or statistics, been able to establish that the Jew is less trustworthy in business than the members of any other group or sect.

The Jew has been regarded as successful in business. We know from common experience that an untrustworthy person cannot long succeed in business. He may have temporary, but never enduring, success. If the Jews, as a class, were untrustworthy, they could not have remained successful in business. The same is true of those Jews who are in the professions. A lawyer or a physician will soon lose his clientele if he is untrustworthy, and his success, if ever he had any, will be short-lived.

Others may declare that their basic reason for antagonism is that the Jews are Communists; others that the Jews are capitalists; others that the Jews are warmongers; and still others that the Jews are pacifists. Some may claim that the Jews are clannish; and others that they forever push themselves forward. Each one of these contradictory accusations can be investigated in turn and be found false.

Others may base their antagonism upon their belief in the absurd charge that the Jews are part of an international conspiracy, as outlined in the infamous "Protocols." This charge has been the "leader" of all the merchandise of hate offered by the anti-Semitic propagandists. The folly of this charge must be apparent to anyone who seriously investigates it. The "Protocols," the foundation for this anti-Semitic charge, as has already been shown, are a fraudulent invention. Even a superficial view of world Jewry should convince anyone that there is no truth at all in this charge. The Jews have no recognized organization or world affairs. They have not even a chief rabbi. They have no bishops, no archbishops, no pope, or any other office of comparable dignity or power. Jewry is divided as much as Christendom, if not more. The Orthodox and the Reformed faiths are as far apart as are the Catholic and Protestant divisions of Christianity. Even on the question of nationalism they have no real unity, for there are Zionists, non-Zionists and anti-Zionists. Furthermore, the numerical strength of the Jews as compared to the population of either Europe, America or the world is inconsequential. The story of a Jewish "world conspiracy" to overthrow existing governments is one of the greatest hoaxes ever perpetrated.

If we say that no one fact is responsible for our antagonism and prejudices but rather the combination of many or all of them, then it must be clear that we are surely the unconscious targets of false propaganda, and that we have become the victims of the poison of hate, though we were warned against it. Adolf Hitler, the high priest of false propaganda, said:[1]

> The very enormity of a lie contributes to its success ***the masses of the people easily succumb to it as they cannot believe it possible that any one should have the shameless audacity to invent such things***even if the clearest proof of its falsehood is forthcoming, something of a lie will nevertheless stick.

[1] *Mein Kampf*, orig. ed., p. 252.

The Effect on the General Public

A CULT which is founded upon a deep-rooted antagonism against any group of citizens affects not only the designated victim but the general public as well. For such a cult flourishes chiefly through strife. It must forever seek to create conflict, and to unite the dissident, the malcontent, and the frustrated by holding out false panaceas for their various ailments.

The result is a nationalistic megalomania, with every one of the consequences of that type of warped mental attitude. Invariably it creates demagogues, who gnaw at the vitals of government. It encourages the multiplication of falsehoods and frauds. It persuades the public to disregard truth and honorable conduct. It places a premium upon public chicanery and deception. It destroys the appeal of religion for those who seek spiritual peace and solace. It revives the superstitions, bigotry, and intolerance of the Dark Ages. It exploits false issues for political purposes to divert the public from the real political and economic issues. Such cults have been used by governments who felt their stability threatened. They have also been exploited by the opponents of constituted government. The unsuspecting public has also been the victim of these frauds.

All students of anti-Semitism, who have seriously and objectively considered the problem, agree that this question is linked with the broader issue—the conflict between the forces of reaction and oppression and those of democracy and liberty. In their cunningly devised pattern of anti-Semitism the Nazis constantly refer to the Jewish question when they abuse democracy. The very existence of the anti-Semitic cult is an attack upon tolerance, which is one of the integrating factors in democracy. Every antagonist of democracy knows that anti-Semitism is a vulnerable spot in the democratic armor. It requires no great vision to foresee that. Were anti-Semitism permitted to develop, similar attacks would affect other groups in our society and, ultimately, the soul of democracy would be destroyed. Raymond Kennedy of Yale University has said:[1]

> Strange as it may seem, the enemies of democracy, for all the suffering they have caused the Jews, may well be performing a service for them and for the democratic powers without realizing it. By their continuous identification of anti-Semitism with their cause, they are making us see more and more clearly that intolerance is itself an enemy of democracy.

> . . . The record of the post-war period in Europe demonstrates clearly that intolerance, of which anti-Semitism constitutes an important element, has no place in a society based on conceptions of toleration, freedom, and equality of opportunity for all men and, indeed, is actually a source of danger for such a society. Unless we are willing to examine ourselves and our ways as a people in order to discover and, if possible, remedy our faults and our deficiencies, we are neither honest nor wise.

Not only is the anti-Semitic cult itself reactionary, but its active promoters have proved to be, in every instance, the worst reactionaries. If an active anti-Semite bases his antagonism upon religious grounds, then he clearly identifies himself as a reactionary in theology. If he is an antagonist of the Jew upon economic grounds, he is no doubt a reactionary in the field of economics. If he bases his antagonism against the Jew upon racial grounds, he is in all probability a reactionary nationalist and is motivated by the pagan herd spirit within him. Throughout the ages the votaries of personal liberty, of democracy and of equality, have been the staunchest warriors against every form of anti-Semitism. Every person who is intellectually honest must concede that anti-Semitism is irreconcilable with the doctrines of democracy and equality.

It is impossible to rationalize the theory of anti-Semitism, whether the theory emanates from ethnocracy or religiosity, because it is palpable nonsense.

[1] *The Position and Future of Jews in America*, from "Jews in a Gentile World."

Reaction of the Jew

THE use of false, contemptuous accusations, scurrilous attacks, forgeries, libels, and vile fictions created for the purpose of stimulating hate and ill will against the Jew, is but a bloodless persecution.

The Jewish people have always taken pride in their past. They regard their good name as priceless, and have tenaciously held to their sacred ideals. They have withstood the "hate persecution" only because they have possessed a great spiritual reserve in their religion. A people without such resources would long ago have become resigned to the age-old conflict and would have ended the struggle with, "What is the use?"

The Jew has made every effort to discover the cause of Christian hatred. The hatred of pagans he can understand and even rationalize, for pagans are opposed to the belief and worship of God and to the doctrine of the brotherhood of man. The Christian, however, worships the same God and hopes for the realization of the brotherhood of man as fervently as does the Jew. The Jew can understand the hatred of the Christians in those centuries when superstition, bigotry, ignorance and despotism ruled. Many others whose faith failed to secure the approval of the Church, or the contemporary ruler, were similarly hated and persecuted. Since the present age is "enlightened," and superstitions have given way before the rule of reason, since democracy has replaced despotism in many lands, and freedom of religion and thought have overcome bigotry, and science may now search peacefully in the laboratories of truth, why this hatred should live on is an insoluble riddle.

The Jew has met every accusation with the truth, and the greatest scholars of Christendom have so attested. If the accusations against him were founded upon realities, then he might seek a remedy. Since they are fictions, he is almost helpless.

It is difficult to understand why the conduct of a few should be charged against the entire group and be labeled "Jewish," when such a name-calling practice is not applied to any other group. Why should the international banker be labeled "Jewish," when there are no more than five or eight Jewish bankers in this class, while there are perhaps one hundred such bankers of the Christian faith, and when the Jews engaged in this profession are an infinitesimal fraction of the entire Jewish group.

A convincing fact that the criticism against the Jews is unjustified is that the anti-Semite supports his charges by nothing more than fictions and libels. If there were a real basis for the criticism, there would be no necessity to invent fictions and libels. The Jew is naturally bewildered when he searches fruitlessly for the facts upon which anti-Semitism is founded. Instead of facts he finds accusations which are based upon fictions, pure inventions, or absurd conjectures.

The anti-Semitic cult is emotional and its thinking is not based upon reason. The indictment that the Jews were responsible for the crucifixion of Jesus is one basic cause for the hatred. Of course, anti-Semites will deny that this accusation is an important factor in their present antipathies. Can those afflicted with emotional hatred accurately diagnose, or even trace, the origin of their hatred? A victim or sufferer from an emotional disturbance must first be cured entirely, or be released from the emotion, before he can rationalize even as to the origin or the basis of his former condition.

Jews of every strain, Orthodox as well as Reformed, are certain that the Jewry of Palestine could not justly be charged with the Crucifixion, and that Jews of later periods certainly could not be held responsible for what had gone on centuries before they ever saw the light of day.[1]

[1] Those who seek a more scholarly discussion of this subject should read *The Christian-Jewish Tragedy*, by Dr. Conrad Henry Moehlman, professor of the History of Christianity at the Colgate-Rochester Divinity School, published by The Printing House of Leo Hart, Rochester, N. Y., 1933.

It has been said that this hatred arises because the Jew is *unlike* the non-Jew. Zangwill said that "there is a universal dislike for the unlike." There are Jews who are like the general public, and there are others who are not. There are Jewish groups unlike other Jewish groups. There are also non-Jewish groups unlike other non-Jewish groups. In the general conception of the non-Jew, however, all Jews are considered unlike the general public. Assuming this to be true, what can be the reasons for this distinction?

The Jew was persecuted for many centuries. He was herded into the ghettos; by law he was compelled to wear a yellow badge on his outer garment to identify him as a Jew; for the same purpose he had to wear certain headgear; he was denied the privilege of owning or cultivating land; he was denied the right to engage in handicraft; he could not join the guilds. Ordinary vocations and avocations were denied to him, and he was regarded as no more than the chattel of the ruler. These and many other impositions and deprivations left their indelible impressions upon him.

Contributing to this "unlikeness" of the Jew was his observance of special laws and the regulations of his religious faith. His Sabbath was and is the seventh day of the week, in accordance with the Biblical injunction. The Christian Sabbath is Sunday, the first day of the week. The holy days and feast days of the Jew were on different days from those of the Christian. His religious services and prayers, except in the Reformed temples, were conducted in Hebrew, just as those of the Catholic church are conducted 'i Latin. His dietary laws, limiting the kinds of food and commanding that they be prepared in a special manner, which have been observed strictly by the orthodox Jew for hundreds of years, also contributed to the notion that the Jew was "unlike." I am not an orthodox Jew, but I have the greatest admiration and respect for those who observe the dietary laws in the faith that they are divine laws which must not be transgressed. (Jews of the Reformed temples believe that the dietary laws were necessary in former, and more primitive, times for the preservation of health and need not necessarily be observed today.) All these "unlike" elements distinguished the Jew from the general public and were responsible for the charge that the Jew was "unlike" non-Jews.

But why hate because some group is unlike our own? Must we necessarily dislike the unlike? In Arabia the Christian and Jew are both disliked because they are "unlike." If an Islamic sect were to settle in the United States and were to continue the practice of Mohammedanism, it would be disliked because it was "unlike," though it were the very best group in the land.

I have heard certain Jews maintain that if all Jews practiced the highest standards of morals, ethics and demeanor, anti-Semitism would surely vanish. But such conduct would also make the Jews exceedingly "unlike," and, consequently, they would be as much disliked as is the "teacher's pet" in school. Such an ambition disregards entirely the fact that Jews are human and are subject to the frailties common to all men.

Another cause for the general impression that the Jew is "unlike" is the peculiar caricature of him in vogue for many years. In addition, the literature of the past, produced amidst superstition and bigotry—as well as the literature still written for children—plus the incessant barrage of hate propaganda, has fostered the impression that the Jew is not like other men.

The penalty of being "unlike," even when being "unlike" is actually to be better, will be imposed until the moral philosophy of the world applies the methods by which physical science has attained its present standard. Though moral philosophy may never reach the standards attained by the sciences, it may, however, advance human behavior by insisting on rules of conduct compatible with known truths.

Dr. George A. Dorsey said:[2]

How has progress been made in medicine, in chemistry, in physics, in engineering, in all the respects in which

2 *Why We Behave Like Human Beings*, p. 476.

progress has been made? By doubts, by questionings, by testing of hypotheses, by solution of problems, by *critical* activity in the human cortex.

If society wishes to make progress in social behavior, in moral philosophy, and in group interrelationships, it must discard its emotional attitudes, make critical examinations of general beliefs, and test assumptions with the acids of truth. Only when this is done will society be freed from the curse of anti-Semitism.

Is There an Objective?

UNTIL the nineteenth century, the apparent objective of anti-Semitic persecution was the conversion of the Jew to Christianity. But the strategy of force employed for this purpose was without reason, and certainly unjustified by the meager results. Force applied against an individual, or against a group, can never "create" faith. Mind and spirit revolt against such coercion. Religious faith can be kindled only by examples of love, by good deeds, and by faithful adherence to the highest concepts of morality. Anti-Semitism, on the other hand, has always created within its victims an abhorrence against those who incited it. Occasionally, when human endurance was exhausted, extreme cruelty against the Jew did procure confessions and baptism, but never could it, by any means, convince anyone of the merits of the Christian faith. *The doctrines of Christianity and repression of the Jew are diametrically opposed to each other.* Christian scholars have repeatedly said that anti-Semitism is un-Christian. No good Jew or liberal Christian has ever been able to rationalize these mental processes by which devout and true Christians can participate in anti-Semitic activities or feelings. There are men and women who deny vehemently that they are anti-Semites, but who nevertheless preach the doctrines of anti-Semitism.

For years a notorious priest has expounded his hate of the Jew, yet he has proclaimed publicly that he is not an anti-Semite. He claims that he is attacking "the atheistic Jew." Why does he not attack "the atheistic Catholic," or "the atheistic Protestant"? The trick is too obvious.

A Protestant preacher, a renowned hate-monger, declaims that he is not an anti-Semite, but he uses the fraudulent "Protocols" in his harangues and distributes the "Silver

Shirt," an anti-Semitic publication, and the long-exposed spurious "Benjamin Franklin Prophecy."

From a reliable source I have the following story:

On a Christian holy day in a small town in Russia, during the regime of the late Czar, a priest delivered a powerful sermon in which he indicted the Jews for the crucifixion of Jesus. With venom spurting at every phrase he recounted the hardships and the miseries of the underprivileged Russian peasant. He aroused his people until rumbling was clearly audible in the congregation, for he had done his best to agitate them. Instinctively the priest knew that, carried away by their passions, they were about to act as he had prompted them to act. Suddenly groups of men rose and stormed toward the exit. Immediately the priest left the altar and ran to the exit. He raised his crucifix high and demanded that all stop and listen to him. Then he said: "You must not go out to kill the Jews. Remember, we are Christians and we are forbidden to kill. What I have said to you about the Jew is all true and they deserve cruel death and destruction, but we, as Christians, must not kill or destroy them."

Fortunately, that day he averted the objective of the anti-Semitism he had aroused. He had filled the hearts of his people with murder and then had stayed the hands that would have committed the crime. More often than not, the agitators have not stayed the hands that were bent upon mischief against the Jews.

Who is an anti-Semite? Is it only the one who carries his anti-Semitism to the final objective? Is it only the one who, in his zeal, would lift the dagger or the bludgeon and participate in a pogrom against the Jews?

Anti-Semitism is a mental attitude. Anyone who preaches or fosters mass hatred against the Jews is an anti-Semite, no matter how eloquently he denies it. Anti-Semitism is a psychological condition, whose manifestations are clearly recognizable. One who repeats vicious libels and fictions against the Jews; one who harangues them for shortcomings and faults common to all men, Jews and non-Jews; one who is inclined to believe *any* accusation against the Jew without an effort to isolate the facts; one who hates his fellow man simply because the other happens to be a Jew; one who claims friendship and esteem for individual Jews whom he knows, but who hates the Jewish mass; one who will charge all Jews with the derelictions of any individual Jew; one who in appraising the individual does not consider his particular merit or demerit, but only that he is a Jew—such a one is an anti-Semite.

If such mental attitudes harmonize with the true Christian faith, then I must confess that my concept of the Christian faith is certainly wrong.

The British Council of Churches recently issued this statement, "The Council affirms that anti-Semitism of any kind is contrary to natural justice, incompatible with the Christian doctrine of man, and a denial of the Gospel. Malicious gossip and irresponsible charges against the Jews, no less than active persecution are incompatible with Christian standards of behavior."

Modern anti-Semitism has changed its objective. It is no longer used to force conversion to the Christian faith. In fact, though a so-called "Jew" may be a Christian in faith, he will still be subject to anti-Jewish repressions and penalties. Nazi anti-Semitism classified anyone a Jew if either of his grandparents was a Jew, although the parents, as well as the victim, may have been devout Christians from the day of their birth. The Nazi doctrine of anti-Semitism has revolutionized the objective of the cult. According to the Nazis, it now takes three generations of both paternal and maternal ancestry of "Christians" to turn a Jew into a non-Jew.

Anti-Semitism is the barometer by which the intelligence of the public may be measured. Every acute hysteria of anti-Semitism has been initiated by a book burning. Throughout the Middle Ages when the order for a public burning was proclaimed, the Jew knew that anti-Semitism would soon be on a rampage. As a prelude to his anti-Semitic savagery, Hitler ordered the burning of all books which conflicted with his ideology. He did not limit the burning to books by Jewish authors, but included all books which promoted democracy, humanitarianism or any advance in moral philosophy. The delusion that knowledge and progress can be destroyed by burning the books dates back to the Dark Ages. The burning of books is a symbolic execution of reason and knowledge. A story apropos is told by the sages:

Rabbi Hanina, in violation of the decree of the ruler, was publicly teaching the Law from the scroll of the Torah, which consists of the five books of Moses. He was arrested by the Romans and was condemned to death by fire. The court ordered a funeral pyre for him and had the scroll of the Torah wrapped around his body. As the flames leaped up they consumed the parchment of the Torah and Rabbi Hanina was surrounded by tongues of fire. One of his disciples called to him, "Rabbi, what seest thou?" and the martyr replied, "The parchment is burning but the letters of the Torah soar higher and higher."

The sages commented on this legend, saying that while the scrolls of the Torah could be destroyed, the spirit of the knowledge they contained was immortal and indestructible.

What is the real purpose, or objective, of anti-Semitism? If more people would ask themselves this question and answer it honestly within their own consciences, the number of anti-Semites would decrease.

The Nazis are bold and *admit* that their objective is the destruction of the Jew and Judaism. All the Jewish temples in Germany have been destroyed by fire, and it will not be difficult to liquidate the remaining German Jews, who originally numbered 550,000. When this is done—what next? Destroy the "Jewish-Christian" faith and wipe out its priests, nuns, monks, ministers, and preachers? All religion is a myth they say; "blood and soil" are the only realities. All religion is a sedative, they rant; the fantasy of the infant mind; strong men and healthy nations do not require the solace of religion. The fetish of the Arabian desert and the pest-ridden Palestine have cursed mankind too long; they say they will again light the fires on the hilltops in tribute to Wotan and Thor. The world they will create will be only for the "superman." The weak, the humble, the resigned are a burden, and should be destroyed; then the strong and the mighty will rule the destiny of the world!

This paranoia is neither a sudden, nor a passing, insanity. It is the result of many years of development in German philosophy, the basic tenets of which were anti-Semitic long ago. It is the fruit of the teachings of anti-Semitism. Can anyone be so naïve as to think that the liquidation of the 550,000 Jews in Germany is the Nazi goal? If these men, women and children had all been concentrated into a small corner of Germany, they would have made a community no larger than Minneapolis. Anti-Semitism is only the first line of attack.

Ernst Juenger boasted that the Nazi power "is the most decisive anti-Christian force that has yet appeared."

Very few, either here or in Europe, would now claim that the objective of their anti-Semitism is to convert the Jew to Christianity.

None, except the Nazi, would claim that the purpose and objective is to exterminate and kill the Jew.

There can be only one other objective left and this may still be concealed in the minds of the anti-Semites of this country. This is to deprive the Jew of equal rights, to create for him an inferior citizenship, to deny him the constitutional rights guaranteed to all citizens, and thus completely to undo the work of the fathers of our republic and to strangle our democracy. Any man who fosters such ideas is himself unworthy of American citizenship and is a traitor to the most sacred American ideals. No man of ordinary common sense can believe that the people of America would countenance such a nefarious program. Even those in whose minds lurks a deep-seated antipathy against the Jew would understand that when we once destroy the rights of one group in America, we invite others to destroy the rights of the remaining groups. Were such a fantastic campaign to be carried out, how long would it be before some other religious group would be dealt with in similar fashion? If the Protestants were in the great majority, they might agitate that the Catholics be treated as basely as the Jews had been; if the Catholics were in the great majority, they might conceivably claim that all non-Catholics should be deprived of citizenship and of equal rights. Anyone who would thus pervert the cardinal principles of America is a saboteur of democracy. It is these individuals who usually parade in public as "super-patriots."

It may seem that even this analysis is entirely unnecessary; that such a proposal, on the part of anti-Semites, is so ludicrous that it should not be taken seriously. Although it has already been proposed by certain groups of anti-Semites, my purpose in calling attention to it is to analyze every reason for and to record every possible objective of anti-Semitism.

If the purpose and objective of anti-Semitism in this country is *not* to annihilate the Jews, if its purpose and objective is *not* to convert them to the Christian faith, and if it is *not* to deprive them of their American constitutional rights—then there is no purpose or objective to anti-Semitism. With the exception of the few entirely bereft of their reason, those who harbor anti-Semitic feelings cannot present any real or logical reason for their anti-Semitism.

It should therefore be clear to every thinking person that anti-Semitism is an expression of hatred, the seeds of which were planted in the days of childhood when the mind was subtly conditioned for the reception of libels and fictions. But it is without definable end, without purpose, and without objective.

Our Country at War

AFTER the first World War there was a lively hope that antagonism against minority sects and groups would not appear again in America. The loyalty and patriotism of Protestant, Catholic, and Jew had been demonstrated so clearly that it was taken for granted that if this country should ever again be engaged in war no one would dare to reflect upon the patriotic devotion of the Jew.

In 1918, the total population of the United States was 103,000,000.[1] The Jewish population was 3,300,000, or 3.2 per cent of the total population. The number of men mobilized in the first World War was 4,355,000, or 4.3 per cent.[2] Of this mobilization 250,000 were Jews, or 7.5 per cent of the total Jewish population. Thus, while the general population had contributed 4.3 per cent to the mobilization, the Jews had contributed 7.5 per cent of the entire Jewish population. Jewish casualties in that war ranged between 13,000 and 14,000; 3,400 were fatalities.

The most outstanding and precious military distinction conferred by our government is that of the Congressional Medal of Honor. Three Congressional Medals of Honor were awarded to Jewish soldiers. The Distinguished Service Cross was awarded to 150 Jewish soldiers, the French Médaille Militaire to four American Jewish soldiers, the Croix de Guerre to 174 American Jewish soldiers.

There were 10,000 commissioned officers of the Jewish faith: more than 100 colonels and lieutenant colonels, 500 majors, 1,500 captains and over 6,000 lieutenants. In the Navy there were 900 Jewish commissioned officers. The highest rank was attained by Rear Admiral Joseph Straus. The Marine Corps had 100 Jewish commissioned officers, including Brigadier General Charles H. Laucheimer. Only

[1] *American Jewish Year Book*, Vol. 22, p. 362.
[2] *Universal Jewish Encyclopedia*, Vol. 9, p. 603.

when the percentage of the population of Jews in this country, namely 3.2 per cent, is considered, can the full import of these figures be appreciated. More than 1,000 citations of valor were awarded to Jews in the American armed forces.

In the annals of the American army these names will always be remembered for outstanding bravery: Clarence Baer, Joseph Berg, Abe Levinson, Merrill Rosenfeld, Morris Silverberg, George Westenberg, Bernard Neitelbarren, Sam Arnstein, Axel Bergman, Peter Zion, Isaac Hirsch, Gilbert Max, Louis Gerstein, Julius Goldstein, Samuel Block, Jacob Kaplan, Nathan Lieberman, John Blohm, Sidney G. Gumpertz, Julius Toelken, William Shefrin, Jacques Swaab, Roy Manzer, Louis Bernheimer and Julius Ochs Adler.

The citation of Julius Ochs Adler read:

During the night the regiment in which Adler had risen to be a major suddenly came under heavy shell fire of the enemy and the companies were ordered to dig in. He showed coolness, special devotion, and care of his men, calmly walking up and down in front of his command, preventing panic, and indicating to individual men where best to seek shelter. During this critical time he gave little thought to personal danger, and his action undoubtedly greatly reduced the number of casualties. During the advance in the Argonne Forest, this officer showed marked leadership and efficiency, and exhibited great coolness under fire, in leading his troops against the enemy, although time and time again superior forces of the enemy confronted him; and his company, although greatly depleted by casualties, inspired by his courage and example, was the first to reach the objective at St. Juvin, capturing approximately fifty prisoners. He was ever ready to go forward, however great the odds seemed against him.

One of the most thrilling chapters of World War I was that of the "Lost Battalion." Whittlesey, a Yankee and a brilliant soldier, was the major in command. His forces were trapped in Argonne Forest. The division to which the "Lost Battalion" belonged had been recruited from the New York

City tenement district and, consequently, was largely composed of Jews. Through an error this battalion was entirely cut off from our other armed forces. The enemy had encircled the men. The food and water were gone. Only two of the medical detachment had survived the slaughter. The Germans delivered an ultimatum—surrender or death—and demanded that the battalion give up. Whittlesey spurned the offer.

General Pershing later presented the Distinguished Service Cross to Abraham Krotoshinsky, an immigrant youth of this battalion. The story as then told is as follows:

> The place was the Argonne Forest, full of "bloody angles." Krotoshinsky belonged to the "Lost Battalion." Surrounded by the enemy and cut off from the rest of the American Army, it ha_ _ecided to die rather than surrender. Runner after _ner was sent out. They were all volunteers, to qu_ from the first despatch, "to get through the enem_ _ lines and bring relief." Every man was a target a_ _on as he went "over the top." It was the valor of _ _d blood that made him run the risk. No man had gone through, for there was no cheer of relieving troops, no signal of aid coming. When the call for a volunteer was made again. Krotoshinsky spoke first, stepped up to the ordeal, went over in full view of the enemy, and was off to save the "Lost Battalion." The story of Abraham Krotoshinsky is one of the sagas of the First World War.

Many superlative acts of bravery were performed by American soldiers in this long conflict. These soldiers were Protestants, Catholics, and Jews, but never did any officer ask the volunteer, ready to face death to save his comrades, "Are you a Protestant, Catholic or Jew?" They were all American soldiers.

In similar manner has the American soldier given a good account of himself in every American war from the Revolutionary conflict to the present holocaust. The participation of the Jews in the Revolutionary War has been noted in a previous section. It is beyond my purpose to give a full account of Jewish participation in the other wars. We shall mention only a few of the names of Jews engraved upon the military history of America.

The career of Commodore Uriah Levy in the early history of the American navy is worthy of note. He enlisted as a boy and distinguished himself early by his reckless daring and courage. During the War of 1812 he was taken prisoner by the English, but ultimately he found his way back to America. Before the war was over he distinguished himself again by capturing many enemy ships and earned the recognition of the national Navy.

Captain John Ordroneaux, a French Jew, also performed outstanding service in the War of 1812. A chapter in *The History of the American Navy* by Edgar Stanton Mackley is devoted to his career. Mark Twain said: "The slur upon the Jew cannot hold up its head in the presence of the figures of the War Department."

During the Civil War more than 1,000 Jews enlisted in the Union cause from Illinois alone. Altogether six thousand Jews entered the military forces of the Union, considerably more than their percentage compared to the total Jewish population. Among the outstanding soldiers were General Edward S. Solomon, who fought at Gettysburg; General Leopold Blumenberg, who lost a leg at the Battle of Antietam; Captain J. B. Greenhut, a brilliant soldier; and Leopold Karpeles, a Medal of Honor man. Lieutenant Max Sachs from the Indiana Volunteers, although surrounded, fought the enemy until death, but by his heroism he saved a large portion of his scattered troops.

The Jew of the North and the Jew of the South fought against each other as patriotically as did the soldiers of other denominations, whatever their faith or creed or relationships.

One of the prominent leaders of the Confederacy was Judah P. Benjamin, who had been a United States Senator. He became Attorney General of the Confederacy and later served as Secretary of State. Upon the defeat of the Confederacy, he started his career over again as a lawyer in London although he was advanced in years. He later became one of the leading lawyers in England. Despite his busy life he found the time to write that classic of legal literature known as *Benjamin on Sales.*

Dr. Simon Baruch was Surgeon General on the staff of General Robert E. Lee. After the war Dr. J. A. Wyeth in an address to the New York Academy of Medicine said: "The profession and humanity owe more to Dr. Baruch than to any other man for the development of the surgery of appendicitis. He put hydropathy upon a scientific basis."

The number of Jews who participated in the Spanish-American War is a matter of record. Colonel Theodore Roosevelt said:

> I remember once General Howard mentioning to me the fact that two of his brigade commanders upon whom he had special reliance were Jews. In Santiago, when I was myself in the army, one of the best colonels among the regular regiments, and who fought beside me, was a Jew. One of the commanders of the ships which in the blockade of the Cuban coast did so well was a Jew. In my own regiment I promoted five men from the ranks for valor and good conduct in battle. It happened by pure accident (for I knew nothing of the faith of any one of them) that these included two Protestants, two Catholics, and one Jew; and that was not without its value as an illustration of the ethnic and religious make-up of our nation and of the fact that if a man is a good American, that is all we ask—without thinking of his creed or his birthplace.

In the Present War

The fact that this country is engaged in a global war is no deterrent to the anti-Semite, who carries on his private campaign of hate. From the very start of the war the rumor-mongers have been busy circulating unfounded accusations against the American Jew. They have charged that the Jew received better treatment from draft board officials; that, through influence, he was placed in preferred positions; that he was shirking his duty as an American citizen wherever and whenever possible. Of course, there were no facts whatever, but that did not stop the flow of rumors.

The device of humor was employed to convey the same thought to the public. Doggerel, which appealed to many as purely humor, was invented, but the intent and effect were to carry on the propaganda of anti-Semitism. Many who disseminated this propaganda were innocent of any intentional wrong for they saw it only as humor and did not understand that this, too, was a cunning trick of those who mean to divide America and to sap our national strength.

One sample of this class of propaganda which flooded this country was known as "World War Number Two" and was printed upon stickers. It read:

First man killed——Mike Murphy
First man to sink a Jap Warship——Colin Kelly
First man to down 5 Jap planes——Eddie O'Hara
First man to get four new tires——Abie Cohen.

I would like to take the author and all those who hav helped him to circulate these venomous lines on a litt journey to some of the Cohens, his fellow citizens, whom so lightly maligned. I would first stop at the house f Sergeant Schiller Cohen in New York City. He is twe three years of age and holds the Distinguished Flying C ss, the Air Medal, ten oak-leaf clusters, and a squadron ta- tion. He was with the first American aircraft to bomb azi- held Europe. He flew with the first Fortresses to attack emy territory in North Africa and participated in the op ning aerial assault on Italy. Altogether, he flew on fi y-two bombing missions and has to his credit two hund 1 and fifty-two hours of air combat.

In Brooklyn we will visit the home of Lieutenant Jack Cohen, who participated in twenty-five operational flights, received the Air Medal and also the Distinguished Flying Cross as a member of a unit which shot down twenty-four Japanese planes.

We will go to Belmar, New Jersey, the home of Captain Marion Y. Cohen, who was one of the first seven men to receive the new Legion of Merit award for exceptionally distinguished service in the Navy. He was specially honored for his skill in handling convoys in submarine-infested waters.

In Dorchester, Massachusetts, we will go to the home of Private Saul D. Cohen, who received the Purple Heart and the oak-leaf cluster for his services in the South Pacific.

In Lawrence, Massachusetts, we will visit the home of Sergeant Mitchell Cohen, who received the Purple Heart for bravery under fire and wounds received in action in the Far East. He has been in the Army more than fourteen years.

In Hazleton, Pennsylvania, we will go to the home of Sergeant Harry Cohen, who served at Pearl Harbor and was later killed in plane combat in the Southwest Pacific.

In Philadelphia we will visit the home of Sergeant Robert J. Kohn, who received the Air Medal and oak-leaf cluster for heroism in North Africa, where he was an aerial gunner.

In Pulaski, Tennessee, we will go to the home of Lieutenant Stanley Cohen, who was awarded the Distinguished Flying Cross and the Air Medal and special citation. He participated in one of the longest bombing missions ever attempted, the three-thousand mile flight from New Delhi to Japanese-held objectives at Bangkok. He is a navigator attached to a bombardment group.

In St. Louis we will go to the home of Captain Joseph B. Cohn, who was awarded the Silver Star and Purple Heart for heroism in North Africa.

This list of Cohens could be multiplied many times. These Cohens were not thinking of new tires nor of the vile scurrility of the hate-mongers, who claimed to be patriots, at home. The authors and purveyors of this insulting literature should have known that the Cohens were out on the first line to save the freedom and liberty which they were enjoying. It will be noticed that we have merely mentioned Jews by the name of Cohen. There are many thousands of Jews on every battlefront who bear other names. The records of the Smiths and the Joneses, the Kellys and O'Malleys, doubtless equal that of the Cohens and the Levys; but the Cohens and the Levys not only have to fight the foreign enemy but also the cowardly enemy at home.

In an address on June 30, 1942, Senator Barbour of New Jersey said of the Jews in the present war that Private Louis Schleifer was the first boy from New York to lose his life; that the first man from the state of Delaware to lose his life was Sergeant Harry Fineman, and that among those who left Philadelphia to make the supreme sacrifice were Corporal Theodore W. Lewis and Private Jack Feldman. Connecticut's first casualty was Kenneth Harold Messenger, and the first boy to be returned to the United States for burial from the Pacific battle zone was Sergeant Herbert Keilson—all Jewish boys.

In the Atlanta *Constitution* on July 13, 1942, Ralph McGill said:

> I have sought and obtained some official records which ought to be of interest to fair-minded persons willing to know the truth and to be on guard against the agents of hate and disunion.
>
> The *American Bar Association Journal* for February reports that the first known fatality among the membership of the American Bar Association was Ensign Robert L. Leopold of Louisville, Kentucky.
>
> The first known casualty from the membership of the Chicago Bar Association was Captain Irving Maddelson.
>
> The first Japanese battleship sunk in the war was that one to which Captain Colin Kelly piloted his ship through heavy fire within bombing range. The bombardier in that plane, who aimed the bombs and released them, was a Jew, Corporal Meyer Levin.
>
> The first fatality from Minneapolis was Ensign Ira Weil Jeffery, who received a posthumous reward for valor.
>
> Among the first fatalities from Chicago was Sherman Levine, who died at Pearl Harbor.
>
> Perhaps the youngest boy in action at Pearl Harbor was Morris Samuelson of New Orleans, who was a gunner and fired more than 250 rounds at the Japanese. He has since been mustered out because it was discovered he falsified his age when enlisting.
>
> The first Delaware fatality was Sergeant Harry Fineman of Wilmington.
>
> The first applicant for membership in the American

Gold Star Mothers of this war was Mrs. Gertrude Kram, of New York, whose 18-year-old son, a gunner with a Navy crew aboard a tanker, was killed in the torpedoing of his ship. She herself was the daughter of a Gold Star mother.

The first American soldier brought home for burial was Sergeant Herbert Keilson of the United States Marines, who was killed aboard a cruiser during an attack on the Gilbert and Marshall Islands some months ago.

One of the youngest war mothers in America is Mrs. Michael Newman of Oregon, whose 17-year-old son enlisted, with her permission, with the Marines.

Lieutenant Commander Solomon Isquith recently was awarded the Navy Cross for "extraordinary courage and disregard for his own safety" while directing the abandonment of the U.S.S. *Utah* when it capsized during the attack on Pearl Harbor.

Private Leonard Yor, of Columbus, recently was honored on the "They Live Forever" program. He received the Order of the Purple Heart for bravery while machine-gunning Japanese during the December 7th attack.

Three young Jews were aboard the aircraft carrier *Lexington*. Lieutenant Commander Max Silverstein was in command of the destroyer *Sims* when it was sunk in the Coral Sea engagement and was killed in the fight.

An interesting editorial in the Lawrence *Bee*, Lawrence, Massachusetts, read:

> When next you are a patient listener to one of those anti-Semitic tirades, remember, if you please, 60 Jewish boys from Lawrence who were in this country's armed forces in 1917-1918, and 120 who are in the present cataclysm.
>
> And this is all the more remarkable when you realize that in 1917-1918 the Hebrew population in Lawrence was about 5,000, while the most optimistic give 3,500 as the number of persons of Hebrew origin in our fair city at the present time.
>
> In other words there are twice as many Jewish boys from Lawrence in the armed forces of this country now as there were in the 1917-1918 World War and still the

local Jewish population is only slightly more than half what it was during the first World War.

Greater love hath no man than to give his life for his friend.

This war differs from all previous wars in recent centuries as far as Jews are concerned. In the last World War German and Austrian Jews fought in the armies of their countries, just as the American and English Jews fought in the armies of their countries. Jew fought against Jew in these previous wars the same as did Christian against Christian. In the present war *all the Jewish soldiers are fighting with the Allies*. There are no Jews in the Japanese forces. There certainly are none in the German forces or in the forces of any of the Axis armies.

Jews in this war are fighting with the forces who are defending the democracy, liberty and integrity of all humanity. Up to June 30, 1943, four hundred and sixty-four American Jews had made the supreme sacrifice on various fields of battle.

At Pearl Harbor, the first onslaught upon America in the present war, seven Jews were cited for bravery and were awarded decorations for gallantry. In the Philippines conflict sixteen Jews were cited for similar performance. In the South Pacific warfare twenty-nine Jews were awarded these honors. In New Guinea eleven Jews received like distinction. In the Solomons twelve Jews were cited for conspicuous service. In the Aleutians six Jews likewise distinguished themselves. In the North Atlantic conflict ten Jews received awards for outstanding bravery and four other Jews were mentioned. In the battle of the skies over Europe seventeen Jews received the Air Medal and oak-leaf clusters for outstanding merit. In the Middle East six Jews received decorations for distinguished service. In the North African campaign twenty-seven Jews were cited and honored for acts of bravery and distinguished service.

From the romance now a part of the military history of the present war I must limit myself to but a few epic stories. At Sananda in New Guinea a group of Americans, including

217

several wounded, were cut off from the main force. Another company with several medical aides was sent out to procure rations for the trapped unit. Crawling beside Major Bert Zeeff, the company commander, was a medical aide named Hyman Epstein from Omaha, Nebraska. Some little distance away a soldier was wounded in the neck by a machine-gun bullet. The major would not order anyone out to assist him, for he knew that it would mean the sacrifice of another life. However, young Epstein crawled out to the wounded man and gave him first aid, lying on his back. Fortunately, he was able to crawl back safely through a rain of bullets. As evening approached, another man was wounded in the head. Epstein again crawled out to assist him. He bandaged the wounded man's head and, although the Japs poured in a heavy fire he succeeded in getting back. That night the Americans were under heavy fire all along the line, but the question passed from one soldier to another: "Did you see what little Epstein did?" At dawn another man was hit and word went down the line that he was in dire need of medical attention. Again young Epstein went out and rendered first aid. The wounded man finally was able to drag himself in, but Epstein was still out in the danger zone. The wounded man immediately cried, "Somebody's got to go out quick and get him." The officers knew, however, that it would be of no avail as the chances of reaching Epstein were slight. Young Epstein never returned. His buddies paid their own tribute to him: "He was one swell little guy." Major Zeeff said: "In war I guess the best go first. That kid was the best. When they are handing honors around, you can give mine to little Hymie Epstein, and that goes for all of us."

When the final history of the present conflict is written, an important chapter will have to be devoted to the surgeons and physicians of the American forces. Their work has been of supreme importance. In recent years complaints have now and then been voiced that the Jews were in the medical profession far beyond their proper proportion. The truth of the complaint could not always be denied. In choosing a professional career, Jews have preferred the medical profession for hundreds of years. It has always seemed to me that the fact that the Jews were disproportionately represented in this profession should not be a subject for real complaint, for medicine is a profession which demands great sacrifice of personal comfort and entails perhaps more personal danger than nearly any other civilian profession. The Jews are now in this branch of the American forces *far beyond* their proper proportion. Before the war, the Nazis prohibited the Jews from engaging in the medical profession, but shortly after the war began, the Nazis invited the German Jewish physicians who had emigrated to other countries to return and enter the Army in their professional capacity! It is doubtful whether a single physician accepted this invitation and, unquestionably, the German army has suffered appreciably from the lack of sufficient medical personnel.

The Jewish doctors in the American forces have given a splendid account of themselves. One unit known as the Michael Reese Hospital Unit from Chicago, Illinois, landed at Sicily and on the shores of Italy with our first troops. In the Solomons Lieutenant Commander Samuel Isquith, a brother of Commander Solomon S. Isquith, remained at his post while his ship, the *Vincennes*, was sinking after being torpedoed. He was the medical officer, and while the ship was in this dangerous condition he attended the sick and the wounded. It is said that he was the last man to leave the ship. He was finally rescued, but he did not stop his work. His men needed medical aid immediately and he worked for days, without sleep, ministering to the wounded survivors of the cruiser *Vincennes*.

Between Buna Mission and Giropa Point, a company was trapped. Captain Rafael Gamso was the medical officer and, during the entire battle, he administered medical aid to the injured in the field. General Eichelberger praised him for performing "a heroic task far above the normal call of duty."

Captain Nathan Brooks and Lieutenant Julius Gotow were infantry surgeons. In the field hospitals, amidst bombing and attacks, they performed medical operations on the wounded as they were brought in. Sergeant Frederick Kosak, also a medical man, was cited for continuing his work with the wounded in the field, "entirely oblivious of his personal safety."

The duty of chaplains in the Army is also not without its danger. One outstanding episode of the bravery of chaplains will always be remembered. An American cargo transport was torpedoed in the North Atlantic. Four chaplains stood on the deck as the water filled the holds. Two of these chaplains were Protestant ministers, one was a Catholic priest, and the fourth was a Jewish rabbi, Alexander Goode. These four clergymen were ready for the plunge, when suddenly they noticed that four members of the crew were without life belts. Without hesitancy the chaplains removed their own life preservers and forced the sailors to take them. After this the chaplains stumbled across the deck to other crew members and assisted in getting as many of the boys off as they could. The lifeboats were filled and were pushed beyond the ship into open sea. The men in the lifeboats saw the four chaplains huddling together upon the sinking ship. They were all praying—the last prayer of four heroic chaplains. Posthumously the Purple Heart was awarded to each of these ministers.

This account, necessarily abbreviated, of the Jews in the armed forces, cannot be closed without a short statement about Sergeant Meyer Levin, who was the bombardier of the plane piloted by the late Captain Colin Kelly. At the very beginning of this war Sergeant Levin launched the bomb which blasted the Japanese battleship *Haruna* near the Philippines. Captain Kelly, who lost his life in this engagement, received the well-earned plaudits of the American people. But Meyer Levin, as an expert bombardier, who had been schooled in the Army since 1939, was responsible for the accuracy of the release of the bomb which blasted the *Haruna*. Later during the Battle of the Coral Sea, Levin, serving aboard the Flying Fortress, *Chief Seattle,* sank a 15,000 ton Japanese transport. He later engaged in more than sixty combat missions. In January, 1943, he volunteered to take part in a Flying Fortress flight which took off from an advanced operational base in New Guinea. Having performed its mission, the bomber ran into a severe storm on its return trip. The entire crew knew that they would crash. Sergeant Levin crawled out of the bomb-bay and unhooked life rafts. The plane came down and plowed into the waves with great force. The crew, although stunned, freed themselves and managed to reach the rafts, already afloat because of Levin's work. Levin, however, was trapped in the plane. He had worked too long getting the rafts out into the sea, but he had saved his fellow crewmen. He was awarded the Distinguished Flying Cross, the Silver Star, oak-leaf clusters, and, posthumously, the Purple Heart and a certificate of merit.

In Appendix II appear statistics on Jews in the Armed Forces in World War II.

It Is Unreasonable to Hate

To HATE a person because he is of a certain race, nationality, cult, or sect is to be devoid of all reason and sense. By
the accident of birth we are all members of one group or
another. No human being was ever able to choose his
parentage. The devout Catholic born of Catholic parents
would have been Protestant had his parents been Protestant.
The anti-Semitic Protestant would have been a Jew had his
parents been Jews. How then can hatred of an individual
be justified because he happened to be born in a particular
group? If we must have enmity it should be for that which
the individual himself does, or stands for. If a German
subscribes to the doctrine of Nazism and furthers its cause,
we are justified in our enmity toward him because he is
against our democracy. But if a German does not subscribe
to Nazism, nor give it and its purposes his aid and support,
then the accident of his birth should not provoke hatred
against him.

I frequently stroll around the grounds of my home. There
are many trees not transplanted by man but placed there by
Mother Nature. They are beautiful trees. I would not permit
an injury to a single one of them. They are of different
variety—the oak, poplar, birch, pine, maple, and shrubs
such as the elderberry and witch hazel. Each has a different
foliage. All the leaves on the same tree look alike, and yet
each leaf is different—just as different as the lines on the
hands or feet of human beings. Even children of the same
family differ in morals, culture, ethics and merit. Often we
judge an individual member of a sect, cult, nation or race
by our stereotype of the entire group.

If all the trees around my home were pine or oak, the
pleasure of my strolls would be lessened by the uniformity

and the monotony. The variety of the trees provides an added charm to the landscape. We in this land are blessed by our varied culture. It gives us balance and check and such varied culture adds to the color and to the grandeur of our America.

The Complacent Jew and the Complacent Christian

WE HAVE the complacent Jew and also the complacent Christian. The complacent Christian knows that the hatred of the Jew springs from the ignorance and superstition of the Dark Ages; he knows that anti-Semitism is not founded upon reason and that it is definitely un-Christian; he knows that it is un-American; that it is a poison imported from European countries which still carry the curse which infected them through the ages; he knows that anti-Semitism is the antithesis of democracy and, yet, he does nothing to arrest its growth and even, thoughtlessly, promotes and encourages this evil.

He may be present when the most ludicrous accusations are made against the Jew and yet he makes no protest. He may pass on a slander without first investigating whether it is true or not, unconscious of the fact that he is encouraging hatred. He may be a member of a University Club which bars from membership even those whose presence would honor it—men such as Einstein, Freud, Bergson or Ehrlich—merely because they are Jews. He may be a member of a country club which bars his nearest neighbor, whom he holds in highest esteem and who, in culture and in character, would equal any member of his club, merely because that neighbor happens to be a Jew. He may live in certain zones restricted to "Gentiles only," areas which deny residence to Americans of the highest standing and esteem. Under such restrictions men such as Judge Cardozo, Governor Horner, Governor Lehmann, Justice Brandeis, Julius Rosenwald, and hundreds of others would be barred, and, yet, these restriction do not bar, and would not make ineligible, an unsavory Gentile political boss, or a Gentile who was a refined gangster. Of course, such restricted places would not admit unsavory characters if they knew their records. They would distinguish between Gentiles of good character, refinement and culture; but no such test is applied to the Jew. The mere fact that he is a Jew is the bar. The complacent Christian may be the employer of office help, of bank clerks, of salesmen—but he restricts the employment to "Gentiles only."

The effect is that such a complacent Christian puts into action anti-Semitic theory and philosophy and, thereby, accentuates the division of our citizenry and, perhaps, unconsciously, marks the Jew as an undesirable. He lacks the incentive to help cure this social evil.

Now and then an exception is made of some Jew. Such a one feels flattered on being invited into such exclusive organizations when others of like, or of higher culture or social status, are excluded. Such a Jew is a pitiable snob.

The complacent Jew is one who is satisfied with his particular lot. He is self-centered and sees no social evil because he has not personally suffered harm or inconvenience because he is a Jew. Such a one is usually a supercritic of other Jews and contends that if all Jews were perfect there would be no anti-Semitism. He wants perfection among the victims, ignoring the fact that this is an impossible goal as long as Jews, like Gentiles, are human beings. Jews of this class are unrealistic and usually know nothing of the real cause of Jew hatred and are unconversant with post-Biblical Jewish history. If one desires to seek scientifically the real cause of anti-Semitism, he will not find it in the Jew, but in the psychology of the anti-Semite.

Strangely enough, such complacent Jews are shocked when they read in the press that a certain malefactor is a Jew. They feel mortified when a Jew has been guilty of some unsavory business transaction which creates unpleasant notoriety. This very reaction is due to fear that the wrong perpetrated by the individual Jew may be held against all Jews by the public. Therefore his very tranquillity is disturbed. Yet he will not help to cure the evil. Like the majority of non-Jews he fails to understand that the Jews

225

come from every stratum of society and culture; that they come from various countries where they have lived for generations and that they carry with them the culture and the general behavior of the nationals among whom they have lived. A Jew from Bulgaria, Rumania, Tunisia, Poland or Germany is not compared with the non-Jew coming from these same nations.

The complacent Jew is always willing to contribute his share to relieve the distress of the persecuted. However, he fails to take interest in any effort to prevent the recurrence of such persecution.

Can This Hatred Be Cured?

Is THERE an antidote against this poisonous hatred? Many students claim that its roots are so deeply buried in the subconscious mind that truth and reason cannot reach the source; that anti-Semitism is therefore incurable. These students claim that it will persist, though its curve will be up and down at various periods. During economic depression anti-Semitism will be more virulent and during economic prosperity this hatred will be passive.

In his masterly book on anti-Semitism Professor Hugo Valentin leaves us with the query, "Is mankind, as Grillparzei feared, to build its course 'from humanity to nationality to bestiality'?"[1]

Many deep-seated delusions, once universally believed, have been eradicated. Among these were the belief in witchcraft, which existed for centuries; the belief that slavery was instituted by divine will; the sacrifice of humans and beasts, which was practiced for hundreds of years by all peoples, and many other firmly established convictions which have been expelled from the mass mind by a slow process. This hatred and prejudice *can* be eradicated.

Anti-Judaism, or anti-Semitism, injures not only the victim but also those who are possessed by it. No mind can function properly if it is infected with hatred. In the mind hatred acts as poison does in the blood stream. Were all Jews to be eliminated, it would not cure the evil—for this hatred would then be directed against some other group. Though a noxious weed may defile and despoil the vegetation in a field, the weed will flourish until it is itself destroyed. The psychosis of hatred will not be cured by the elimination of the object of the hate. On the contrary, it will become fortified for new attacks and conquests.

[1] *Anti-Semitism*, Victor Gollancz, Ltd., 1936, p. 307.

Never has an all-out effort been made against this hatred. Individual non-Jews, such as Lessing, Dohm, Pius XI, Zola and others, have hurled their denunciations against it, but there has been no concerted effort to direct the mass mind from the hatred to the proper channels of truth and reason. *One hundred leaders of progressive thought in America, properly organized and backed by the churches and the newspapers, could destroy this monster and render a lasting service to our country and to humanity at large.*

Every accusation against the Jew can and should be answered by absolute truth. Students of the subject are agreed that anti-Semitism, the all-inclusive hatred of the Jew and Judaism, is the weapon of reactionary movements. It always has been and is today. There is nothing to fear from truth, but everything from ignorance. The professional hate-mongers repeat libels which they know have been proven false time and again. The people who listen to them can be reached by effectively organized effort. When scurrilous accusations and libels no longer find reception, the hate-mongers will be out of business.

The origin of hatred against the Jew has been explored by many students, but the results of their studies have differed. The axiom that "removing the cause removes the effect" applies only where there is a factual cause, but it does not apply where the effect is based upon a pure fiction, which exists only in the mind. This type of prejudice can be eradicated only by its possessor.

The almost universal belief in witchcraft is an example. People suffered greatly from pranks of nature, the frost which killed the fruit of the vineyards, the storms which demolished the ripening crops, and the great droughts which destroyed vegetation. Men thought that some evil spirit must have brought this suffering upon mankind. This evil spirit could not be seen; therefore, it must reside in concealment in a human body. Suspicion was cast upon this or that human being as the carrier of the evil spirit. It would be claimed that X was seen loitering in the field after dark; or that he was seen with a lantern before sunrise;

or that he would make strange marks with chalk upon the wall—this was enough to establish that X was a witch. After a manner of trial X was condemned to death. Thousands of cases can be cited of people who were condemned to death for witchcraft when the evidence was just as unrelated to the charge. But what difference did it make what evidence there was to support the charge, since there never was any witchcraft? Men renowned for wisdom, calm judgment and sagacity believed in witchcraft and that certain human beings were really endowed with the power to bring the whole world to destruction. Now, however, the world knows that there never were any witches and there never was any witchcraft. It existed only in the mind. It was a delusion. How did mankind, after so many centuries, overcome this delusion? Certainly not by destroying the original cause, the pranks of nature, but by the rational process of establishing the fact that no human being can control the destructive powers of nature.

The delusion irrationally based upon fact may be cured or corrected more easily than a delusion which is based on fiction. Factual conditions may be corrected, thus eliminating the irrational delusion, but a fiction, with its existence only in the mind, cannot so easily be destroyed. The fiction and its resulting mental delusion can be corrected or destroyed only with the co-operation of its possessor—a difficult task, indeed.

The mental condition of those possessed by these delusions is protected by a natural resistance against every change, for an emotional condition is involved. The belief in witchcraft existed for more than four thousand years. The belief in the doctrines of anti-Semitism is akin, in its mental patterns, to that of witchcraft. It differs only in the fact that the anti-Semitic accusations are changed from time to time. As one falsehood is exposed, another is invented.

When it became known that the fraudulent "Protocols" were a plagiarism of Maurice Joly's book, *Dialogues in Hell,* the anti-Semitic brethren claimed that Joly himself was a Jew and that, of course, he must have known of the "Protocols" and therefore incorporated them in his book! But this was another fraudulent invention. Joly's biographical data reveal that he was a Catholic without Jewish antecedents and simply a French anti-Semite. The next invention to re-establish the authenticity of the "Protocols" is awaited with interest. It is strange that no anti-Semite has ever disclaimed or discredited a single one of the exposed falsehoods of anti-Semitism. It seems that the hundreds of fraudulent accusations against the Jews are sacred household gods in the sanctuary of anti-Semitism.

The Corrective

ANTI-SEMITISM, in the main, is a social and psychological muddle. Its ingredients are an agglomerate of savage herd spirit, superstition, bigotry and sophistry. It is nurtured and utilized either for political power, or for economic aggression, or as a religious dogma, or yet to encourage a return to feudalism; or finally, for personal aggrandizement. In any case, it is a threat against orderly and sensible progress in mass behavior.

It is incompatible with the doctrine of the brotherhood of man which has been espoused by every religion. It deprecates the tenets sponsored by these religions. The maxim *Falsus in uno, falsus in omnibus* has its effect, perhaps unconsciously. Any religious body which promotes or fails to negate anti-Semitism actively will be better in the long run to discard the doctrine of the brotherhood of man. Erasmus said wryly: "If it is Christian to hate the Jews, then we are true Christians."

Anti-Semitism can be corrected through the efforts of the non-Jew.

The fictitious stereotype of the Jew, pictured to the mind from early childhood, must be discarded. The charge that the Jew is a deicide must be revised by a corrected view of the historic episode at Calvary. The appraisal of the social behavior of the Jew must be the result of a truthful and correct analysis of his credits and his debits; the rules by which the major group are judged must also be applied to the Jewish group. The stereotype of the Jew in the mass mind must be replaced by a picture of the Jew of reality.

The Jewish group also has its duty—it must be ready constantly to furnish the facts to disprove the libels. It must, as far as any group can, control the individuals, and use its moral power to the end that individuals, by their conduct and action, incur no reproach. In every possible way it must strive to dissipate the notion that the Jew differs from the general public in any manner except in his religious faith. In business, politics and social life he must continue to assimilate, notwithstanding the fact that he has been rebuffed and has been charged with being clannish. He must be tolerant toward every other minority group, either religious or racial. He must not permit his resentment against anti-Semitism to react against those who express anti-Semitic sentiments, but on the contrary, he must remember that many of these individuals are the victims of this fraud and not the creators of it. He can try to enlighten such individuals, and he must make a great effort to correct their attitudes, unless they are anti-Semites for selfish motives, or are mentally deranged. The greatest handicap to corrective work by the Jew is the difficulty in reaching or contacting the anti-Semite. It reminds one of the preacher who at every church service stresses the necessity of attending religious services, but still fails to reach the absentees. The Jews could not use militant measures in reprisal against anti-Semites. Reprisal in any form is not a corrective, and often aggravates the wrong.

The Jew must co-operate in every manner compatible with his dignity, with his neighbors and his fellow citizens. He must adhere to his religious faith; spiritual strength and solace are especially necessary for a minority sect. For the good of all mankind, the Jew must continue to be "the people of the book." He must continue to contribute to the advance of civilization.

It is of great importance that the leaders of mass thoughts should not lose sight of the power of Public Opinion. No law ever devised by the genius of man can leash the might of Public Opinion; no government can withstand its pressure; no army can conquer its invisible power, which can be directed for the good of the world, or be diverted to evil.

Public Opinion is like a mighty ocean whose waves touch all the shores of human passion. At times this ocean is calm and peaceful, carrying on its heaving bosom ships laden

PART V

THE HARVEST

"As WE sow, so do we reap," is an axiom also applicable to national, intergroup and social mass conduct. Man has sown the seed of religious intolerance—we are reaping the noxious growth of hatred, which is the poison in the storehouse of human emotions. The hatred of the Jew is a long and cruel story. The hatred is, in fact, directed against the things said about him, and not against the real Jew. It is the imaginary Jew, and not the Jew of reality, who is hated.

Who has not frequently heard expressions like these: "I know quite a number of Jews for whom I have the highest respect, but as a group—" or "Some of my best friends are Jews, but as a group—." What is really meant is that the mental picture of the Jew, the Jew depicted in the literature of the past, the Jew as portrayed by anti-Semitic propagandists, is abhorred, but the Jew who is personally known is usually respected.

The mental photograph of the Jew is "superimposed." This mental picture was not taken by a lens which reflected the real Jew. It is the picture of the Jew made by those whose every objective was so to depict the Jew as to arouse contempt and hatred for him. This picture has been deeply imprinted on the subconscious mind. Even the "best-friend Jews" cannot erase this false mental picture of the Jew at large.

Had the imaginary Jew really been the Jew of fact, he could not have survived to this day. No group of people can long endure in a sub-moral life. Even if they withstood the attacks from without, they could not survive the decay from within.

Since his dispersion nearly two thousand years ago, the

Jew has withstood the bitterest persecutions without aid from others. No militancy could avail him against the foe. He had no army, no sword, no shield, to parry the blows of these twenty centuries. Today, though civilization has advanced to the outposts of a new era, he is still the victim of inhuman barbarities.

No people, base of heart, subnormal in morals, false in ideals, or insensitive of soul, could have thus endured to this day, and have maintained their place with dignity in the family of humankind. The story of the Jew in the past two thousand years is an heroic epic.

Will the hatred, prejudice and persecution of the Jew continue? It depends upon the will of the Christians.

From the seeds of falsehood we have harvested the thorns of hate and the thistles of remorse.

From the seeds of truth we may harvest brotherly understanding and good will.

EPILOGUE

Judaism Speaks

JUDAISM is the mother of Catholicism and the grandmother of Protestantism. She is old and has reared more than one hundred generations. She has been a pioneer in the faith of one God. When all the world was pagan, she cleared the path in the jungles to the worship of the Father of all mankind. In the present turmoil of a world torn by the cruelty of war, when truth, justice and mercy are banished, she speaks:

"I am old, yet I have never seen the righteous forsaken. I am the oldest in the faith of the Eternal and I received the moral code as a heritage for the benefit of all the children of man. The homestead of the faith of the patriarchs, Abraham, Isaac and Jacob, is my spiritual abode. It has withstood the ravages of time and the bitter onslaught of my enemies. You, my daughter and granddaughter, have wanted me to live with you in your mansions of faith. I believe that it is better that I remain in my old homestead. I can be of greater good there to mankind, and in the old homestead I know that I shall have my spiritual peace and solace. Both of you have many in your households. Both of you may share with me, as you have always done, in the moral and spiritual goods of my household. You have taken these treasures into your own home and that is as it should be. My prayer is that you and the members of your household use them. These treasures are not merely antiquities to be admired; they must be employed every day. I demand that the children in my home use them in every affair of life. There are a few who are weak and frail and who transgress. Some in your household may do likewise. These treasures are wonderful—the more they are used, the more valuable they become. They never wear out. Their only value is in their use. They are old and yet they seem new every day. These treasures are the divine commandments, the psalms, the prophecies, the lessons of justice, truth, mercy and righteousness given to Israel as the custodian, but dedicated to the use of all humankind.

"Out of my household came Moses, Joshua, Isaiah, Jeremiah, Ezekiel, Amos, Micah and those other great messengers of the Divine. In later years came Peter, Paul, Matthew, Mark, Luke, John and Timothy. Jesus and his mother were of my household. Jesus observed my laws and ordinances as prescribed in the 'Torah.' Did not Jesus say:

> I am not come to destroy the Torah, nor am I come to destroy the words of the prophets, but to fulfill; For I say unto you: heaven and earth shall pass away before there shall be changed one jot or tittle of the Torah, and before all that is written therein shall be fulfilled.

"I have had many sorrowful and bitter experiences. Mighty armies have destroyed my Temples. I have been exiled to foreign lands. I have suffered inhumanities and cruelties. But because I carried always with me the sacred heritage of my faith I have never been vanquished. I fancied that the Ghetto walls were the wailing walls of my Ancient Tabernacle and that the funeral pyres of persecution were the burning bush through which Moses heard the voice of God, and that the torture chambers were the hardships of slavery in Egypt before Pharaoh let my people go.

"You, my daughter and granddaughter, have also suffered, but chiefly by the strife between you. You have thought evil one toward the other. This should not be. Remember the teaching of Malachi—'Have we not all one Father? Hath not One God created us?'

"You, too, have often neglected the commandment to honor your father and mother. You have often failed to respect your old mother. However, I have never failed to love you.[1] Of course, mothers always love and this love is

---

[1] Universal Jewish Encyclopedia, Vol. 3, p. 190; Vol. 6, p. 87.

often made more sacred by bitter tears. You know that God did not place the duty of a mother to love her children in the Ten Commandments; He knew that it was not necessary. Though old, I will to live and I must continue to live until the day comes when justice and mercy shall rule over all, when truth shall not be denied, when all men shall be brothers and all shall acknowledge God the father of mankind. Truth, justice and mercy by all and for all is the highest moral concept.

"There is a legend in Rabbinic lore, that on one occasion God Himself prayed and His prayer was: 'Be it my will that my justice be ruled by my mercy.' What a wonderful family humankind would be if all would practice justice and administer the same with mercy!

"I have one passion which has urged me on throughout these centuries. In this I know you both will join with all your heart and soul—that is, to speed the day, foretold by the prophet, when the sword will be beaten into plow-shares and the spears into pruning-hooks. With this ancient prayer I close——May the Lord's countenance be upon you and grant you peace!"

APPENDIX

I

SEVEN HUNDRED JEWS WHO HAVE MADE NOTABLE CONTRIBUTIONS TO MODERN CIVILIZATION

Limitations of space make it impractical to give more than an "honor roll" of distinguished names in the fields of modern arts and sciences. Many figures of the past, from Paul and Philo to Maimonides and Ibn-Gabirol, as well as important modern figures, have been omitted in order to allow for adequate representation from many categories. Furthermore, contributions such as those of great Jewish religious leaders, educators and others, whose labors affected principally the Jewish community, have not been acknowledged here.

ARCHITECTURE

ADLER, DANKMAR (United States) 1844-1900. Designed Chicago Stock Exchange; headed firm which erected first steel-construction skyscrapers in United States.

ALSCHULER, ALFRED SAMUEL (United States) 1876. Improvements in building construction.

KAHN, ALBERT (United States) 1869-. Designed Ford motor plant; General Motors Building; Construction projects in U.S.S.R.

KAHN, ELY JACQUES (United States) 1884-. Jay-Thorpe Building; Industrial Arts Building at Century of Progress Exhibition. "Design in Art and Industry."

KLERK, MICHEL DE (Holland) 1884-1923. Model apartment house architecture.

MENDELSOHN, ERICH (Germany) 1887-. Exponent of expressionism in architecture. Designer of the "Einstein Tower."

* Denotes Jewish extraction.

MESSEL, ALFRED (Germany) 1853-1909. Pioneer in modern architecture; constructed first building made entirely of steel and stone.

NACHTLICHT, LEO (Germany) 1872-. Pioneer in modern architecture. Designed "Gurmenia Haus," Berlin.

ART

ALTMANN, NATHAN (Russia) 1889-. Painter and sculptor. Portraits of Peretz and Dr. Pasmanik; busts of Lenin and Lonacharski.

ANTOKOLSKI, MARK (Russia) 1843-1902. Sculptor. First sculptor to introduce reality into Russian art. "Jewish Tailor," "Ivan the Terrible," "Peter the Great," "The Dying Socrates."

ARONSON, NAOUM (Russia, France) 1872-1943. Sculptor. "Tolstoi," "Russia," "Young Russia," "Beethoven," "Dante," "Eve."

240

AUERBACH-LEVY, WILLIAM (United States) 1889-. Painter. "The Scholar," "Motke."

BAND, MAX (France, United States) 1900-. Painter. "Hannah and Samuel," portrait of President Roosevelt, "Boy with Lead Soldiers."

BEER, SAMUEL (France) 1846-1912. Sculptor. "Albrecht Durer," "Washington Irving."

BENDEMANN, EDUARD JULIUS (Germany) 1811-1889. Painter. "The Jews Mourning in Exile," "Jeremiah at the Fall of Jerusalem." Illustrated Lessing's "Nathan der Weisse."

BERNSTAMM, LEOPOLD B. (Russia, France) 1859-1939. Sculptor. "The First Arrow," "Christ and the Woman."

BERNSTEIN, THERESA United States) 1903-. Painter. "Girlhood," "Outing on the Hudson," "Lilies of the Field."

BIHARI, SANDOR (Hungary) 1856-1906. Sculptor. "Self Portrait," "Cross-Fire."

BLUM, ROBERT FREDERICK (United States) 1857-1903. Painter. Pioneer in American mural decoration.

BRACKMAN, ROBERT (United States) 1896-. Painter. "A Girl and Still Life," "The Mask."

BRENNER, VICTOR DAVID (United States) 1871-1924. Sculptor and medalist. Design for the Lincoln penny, seal of the New York Public Library, portrait medallions of Theodore Roosevelt, Carl Schurz, and Whistler.

BURLIN, PAUL (United States) 1886-. Painter. "Indian Mother," "Nomad Girl," "Stone Age."

BUTENSKY, JULES (United States) 1871-. Sculptor. "Universal Peace," "Exile."

CHAGALL, MARC (France) 1887-. Painter. "The Village and I," "The Betrothed," "Artist's Wife."

COHEN, KATHERINE (United States) 1859-1914. Sculptress.

"Abraham Lincoln," "General Beaver," "Romola."

COOPER, SAMUEL (England) 1609-1672. Painter. Famous for miniatures; portrait of Cromwell.

DAVIDSON, JO (United States) 1883-. Sculptor. Portrait busts of Marshall Foch, Anatole France, Woodrow Wilson, Walt Whitman.

DONATH, GYULA (Hungary) 1850-1909. Sculptor. "Genius of Death," "Queen Elizabeth."

ENGEL, JOZSEF (England, Italy) 1815-1901. Sculptor. "Fight of the Amazons," "Achilles Surrenders," "Apollo and the Hours."

EPSTEIN, JACOB (England, United States) 1880-. Sculptor. "Christ," "Day and Night," "Oscar Wilde Memorial," "Strand Figures."

EZEKIEL, SIR MOSES JACOB (United States) 1844-1917. Sculptor. "Jefferson Monument," "Religious Liberty," "Christ in the Tomb."

FIORINO, JEREMIAS (Germany) 1797-1847. Painter. Miniature portraits on porcelain and ivory.

FRIEDLANDER, FRIEDRICH (Austria) 1825-1901. Painter. "Death of Tasso," "Strawberry Sellers."

FROMKES, MAURICE (United States) 1872-1931. Painter. "The Spanish Mother," "The Madonna of the Road."

FUCHS, EMIL (Austria, United States) 1866-1929. Sculptor and painter. Sculpture: "Mother Love," "Paderewski," "Little Mabel." Paintings: "A Lady in Blue," "Tom O'Shanter."

GERTLER, MARK (England) 1892-1939. Painter. "Apple Woman and Her Husband," "Agapanthus."

GLICENSTEIN, ENRICO (United States) 1870-. Sculptor. "The Wanderer," "Old Prophet," busts of Balfour and Zangwill.

241

GROPPER, WILLIAM (United States) 1897-. Painter and cartoonist. "The Senate."

GROSS, CHAIM* (United States) 1904-. Sculptor. "An Alaskan Snowshoe Mail Carrier."

GRUN, MORITZ (England, France) 1868-. Painter. "Overhauling the Nets," "Peaceful Moments," "Brittany Interior," "First Start in Life."

GRUNEWALD, ISAAC HIRSCH (Sweden) 1889-. Painter. "Comrades," "The Spring," "Pascin," "Le Petit Déjeuner," "Norvegienne."

GUNZBERG, ILYA (Russia) 1860-. Sculptor. "Don Quixote," "Tolstoy."

GUITTMAN, JACOB (Austria) 1815-1858. Sculptor. "Peasant at His Plow," "Faith, Hope, and Love."

HALPERT, SAMUEL (United States) 1884-1930. Painter. Pioneer in modern art.

HANNAUX, EMANUEL (Paris) 1855-1934. Sculptor. "Le Bûcheron," "L'Enfant Prodigue," "Le Poète et La Sirène."

HERMAN, LIPOT (Hungary) 1881-. Painter. "Mother at the Table," "The Lovers."

HOROWITZ, LEOPOLD (Germany) 1838-1917. Painter. "The Ninth of Ab," "The Polish Tutor," "The Harmless War."

ISRAELS, ISAAC (Holland) 1865-. Painter. "Military Burial," "Knights of the Rotten Row."

ISRAELS, JOSEF (Holland) 1824-1911. Painter. "The Zandvoort Fisherman," "Alone in the World," "A Frugal Meal," "Toilers of the Sea."

IVANYI-GRUNWALD, BELA (Hungary) 1867-1940. Painter. "Casting Lots," "Awakening of Spring," "Women Bathing."

JACOBY, CARL (Germany) 1853-. Painter. "Grace," "In the House of Mourning."

KALISH, MAX (United States) 1891-. Sculptor. "The End of the Day."

KANTOR, MORRIS* (United States) 1896-. Painter. "Lighthouse."

KEYSER, ERNEST WISE (United States) 1875-. Sculptor. Barry memorial, "Admiral Schley," "Lady of the Lotus."

KISLING, MAURICE (France) 1891-. Painter. "Charrette."

KROLL, LEON (United States) 1884-. Painter. Murals in Department of Justice Building at Washington, and War Memorial Hall at Worcester.

LASZLO, PHILIP A. (England) 1869-1937. Portrait painter. Portraits of King Edward VII and Queen Alexandra.

LEVITAN, ISAAC ILYITCH (Russia) 1860-1900. Painter. Father of Russian landscape painting. "Autumn Day in Sokolniki," "The Needy," "Autumn."

LEVY, RUDOLF (Germany) 1875-. Painter. Leader in German impressionist movement.

LICHTENAUER, JOSEPH (United States) 1876-. Mural painter.

LIEBERMAN, MAX (Germany) 1847-1935. Painter. Impressionist; founder of the "Secession." "Net-Menders," "The Rope-Walk," "The Cobbler's Shop," "Woman with Goats."

LIGETI, MIKLOS (Hungary) 1871-. Sculptor. "Tree of Knowledge," "The Burying of Christ," "Lajos Kossuth."

LOEB, LOUIS (United States) 1866-1909. Landscape painter. "Temple of the Winds," "Miranda," "The Siren," "The Dawn," "The Joyous Life."

LOZOWICK, LOUIS (United States) 1892-. Artist. Paintings and graphic productions on dynamics of machine age.

MAGYAR-MANNHEIMER, GUSTAV (Hungary) 1859-1937. Painter. "Venus and Tannhauser," "Storm Over Lake Balaton."

242

MANIEVICH, ABRAHAM AN-SHELOVICH (Russia) 1833-. Painter. "Through the Branches," "Autumn Symphony."

MARCEL-IANCU (Rumania) Date of birth unknown. Painter and architect Dadaist school. "Abstract Transformations."

MAREES, HANS VON* (Germany) 1837-1887. Historical painter. "The Esperids," "Saint Hubert," "The Three Ages of Life."

MENGS, ANTON RAPHAEL (Germany) 1728-1779. Painter. "Holy Family," "Aurora and the Four Seasons," "The Apotheosis of Trajan," "The Temple of Fame."

MENGS, ISMAEL ISRAEL (Germany) 1688-1764. Miniature painter. "Portrait of a Merchant," "A Lady."

MIELZINER, LEO (United States) 1869-1935. Painter. Portraits of Woodrow Wilson, Harlan Stone, Calvin Coolidge.

MODIGLIANI, AMEDEO (France) 1894-1920. Painter. Leader of École de Paris.

MOSLER, HENRY (United States) 1841-1920. Painter. His "Le Retour," the first American picture ever bought for the Luxembourg. "A Wedding Feast in Brittany," "Spinning Girl," "Saying Grace."

MYSLBEK, JOSEF V. (Czecho-slovakia) 1848-1922. Sculptor. "Bedrich Smetana," "Devotion," "St. Wencelaus."

NADELMAN, ELI (United States) 1885-. Sculptor. "La Mysterieuse," "Hostess."

NUSSBAUM, JACOB (Germany) 1873-1936. Painter. "Schiller-Platz," "Hauptwache."

OPPENHEIMER, MAX (Austria) 1885-. Painter. "Dur," "Pieta," "Orchestra," Daily Life."

ORLOFF, CHANA (France) 1888-. Sculptress. "Femme Assise," "Eve," "Turkey."

OSTROWSKI, SAMUEL

(France) 1896-. Painter. Portrait of art historian, Adolf Bazler; "Boulevard Montparnasse." Noted for paintings of French scenes.

PAEFF, BASHKA (United States) 1893-. Sculptress. "Boy and Bird," "Laddie Boy."

PASTERNAK, LEONID O. (Russia) 1862-. Painter and etcher. "A Letter from Home," "Tolstoy in the Family Circle."

PHILLIPS, JAY CAMPBELL (United States) 1873-. Painter. "The First Born," "Paradise Bay."

PISSARRO, CAMILLE (France) 1830-1903. Painter and graphic artist. Creator of the analytical technique of classic impressionism. "Bather in the Woods."

PISSARRO, LUCIEN (England) 1863-. Painter and engraver. Founded Eragny Press.

RAPPAPORT, MAX (Germany) 1884-1924. Painter. "Actress in Green Dress," "Woman Asleep."

RHEINHOLD, HUGO (Germany) 1853-1900. Sculptor. "Ye Shall Be as God," "On the Road."

RIES, TERESA FEODOR-OWNA (Austria) 1874-. Sculptress. "The Witch," "Death," "The Kiss."

RIVERA, DIEGO* (Mexico) 1886-. Mural painter. "The Fall of the Aztec Empire," "Going Down the River."

ROSENTHAL, LOUIS (United States) 1888-. Sculptor. "Spirit of Test," "Invocation," "Industry."

ROTHENSTEIN, SIR WILLIAM (England) 1872-. Painter. "The Browning Readers," "Jews Mourning," "The Sculptor."

SCHATZ, BORIS (Palestine) 1866-1932. Sculptor. "Jeremiah," "The Mother of Moses."

SUSSMANN-HELLBORN, LOUIS (Germany) 1828-1908. Sculptor. "Domroschen," "Trunkener Faun."

SIMON, LUCIEN (France) 1861-. Painter. "Circus," "A Group of Painters," "The Procession at Penmarc's," "Old Household."

SOYER, RAPHAEL (United States) 1899-. Painter. "Suzan," "Street Scene," "Furnished Room."

STERNER, ALBERT EDWARD (United States) 1863-. Painter. Illustrations for "Prue and I," "The Blue Stocking."

TISCHLER, VICTOR (Germany) 1890-. Painter. "Max Reinhardt."

URY, LESSER (Germany) 1861-1931. Painter. "Jerusalem," "Man," "Jeremiah."

VEIT, PHILLIP (Germany) 1793-1877. Painter. Collaborated on many frescoes in Vatican.

WARSHAWSKY, ABEL (United States) 1883-. Painter "Bridge at Avignon," "House of Balzac," "Bay of Carmel."

WEYL, MAX (United States) 1837-1914. Painter. "Approaching Night," "Lovers' Lane," "Indian Summer Day."

WOLFSFELD, ERICH (Germany) 1884-. Painter and etcher. "The Archers," "The Blind Mendicant."

WOLLHEIM, GERT (Germany) 1894-. Painter. "Departure from Dusseldorf."

WOOLF, SAMUEL J. (United States) 1880-. Painter. Portraits of Mark Twain, John Finley.

ZACK, LEON (France) 1892-. Painter. "Job and His Friends."

ZOFFANY, JOHANN (England) 1733-1810. Portrait painter.

ASTRONOMY

BEER, WILHELM (Germany) 1797-1850. Valuable observations of Mars. With Madler, made first complete cartographical representation of the moon.

BERMAN, LOUIS (United States) 1903-. Determined temperature of stars.

HERSCHEL, CAROLINE LUCRETIA (Germany)* 1750-1848. Discovered comets and three nebulae.

HERSCHEL, SIR WILLIAM (England)* 1738-1822. Discovered planet Uranus and sixth and seventh satellites of Saturn; proved that sun is a movable star. His studies the first proof that Newton's law of gravitation was valid outside the solar system.

BERSON, ARTHUR (Germany) 1859-. Meteorologist. Investigated nature of the upper atmosphere.

HIRSCH, ADOLF (Switzerland) 1830-1901. Researches in weighing the earth.

LOEWY, MAURICE (France) 1833-1907. Devised equatorial coudé for astronomical observation.

SCHWARZSCHILD, KARL (Germany) 1873-1916. Astronomer and mathematician. Invented instrument for the actinometric photography of stars, and Zenith camera for topography.

BOTANY

AARONSOHN, AARON (Palestine, United States) 1878-1919. Agronomist. Discovered Palestinian "wild wheat," used in United States and elsewhere to strengthen the cultivated plant.

COHN, JULIUS FERDINAND (Germany) 1828-1898. Founded the science of bacteriology; developed the theory of bacterial causes of infectious disease. First to use the word "bacillus."

PRINGSHEIM, NATHANIEL (Germany) 1823-1894. Scientific study of algae. Discoveries in morphology and physiology of plants, especially in reproduction and evolution.

SACHS, JULIUS VON (Germany) 1832-1897. First to show importance of transpiration in plants; researches on plant metabolism.

TAUBENHAUS, JACOB J. (United States) 1884-1937. Plant pathologist. Research on root rot of cotton plant.

ALSBERG, CARL LUCAS (United States) 1877-1940. Opened new field in biochemistry affecting nutrition. Contributions to mass feeding and national food supplies.

ARNSTEIN, HENRY (United States) 1886-1934. Process for production of motor fuel alcohol from waste products; and process for production of compressed yeast.

BERTHEIM, ALFRED (Germany) 1879-1914. Synthesis of organic arsenic compounds. Assisted in synthetic production of salvarsan.

CARO, HEINRICH (Germany) 1834-1910. Revolutionized dye industry. Discovered aniline red, induline, Manchester brown, eosin, Victoria blue. Codiscoverer of phosgene.

CARO, NIKODEM (Germany) 1871-. Developed process for fixation of nitrogen and organized the cyanamide industry. His discovery made possible wide use of calcium cyanamide fertilizer.

COHEN, ERNST J. (Holland) 1869-. The allotropic forms of tin. Important piezochemical studies.

COHEN, JULIUS B. (England) 1859-1935. Studies on city smoke and air.

DARMSTADTER, LUDWIG (Germany) 1846-1927. Improved method for manufacture of sulphuric acid.

DUBIN, HARRY EMIS (United States) 1891-. Processes for preparation of vitamins.

ERRERA, JACQUES (Belgium) 1896-. Awarded Francqui prize for researches in molecular physics.

FAJANS, KASIMIR (Germany, United States) 1887-. Discovered element Uranium X2. Formulated law of radioactive displacement of elements in the periodic table.

FRANK, ADOLPH (Germany) 1834-1916. Founded German potash industry and developed carbide and acetylene industries. Discovered use of alkali metals and oxides in atmospheric nitrogen fixation.

FRIEDLANDER, PAUL (Germany) 1857-1923. Produced thioindigo synthetically; discovered chemical composition of antique purple.

FUNK, CASIMIR (Germany, England, United States) 1884-. Discovered "vitamins."

GOLDSCHMIDT, GUIDO (Germany) 1850-1915. Research in papaverin and its compounds.

GOLDSCHMIDT, VICTOR (Norway) 1888-. Formulated crystal chemical laws; developed arc spectrographic analytical methods.

GOMBERG, MOSES (United States) 1866-. Discovered trivalent carbon.

GRUNEBERG, HERMANN (Germany) 1827-1897. Developed process for potash recovery for use as fertilizer.

GRUNSTEIN, NATHAN (Germany) 1877-. Method for producing synthetic acetic acid important in indigo and artificial silk industry.

HABER, FRITZ (Germany) 1868-1934. Discovered means of fixing atmospheric nitrogen. Process for producing synthetic ammonia on commercial scale revolutionized industry and agriculture. Awarded Nobel prize for chemistry in 1918.

LEVENE, PHOEBUS (United States) 1869-1940. Contributed to knowledge of enzymes, hormones, and vitamins.

LEWKOWITSCH, JULIUS (England) 1858-1913. Developed industrial technology of fats and oils. "Chemical Technology and Analysis of Oils, Fats, and Waxes."

LIEBEN, ADOLF (Germany) 1836-1914. Discovered chloro-acetals and dichloro-ethers: iodoform reaction for ethyl alcohol used in urinalysis.

LIEBERMANN, CARL THEODOR (Germany) 1842-1914. Synthetized alizarin.

LINDO, DAVID (West Indies) 1833-1899. Collaborated on Lindo-Sladding method of determining nitrogen content of fertilizer.

LIPPMAN, EDUARD (Austria) 1842-1919. Research in preparation of homologues of quinine.

LOWY, ALEXANDER (United States) 1889-1941. Method for safeguarding bank vaults; research on improvement of dyestuffs.

LUNGE, GEORG (Germany) 1839-1923. Perfected various chemical processes, introduced methyl orange as an indicator; invented the nitrometer and the gasvolumeter.

MARCKWALD, WILLY (Germany) 1864-. Instrumental in discovery of radium. Discovered phenomenon of "phototropy."

MELDOLA, RAPHAEL (England) 1849-1915. Coal tar dyes.

MENDEL, LAFAYETTE B. (United States) 1872-1935. Pioneer work in vitamins, particularly vitamin A.

MEYER, LOTHAR JULIUS (Germany) 1830-1935. Known for work in development of Periodic Law; evolved the atomic volume curve.

MEYER, VICTOR (Germany) 1848-1897. Discovered the oximes and thiophene; devised method for determining vapor densities.

MOND, LUDWIG (England) 1839-1919. Perfected Solvay process for manufacture of ammonia soda. Invented the Mond producer-gas plant. Discovered nickel-carbonyl.

NEUBERG, CARL (Germany) 1879-. Discovered butyglycerin, important in preparation of synthetic rubber.

STIEGLITZ, JULIUS (United States) 1867-1937. Established interdependency of chemistry and medicine. Extensive research in organic and inorganic chemistry.

VON TOCH, HERMANN (Austria) 1829-1861. Discovered kerosene oil.

VON BAEYER, ADOLF* (Germany) 1835-1917. Molecular structure of indigo; made indigo synthetically. Discovered cerulein, eosin, and indol (dyes). Awarded Nobel prize for chemistry in 1905.

WALLACH, OTTO (Germany) 1847-1931. Awarded Nobel prize in 1910 for research on terpenes and contributions to organic chemistry.

WEIZMANN, CHAIM (England) 1873-. Discovered new method of obtaining acetone, of great importance to Allies during World War I.

WILLSTATTER, RICHARD (Germany) 1872-. Awarded Nobel prize in 1915 for study on plant coloration and chlorophyll, and chemical composition of enzymes.

WOOLF, ALBERT E. (United States) 1846-1920. Discovered now widely used method of purifying drinking water; introduced hydrogen peroxide as antiseptic and bleaching agent.

ENGINEERING AND INVENTION

ABRAHAM, RUDOLF (Germany) 1857-1925. Inventor. Hydropulsor and aquapulsor machines, utilizing water power and ocean tides.

ARNSTEIN, KARL (Germany, United States) 1887-. Engineer. Chief construction engineer of Zeppelin works; designer of dirigible "Los Angeles."

ARON, HERMANN (Germany) 1845-1913. Inventor. Electric meter. Pioneer in wireless telegraphy.

ARONS, LEO (Germany) 1860-1919. Inventor. "Aronsian tubes" making electrical vibrations visible. Quicksilver steam lamp.

246

ARTOM, ALLESANDRO (Italy) 1867-1927. Inventor. System of military telegraphy. Radio-goniometer direction finding instrument used in aerial service.

AYRTON, HERTHA (England) 1854-1923. Scientist. Work on electric arc and electric searchlight. Invented anti-gas fan used to repel poison gases during World War I.

BECKER, MORITZ (Germany) 1830-1901. Inventor. Machines for processing amber.

BELAIS, DAVID (United States) 1862-1933. Inventor. White gold.

BERLINER, EMIL (United States) 1851-1929. Inventor. Invented loose contact telephone transmitter (also serves as modern radio microphone) thus making the Bell telephone a practical instrument; also the disc record which, in combination with his method for duplicating records in quantity, made possible the Victor Talking Machine. Pioneer on the helicopter.

COHEN, EMIL WILHELM (Germany) 1842-1905. Minerologist. Cohenite nickel compound.

COLORNI, ABRAHAM (Italy) Engineer. Invented quick-firing gun, taximeter and instrument for measuring distances by reflectors.

DUBILIER, WILLIAM (United States) 1888-. Inventor. Mica condensers.

ELLSBURG, EDWARD (United States) 1891-. Engineer. First to raise a submarine from the bottom of the sea.

FLEISCHER, MAX (United States) 1885-. Inventor. Developed animated cartoon.

GOLDMARK, HENRY (United States) 1857-1941. Engineer. Designed locks for Panama Canal and supervised their installation. One of first to use steel in bridges.

GOLDSCHMIDT, HANS (Germany) 1861-1923. Inventor. Thermite process.

GOLDSCHMIDT, RUDOLF (Germany) 1876-. Inventor. Rotating-field alternator for use in radio-telephony.

GOMPERTZ, LEWIS (England) 1861-. Inventor. Expanding chuck. Founded first society for prevention of cruelty to animals.

HUBERT, CONRAD (United States) 1860-1928. Inventor. Flashlight.

JACOBI, MORITZ HERMANN (Germany) 1801-1874. Inventor. Galvanoplastic process of electrotyping; pioneered use of electromagnetism for mechanical purposes.

KITSEE, ISADOR (United States) 1845-1931. Inventor. Refrigerator car; railroad signals; underground telegraph; early wireless set.

KORDA, DEZSO (France) 1864-. Engineer. First produced ferro-silicon in electric furnaces.

KORN, ARTHUR (Germany) 1870-. Inventor. Wireless transmission of pictures.

LANGSDORF, ALEXANDER (United States) 1877-. Engineer. *Principles of Direct-Current Machines; Theory of Alternating-Current Machinery.*

LEVY, LOUIS EDWARD (United States) 1846-1919. Photochemist and inventor. Invented Levytype process of photoengraving.

LEVY, MAX (United States) 1857-1926. Inventor. Half-tone screen.

LIEBEN, ROBERT VON (Austria) 1878-1913. Inventor. Collaborated in invention of radio tube.

MARCUS, SIEGFRIED (Germany) 1831-1898. Inventor. Invented the first automobile, the thermos flask, telegraph relays, and electrical firing of submerged mines.

MARKS, LOUIS BENEDICT 1869-1939. Inventor. Invented the enclosed arc lamp.

MEYERSTEIN, MORITZ (Germany) 1808-1882. Physicist and inventor. Invented spectroscope for the determination of the coefficients of refraction and dispersion, and caliper-spherometer.

MOISSEIFF, LEON SOLOMON (United States) 1872-1943. Bridge engineer. Consultant on Golden Gate Bridge. Developed deflection theory of suspension bridges.

NAUMBURG, ROBERT E. (United States) 1892-. Inventor. Invented device for the blind.

POPPER, JOSEPH (Austria) 1838-1921. Engineer. Pioneer in transmission of electrical power.

RATHENAU, EMIL (Germany) 1838-1915. Engineer. Introduced telephone and electric lamps into Germany; developed method of transmitting high tension current; was first to show how aluminum could be used on an industrial scale.

RIES, ELIAS ELKAN (United States) 1862-1928. Inventor. A. C. Converter making practicable electrical railways. Electric elevator control. Early talking motion picture.

RIES, PHILLIP (Germany) 1834-1874. Inventor. Invented telephone prior to Bell.

SAMUDA, JACOB (England) 1811-1844. Inventor. Atmospheric railway.

SAX, JULIUS (England) 1824-1890. Inventor. Magnetic bells and sounders for fire alarms.

SCHLESINGER, GEORG (Germany) 1874-. Engineer. Pioneer in perfecting machine tools; new methods for erection of modern factories.

SCHWARZ, DAVID (Germany) 1845-1897. Inventor. First rigid airship.

SHALOWITZ, AARON LOUIS (United States) 1892-. Cartographic engineer. Method for determining velocity of sound by acoustic methods.

SILVERMAN, ALEXANDER (United States) 1881-. Inventor. Invented illuminator for microscopes. Pioneer reesarch in chemistry of glass.

SLEPIAN, JOSEPH (United States) 1891-. Research engineer. Developed autovalve lightning arrester to protect cross-country transmission lines, deion circuit interrupter, ignition mercury arc tube.

STEINMAN, DAVID BARNARD (United States) 1886-. Bridge engineer. Consultant on Henry Hudson Bridge, George Washington Bridge, Triborough Bridge.

STEINMETZ, CHARLES PROTEUS (United States) 1865-1923. Electrical engineer. Discovered law of hysteresis, enabling accurate construction of electrical apparatus; developed symbolic method of calculating alternating current largely responsible for rapid progress made in the commercial introduction of alternating current apparatus. Developed lightning arresters to protect high power transmission lines; invented the induction regulator, the method of phase transformation and metallic electric arc lamp.

STRAUSS, JOSEPH BAERMAN (United States) 1870-1938. Bridge engineer and inventor. Constructed Golden Gate Bridge. Inventor of Strauss trunnion bascule and direct lift bridge.

STRAUSS, SIGMUND (Austria) 1875-1942. Inventor. With Robert von Lieben invented the radio amplifier tube cardiotron.

WALDEN, HENRY W. (United States) 1889-. Inventor. First successful American monoplane. Animated electric signs.

ZALINSKI, EDMUND LOUIS GRAY (United States) 1849-1909. Inventor. Pneumatic dynamite torpedo gun; entrenching tool; ramrod bayonet; telescopic sight for artillery; system of range and position finding for seacoast and artillery firing.

LANGUAGE AND ARCHEOLOGY

ASCOLI, GRAZIADIO (Italy) 1829-1907. Philologist. "Saggi Ladini."

BENFEY, THEODOR (Germany) 1809-1881. Philologist. Works on the Veda, on Sanskrit grammar, and on ancient mythologies.

BERNAYS, JACOB (Germany) 1824-1881. Philologist and philosopher. *Die Dialoge des Aristoteles in Verhaltniss zu seinen ubrigen Werken.*

DARMESTETER, ARSENE (France) 1846-1888. Philologist.

DARMESTETER, JAMES (France) 1849-1894. Orientalist. French translation of the *Zend-Avesta.*

GLUECK, NELSON (United States) 1895-. Archeologist. Excavation of Transjordan.

JASTROW, MORRIS (United States) 1861-1921. Semitic scholar. *Religion of Babylonia and Assyria; Hebrew and Babylonian Traditions.*

REINACH, SOLOMON (France) 1858-1932. Archeologist. *Cultes, Mythes, and Religions; Apollo.*

ZAMENHOFF, LAZARUS LUDWIG (Poland) 1859-1917. Philologist. Founded the universal language, Esperanto.

LITERATURE

AGUILAR, GRACE (England) 1816-1847. Novelist. *The Vale of Cedars; Home Influence.*

ANSPACHER, LOUIS K. (United States) 1878-. Playwright. *Tristan and Isolde; Woman of Impulse; Dagmar; This Bewildered Age.*

ASCH, SHOLEM (United States) 1880-. Novelist. *The Nazarene; Three Cities; The Apostle.*

AUERBACH, BERTHOLD (Germany) 1812-1882. Novelist. *Tales of the Black Forest.*

AUSLANDER, JOSEPH (United States) 1897-. Poet. *Riders at the Gate; Cyclop's Eye.*

BAUM, VICKI (Austria, United States) 1888-. Novelist. *Grand Hotel; And Life Goes On.*

BEER-HOFFMANN, RICHARD (Germany) 1866-. Poet and dramatist. *Der Tod Georgs; Jakob's Traum; Altern.*

BEERBOHM, MAX (England) 1872-. Author and caricaturist. *Works of Max Beerbohm; Happy Hypocrite; Seven Men.*

BEHRMAN, SAMUEL N. (United States) 1893-. Playwright. *Comedy of Manners; Serena Blandish; End of Summer; No Time for Comedy.*

BENDA, JULIEN (France) 1867-. Novelist and critic. *Les Sentiments de Critias; Trahison des Clercs.*

BENJAMIN, LEWIS SAUL (England) Pseudonym "Lewis Melville" 1874-1932. Biographer and novelist. *Life of William Makepeace Thackeray; South Sea Bubble.*

BERCOVICI, KONRAD (United States) 1882-. Author. *Story of the Gypsies; Singing Winds; Incredible Balkans.*

BERNARD, TRISTAN (France) 1866-. Playwright and novelist. Dramas: *Le Fardeau de la Liberté; Le Daisy.* Novel: *Les Memoires d'un Jeune Homme Range.*

BERNSTEIN, HENRI (France) 1876-. Playwright. *Le Marche; La Rafale; Le Secret; Le Voleur.*

BLOCH, JEAN RICHARD (France) 1884-. Novelist. *—And Co.; A Night in Kurdistan.*

BODENHEIM, MAXWELL (United States) 1895-. Poet. *King of Spain; Minna and Myself.*

BORNE, KARL 1786-1838.

Journalist. *Die Wage; Briefe aus Paris.*

BRANDES, GEORG (Denmark) 1842-1927. Critic. *Main Currents of 19th Century Literature; Creative Spirits of the 19th Century; William Shakespeare.*

BROD, MAX (Germany) 1884-. Novelist. *The Redemption of Tycho Brahe; Three Loves; Reubeni.*

BRODY, SANDOR (Hungary) 1863-1924. Novelist. *Rembrandt.*

CAHAN, ABRAHAM (United States) 1860-. Journalist and novelist. *The Rise of David Levinsky.*

DAHLBERG, EDWARD (United States) 1900-. Novelist and critic. *Those Who Perish; Bottom Dogs.*

DAVIS, JAMES (Owen Hall) (England) 1853-1907. Librettist. *Floradora.*

DEUTSCH, BABETTE (United States) 1895-. Poet and novelist. *Potable Gold; This Modern Poetry; Thoughts at the Year's End.*

DÖBLIN, ALFRED (Germany) 1878-. Novelist. *Berlin Alexanderplatz.*

ENNERY, ADOLPHE PHILLIP D' (France) 1811-1899. Playwright. (Collaborated with Alexandre Dumas) *Marie Jeanne; The Two Orphans.*

ENRIQUEZ GOMEZ, ANTONIO (Spain) 1602-1662. Playwright, poet and novelist. Play: "*A lo que obliga el honor;*" Novel: *El Siglo Pitagorico y Vida de don Gregorio Guadana.*

ERDOS, RENEE (Hungary) 1879-. Novelist. *Ave Roma; Norina.*

FERBER, EDNA (United States) 1887-. Novelist. *So Big; Show Boat.*

FEUCHTWANGER, LION (Germany) 1884-. Novelist. *The Ugly Duchess; Power; Josephus* trilogy.

FLORIO, JOHN* (England) 1553-1625. Author. Translated essays of Montaigne into English.

FRANCE, ANATOLE* (Anatole Thibault) (France) 1844-1924.

Novelist. *Le Crime du Sylvester Bonnard; Thaïs l'Ile des Pingouins.*

FRANK, BRUNO (Germany) 1887-. Novelist. *A Man Called Cervantes; Storm in a Teacup; The Persians Are Coming; Closed Frontiers.*

FRANK, WALDO (United States) 1889-. Novelist. *Rahab; The Rediscovery of America; The Bridegroom Cometh.*

FRANKEN, ROSE (United States) 1898-. Playwright. *Claudia; Another Language.*

GOLDING, LOUIS (England) 1895-. Novelist. *Magnolia Street; Mr. Emanuel; The Miracle Boy.*

GOLLANCZ, SIR ISRAEL (England) 1863-1930. Critic. Edited "The Temple Shakespeare."

GOODMAN, JULE ECKERT (United States) 1876-. Playwright. *The Right to Live; The Man Who Came Back; Many Mansions.*

GUITERMAN, ARTHUR (United States) 1871-. Poet. *The Laughing Muse; I Sing the Pioneer.*

HALÉVY, LUDOVIC (France) 1834-1908. Novelist. *L'Abbé Constantin.* In collaboration with Meilhac he wrote librettos for Offenbach's operas.

HALPER, ALBERT (United States) 1904-. Novelist. *Union Square; On the Shore.*

HAMMERSTEIN, OSCAR II (United States) 1895-. Librettist. *Rose Marie; Show Boat; Oklahoma.*

HARBY, ISAAC (United States) 1788-1828. Dramatist and critic. *Alexander Severus; The Gordian Knot; Alberti.*

HARDEN, MAXIMILIAN (Germany) 1861-1927. Journalist. Founder, editor of *Die Zukunft.*

HART, MOSS (United States) 1904-. Playwright and librettist. *You Can't Take It with You; I'd Rather Be Right; The Man Who*

Came to Dinner (with George S. Kaufman); *Lady in the Dark.*

HARTE, FRANCIS BRET* (United States) 1831-1902. Humorous writer. *The Luck of Roaring Camp; Plain Language from Truthful James.*

HARTMANN, MORITZ (Germany) 1821-1872. Poet. "Kelch und Schwert." Helped inspire revolutions of 1848.

HECHT, BEN (United States) 1894-. Novelist and playwright. Novels: *Erik Dorn; A Book of Miracles;* Play: *The Front Page* (with Charles MacArthur).

HEIJERANS, HERMANN (Holland) 1864-1924. Novelist and playwright. *The Good Hope; The Rising Sun; A Case of Arson.*

HEINE, HEINRICH (Germany) 1797-1856. Poet. *Buch der Lieder; Lorelei; Reisebilder.*

HELLMAN, LILLIAN (United States) 1905-. Playwright. *Children's Hour; The Little Foxes; Watch on the Rhine.*

HINDUS, MAURICE (United States) 1891-. Journalist. *Russian Peasant and Revolution; Sons and Fathers; Red Bread.*

HEYSE, PAUL* (Germany) 1830-1914. Poet and novelist. Nobel Prize for literature in 1910. *L'Arrabbiata; Kinder der Welt; Hans Lange.*

HERTZ, HENRIK (Denmark) 1798-1870. Poet and playwright. *King Rene's Daughter; Svend Dyrings Hus; The Savings Bank.*

HURST, FANNIE (United States) 1889-. Novelist. *Humoresque; Imitation of Life.*

KAFKA, FRANZ (Germany) 1883-1924. Novelist. *Der Prozess; Das Schloss; Amerika; The Castle.*

KALISCH, DAVID (Germany) 1820-1872. Journalist. Founded the weekly *Kladderadatsch* and created a new dramatic genre, the *Berliner Posse, 100,000 Thaler.*

KARINTHY, FRIGYES (Hungary) 1888-1938. Playwright. *Journey Around My Skull.*

KAUFMAN, GEORGE S. (United States) 1889-. Playwright. *You Can't Take It with You; Of Thee I Sing; Stage Door; I'd Rather Be Right; The Man Who Came to Dinner.*

KERR, ALFRED (pseud. for Alfred Kempner) (Germany) 1867-. Critic. *The New Drama; Die Welt im Drama; Die Welt im Licht; Yankeeland.*

KINGSLEY, SIDNEY (United States) 1907-. Playwright. *Men in White; Dead End.*

KLACZKO, JULIAN (France, Germany) 1828-1906. Publicist. *Two Chancellors; The Oriental Question; Études de Diplomatie Contemporaine.*

KLEIN, CHARLES (United States) 1867-1915. Playwright. *The Music Master; The Auctioneer; The Lion and the Mouse.*

KOBER, ARTHUR (United States) 1900-. Playwright. *My Dear Bella; Having Wonderful Time.*

KOMROFF, MANUEL (United States) 1890-. Novelist. *Coronet; Waterloo.*

KÖRMENDI, FERENC (Budapest) 1900-. Novelist. *Escape to Life; Error.*

LANDSBERGER, HUGO (pseud. Hans Land) (German) 1861-1938. Novelist. *Artur Imh.; Staatsanwalt Jordan.*

LANGER, FRANTIS K (Czechoslovakia) 1888-. No ist and playwright. *Millions; N ght; The Golden Venus.*

LAZARUS, EMMA (United States) 1849-1887. Poet. *Admetus and Other Poems; The Dance to Death; The New Colossus.* Her sonnet is on the base of the Statue of Liberty.

LEE, SIR SIDNEY (England) 1859-1926. Critic. *Life of William Shakespeare; Life of Queen Victoria; The French Renaissance in England.*

LENGYEL, MENYHERT (Hungary) 1880-. Playwright and

scenarist. *Typhoon*; *The Dancer*; *Angel*; *Catherine the Great*; *Ninotchka*.

LEWISOHN, LUDWIG (United States) 1882-. Novelist and critic. *Upstream*; *Midchannel*; *Stephen Escott*.

LOPEZ, SABATINO (Italy) 1867-. Playwright. *La Buona Figliuola*; *Ninetta*.

LUDWIG, EMIL (Germany) 1881-. Biographer. *Bismarck*; *Napoleon*; *Lincoln*; *The Son of Man*.

MALTZ, ALBERT (United States) 1908-. Playwright. *Merry-go-Round*; *Peace on Earth*; *Zero Hour*.

MAUROIS, ANDRÉ (France) 1885-. Biographer.

MENDES, CATULLE (France) 1841-1909. Poet and novelist. *Philomena*; *La Grive des Vignes*; *Lila and Colette*; *Number 56*.

MERRICK, LEONARD (England) 1864-1939. Novelist. *Conrad in Quest of His Youth*; *When the Lamps are Lighted*.

MOLNAR, FERENC (Hungary) 1878-. Dramatist. *Liliom*; *The Play's the Thing*; *The Swan*.

MOMBERT, ALFRED (Germany) 1872-1942. Poet. *Atair*; *Aglow*; *The Creation*; *Aeon*.

MONTAIGNE MICHEL DE* (France) 1533-1592. *Essays*.

NATHAN, ROBERT (United States) 1894-. Poet and novelist. *One More Spring*; *Road of Ages*; *Jennie*.

NEUMANN, ALFRED (Germany) 1895-. Novelist. *The Rebels*; *Guerra*; *Mirror of Fools*.

ODETS, CLIFFORD (United States) 1906-. Playwright. *Waiting for Lefty*; *Awake and Sing*.

OPPENHEIM, JAMES (United States) 1882-1932. Poet and novelist. *Wild Oats*; *Songs for the New Age*.

PARKER, DOROTHY R. (United States) 1893-. Short story writer. *Enough Rope*; *Sunset Gun*; *After Such Pleasures*.

PINERO, SIR ARTHUR

WING (England) 1855-1934. Playwright. *The Profligate*; *The Second Mrs. Tanqueray*.

PASTERNAK, BORIS (Russia) 1890-. Poet. *My Sister Life*; *Themes and Variations*; *Tales*.

POLLOCK, CHANNING (United States) 1890-. Playwright. *The Pet*; *The Adventures of a Happy Man*.

PROUST, MARCEL* (France) 1871-1922. Novelist. *Remembrance of Things Past*.

QUERIDO, ISRAEL (Holland) 1874-1932. Novelist, critic, and playwright. *De Jordaan*; *Toil of Men*; *Saul and David*.

RAPHAELSON, SAMSON (United States) 1896-. Playwright. *Accent on Youth*; *Skylark*.

REVESZ, BELA (Hungary) 1876-. Poet. *Beethoven*; *Tragedy of Ady*.

RICE, ELMER (United States) 1892-. Playwright. *The Adding Machine*; *Street Scene*; *Counselor-at-Law*.

SALTEN, FELIX (Hungary) 1869-. Novelist. *Bambi*; *Florian*; *The Hound of Florence*.

SAMUEL, MAURICE (United States) 1895-. Critic and translator. *The Outsider*; *Whatever Gods*; *The World of Sholem Aleichem*.

SASSOON, SIEGFRIED* (England) 1886-. Poet and essayist. *The Old Huntsman*; *The Heart's Journey*; *Memoirs of a Fox Hunting Man*; *Memoirs of an Infantry Officer*.

SCHNITZLER, ARTHUR (Austria) 1862-1931. Novelist and playwright. *Anatol*; *Liebeliei*; *Der Weg Ins Freie*; *Professor Bernhardi*.

SEGHERS, ANNA (Germany) 1900-. Novelist. *The Seventh Cross*.

SPEWACK, BELLA—

SPEWACK, SAMUEL (United States) 1899-. Playwrights. *Spring Song*; *Boy Meets Girl*.

STEIN, GERTRUDE (United States) 1874-. Experimental writer. *Making of Americans*; *Paris*,

252

France; *Four Saints in Three Acts;*
The Autobiography of Alice B.
Toklas.

STERN, G. B. (England) 1890-.
Novelist. *The Matriarch; Tents of*
Israel.

STERNHEIM, CARL (Germany) 1873-. Playwrights. *Ulrich*
und Brigitte; Die Hose; Fairfax.

STONE, IRVING (United
States) 1903-. Biographer and
novelist. *Lust for Life; Sailor on*
Horseback; Darrow for Defense.

STRUNSKY, SIMEON (United
States) 1879-. Essayist. *The Living*
Tradition.

TOLLER, ERNST (Germany)
1893-1939. Poet and playwright.
Die Wandlung; Man and the
Masses; Blind Goddess.

TRAUBEL, HORACE (United
States) 1858-1919. Biographer and
essayist. *With Walt Whitman in*
Camden.

TUWIM, JULIAN (Poland)
1894-. Poet and playwright. *The*
Dancing Socrates.

UNTERMEYER, LOUIS
(United States) 1885-. Poet and
anthologist. *—and Other Poets;*
This Singing World; Challenge.

VAJDA, ERNEST (United
States) 1886-. Playwright. *The*
Guardsman; Grounds for Divorce.

WASSERMAN, JACOB (Austria) 1873-1934. Novelist. *The*
World's Illusion; The Gooseman.

WERFEL, FRANZ (Germany)
1890-. Novelist. *The Pure in*
Heart; The Forty Days of Musa
Dagh; The Song of Bernadette.

WITTLIN, JOSEPH (Poland)
1896-. Poet and novelist. *The Salt*
of the Earth.

WOLFE, HUMBERT (England)
1885-1940. Poet. *Kensington Gardens; The Unknown Goddess;*
This Blind Rose.

ZANGWILL, ISRAEL (England) 1864-1926. Playwright and
short story writer. *Children of the*
Ghetto; The Melting Pot.

ZARA, LOUIS, 1910-. Novelist.

Blessed is the Man; This Land Is
Ours; Against This Rock.

ZWEIG, ARNOLD (Austria)
1887-. Novelist. *The Case of Sergeant Grischa; Verdun.*

ZWEIG, STEFAN (Germany)
1881-. Biographer and critic.
Marie Antoinette; Erasmus; Mary,
Queen of Scots; Fouché.

MATHEMATICS

CANTOR, GEORG (Germany)
1845-1918. Theory of irrational
numbers and an arithmetic of the
infinite.

CANTOR, MORITZ (Germany)
1829-1920. *Vorlesungen Uber die*
Geschichte der Mathematik.

EISENSTEIN, FERDINAND
(Germany) 1823-1852. Theory of
complex numbers.

GOMPERTZ, BENJAMIN
(England) 1779-1865. Developed
mathematical law of mortality
used in actuarial tables.

GROSSMAN, LUDWIG (Austria) 1854-. The curve of probability of the length of human
life.

HADAMARD, JACQUES
(France) 1865-. Proved the prime
number theorem.

JACOBI, KARL GUSTAV (Germany) 1804-1851. Work on elliptical functions and theory of determinants.

KASNER, EDWARD (United
States) 1878-. Work in conformal
geometry and the mathematics of
relativity. *Einstein's Theory of*
Gravity; Mathematics and Imagination.

LEVI-CIVITA TULLIO (Italy)
1873-1942. Absolute differential
calculus.

MINKOWSKI, HERMANN
(Germany) 1864-1909. Work on
geometry of numbers.

SYLVESTER, JAMES JOSEPH
(England) 1814-1897. Doctrine of
invariants in algebra.

ABRAHAM, KARL (Germany) 1877-1925. Contributed to doctrine of "narcissism"; also work on manic-depressive insanity.

ABRAHAMS, BERTRAM (England) 1870-1908. New treatment for favus.

ADLER, ALFRED (Austria) 1870-1937. Pioneer psychoanalyst and founder of the "individual psychology" school.

AMATUS, LUSITAN (Italy) 1511-1568. Pioneer study on blood vessels; prepared way for Harvey's discovery of circulation of blood.

ASHER, LEON (Switzerland) 1865-. Discoverer of biochemical interchange between blood and tissues.

BAGINSKY, ADOLF (Germany) 1843-1918. Pediatrics.

BARANY, ROBERT (Austria) 1876-1936. Nobel prize for medicine in 1914 for work on psysiology and pathology of human ear. Investigations in the physiology and pathology of brain. Method for objective diagnosis of deafness.

BARUCH, SIMON (United States) 1840-1921. Credited with development of appendectomy. Authority on tropical diseases; pioneer hydrotherapist.

BEER, EDWIN (United States) 1876-1938. Pioneered improved diagnostic and therapeutic methods in urology.

BENEDIKT, MORITZ (Austria) 1835-1920. One of founders of electrotherapeutics and criminal anthropology.

BERG, ALBERT A. United States) 1872--. Performed first operation for volvulus of stomach.

BERGER, EMIL (Germany, France) 1855-. Invented automatic ophthalmoscope.

BERMAN, LOUIS (United States) 1893-. Discovered internal secretion of parathyroid glands. Leading theorist of glandular determination of behavior.

BERNHEIM, HIPPOLYTE-MARC (France) 1847-1919. Study of hypnotism.

BESREDKA, ALEXANDER (France) 1870-. New method of immunization and serum against typhus.

BLUMENTHAL, FERDINAND (Germany) 1870-. Discoveries on chemical and biological nature of cancer.

BORN, GUSTAV (Germany) 1851-1900. New methods in histological research.

BUERGER, LEO (United States) 1879-. Discovered Buerger's disease. Developed Brown-Buerger cystoscope.

BRODIE, MAURICE (United States) 1903-1939. Vaccine for infantile paralysis.

BUMENTHAL, MARK (United States) 1831-1921. Introduced lip reading in United States.

ASPER, LEOPOLD (Germany) 18 Kidney analysis and examina

COHEN, HARRY (United States) 1885-. Invented volsella for intravesical use, clamp tourniquet, and ligature guide for deep abdominal work.

COHN, ALFRED E. (United States) 1879-. Discovered direct effect of digitalis on heart. Discoveries in myocardiac involvement in rheumatic fever.

COHN, HERMANN (Germany) 1838-1906. Founded optical hygiene for school children.

COHNHEIM, JUIUS (Germany) 1839-1884. Discovered the true nature of pus; first to freeze pathological objects for examination; also innovations in microscopical work.

CORIAT, ISADOR (United States) 1875-. Psychoanalyst. Treatment for stammering.

DETRE, LASZLO (France) 1874-1938. Originated antigen

theory in immunology. Discoveries in isolation of tuberculin.

EDER, MONTAGU (England) 1865-1936. Pioneer in psychotherapy; established clinics for school children of London.

BREUER, JOSEPH (Austria) 1842-1925. Discovered with Hering the self-regulatory mechanism of breathing.

EHRLICH, PAUL (Germany) 1854-1915. Theories on nature of toxin and antitoxin; started modern immunology. Science of chemotherapy advanced by his researches on dyes. Introduced treatment of syphilis with "606." Shared Nobel prize for medicine in 1908.

EIGER, MARIAN (Poland) 1874-1939. Discovered the "Eiger cell" in the human heart.

ELSBERG, CHARLES A. (United States) 1871-. Innovations in heart and brain surgery.

EXTON, WILLIAM (United States) 1876-. New methods of diagnosis in urology and diabetes.

FINKELSTEIN, HEINRICH (Germany) 1865-. Pediatrics.

FISHBERG, MAURICE (United States) 1872-1934. Pioneered pneumothorax treatment of tuberculosis in United States.

FLEISCHL, VON MARKOW ERNST (Austria). 1846-1891. Invented haemometer for testing the blood.

FLEXNER, SIMON (United States) 1863-. Serum for cerebrospinal fever; also bacillus of dysentery. Contributed to knowledge of virus of infantile paralysis.

FRANK, ROBERT T. (United States) 1875-. Demonstrated presence of female sex hormone in ovarian follicle.

FRANKEL, ALBERT (Germany) 1848-1916. Discovered cause of croupous pneumonia.

FREUD, SIGMUND (Austria) 1856-1942. Founder of Psychoanalysis. *Totem and Tabu, Wit and the Unconscious.*

FREUND, ERNEST (Austria) 1863-1914. Introduced sodium citrate as an anti-blood coagulant.

FREUND, WILHELM (Germany) 1833-1917. Pioneer in gynecological surgery.

GAERTNER, GUSTAV (Austria) 1855-. Invented kaolin rheostat, the tonometer, the ergostat, and automatic lifesaver for miners.

GOLDBERGER, JOSEPH (United States) 1874-1929. Discovered cause of and cure for pellagra. Pioneer in immunology.

GOLDBLATT, HARRY (United States) 1891-. Pioneer work on effect of ultraviolet rays on fat soluble vitamin; discoveries in kidney surgery and blood pressure.

GOLDMANN, EDWIN (Germany) 1862-1913. First to use pyrol blue in staining connective tissue.

GOTTSTEIN, JACOB (Germany) 1832-1895. Suggested curette for the removal of adenoidal growths.

GROSS, LOUIS (United States) 1895-1937. Studies of rheumatic fever; also of dynamics of the heart.

GRUBY, DAVID (France) 1810-1898. Discovered thrush fungus and trichophyton tonsurans as causes of disease.

GRUENING, EMIL (United States) 1842-1914. Pioneer in surgery; modern mastoid operation.

HAFFKINE, WALDEMAR (France, India) 1860-1930. Method of inoculation against cholera and bubonic plague.

HAJEK, MARCUS (Austria) 1861-1941. Laryngology.

HANOVER, ADOLPH (Denmark) 1814-1894. Introduced microscope into medical research.

HART, ERNEST A. (England) 1836-1898. Treatment of popliteal aneurism. Editor of *British Medical Journal;* leader in social medi-

255

cine, chiefly responsible for the Infant Life Protection Act.

HAUSER, FELIPE (Spain) 1832-1925. Study of cholera.

HAYS, ISAAC (United States) 1847-1925. First corrected astigmatism with cylindrical lenses.

HENLE, FRIEDRICH G. (Germany) 1809-1885. Anatomist; first to describe structure of the kidneys.

HENOCH, EDUARD (Germany) 1820-1910. Pediatrics.

HERCZEL, MANO (Hungary) 1861-1918. Pioneer in abdomen and kidney surgery.

HESS, ALFRED (United States) 1875-1933. Developed cures for scurvy and rickets; discovered method of irradiating food with ultraviolet rays.

HIRSCHBERG, JULIUS (Germany) 1843-1925. First to use electromagnet in extraction of foreign metallic objects from eye.

HIRSZFELD, LUDWIK (Poland) 1883-. Discoveries in study of blood types. Discovered the bacillus of paratyphus C.

HUHNER, MAX (United States) 1873-. Test for sterility.

HYMAN, ALBERT (United States) 1893-. Electrical stimulation method to revive the stopped heart.

ISAACS, RAPHAEL (United States) 1891-. Discovered effect of rays on blood; treatment of pernicious anemia.

ISRAEL, JAMES (Germany) 1848-1926. One of founders of scientific surgery of kidneys.

JACOBI, ABRAHAM (United States) 1830-1919. Founder of pediatrics in United States. Invented laryngoscope.

JACOBSON, JULIUS (Germany) 1828-1889. Operative improvements for cataract and trachoma.

JACOBSON, LUDWIG (Denmark) 1783-1843. Discovered "Jacobson's organ"; invented lithoclast.

JARCHO, JULIUS (United States) 1882-. New methods and instruments in gynecology.

KAHN, MORTON CHARLES (United States) 1895-. Discovered single cell method of isolating bacteria; and the life cycle of the tubercle bacillus.

KAHN, MAX (United States) 1887-1926. Invented Intarvin, valuable in treatment of diabetes.

KAHN, REUBEN (United States) 1887-. Test for detection of syphilis. First to demonstrate immunizing powers of the skin.

KASSOWITZ, MAX (Austria) 1842-1913. Structure of the bones.

KAUFMAN - COSZIA, OSCAR (France) 1891-. Influence of carbon dioxide on diabetes.

KLEIN, SALOMON (Austria) 1845-1937. Ophthalmology.

KLEMPERER, GEORG (Germany) 1864-. Cancer.

KOHN, ALFRED (Czechoslovakia) 1867-. Cytology.

KOPLIK, HENRY (United States) 1858-1927. Discovered the diagnostic spots of measles. First to establish milk stations in the United States.

KOLLER, CARL (Austria, United States) 1857-. Introduced use of cocaine as local anesthetic.

KRAMER, BENJAMIN (United States) 1888-. One of first to discover value of ultraviolet and cod-liver oil treatments for rickets. Methods for detection of calcium, sugar, and sodium in blood tests.

KRISHABER, MAURICE (France) 1833-1883. Discoveries in laryngology and neurology.

KRISTELLER, SAMUEL (Germany) 1820-1900. Obstetrical technique.

LANDSBERGER, RICHARD (Germany) 1864-1939. Founded bio-dentistry and orthopedy of skull and jaw.

LANDSTEINER, KARL (Austria, United States) 1868-. Received Nobel prize for discovery of the human blood groups, which made possible successful blood transfusions; also discovered a serum for infantile paralysis.

LANGSTEIN, LEOPOLD (Germany) 1876-1933. Child nutrition.

LEMPERT, JULIUS (United States) 1891-. New treatment for acute mastoiditis; also new cure for deafness.

LESSER, ERNST (Germany) 1879-. Early work on insulin.

LEVIN, ISAAC (United States) 1886-. Discoveries and inventions for treatment of cancer.

LEWIN, KURT (Germany, United States) 1890-. Representative of "Gestalt" psychology.

LEWISOHN, RICHARD (United States) 1875-. Citrate method of blood transfusion.

LIBMAN, EMANUEL (United States) 1872-. Described Libman's disease and invented method to test intensity of individual's reaction to pain.

LICHTHEIM, LUDWIG (Germany) 1845-1928. Discovered "Lichtheim's disease"; research on hydremia and meningitis.

LIEBREICH, OSCAR (Germany) 1839-1908. Discovered narcotic effect of chloral and healing effect of lanolin. Introduced scientific manufacture of hypnotic drugs.

LOEB, JACQUES (United States) 1859-1924. Pioneer in artificial parthenogenesis.

LOEVENHART, ARTHUR SOLOMON (United States) 1878-1929. Antisyphilitic drugs.

LOEWENSTEIN, ERNST (Austria) 1878-. Methods for immunization against diphtheria, tuberculosis and lockjaw.

LOEWI, OTTO (Germany) 1873-. Pharmacologist. Awarded Nobel prize for medicine for his researches on the chemical nature of the transmission of nervous impulses, and on the structure of the heart.

MAGNUS, GUSTAV (Germany)

1802-1870. Discovered respiration of tissues.

METCHNIKOF, ELIE* (Russia) 1845-1916. Nobel prize in medicine, 1908. Work on theory of immunity. Author of theory of phagocytosis.

MICHAEL, ISAAC (Germany) 1848-1897. Invented cold light apparatus for internal operations.

LEWIN, LOUIS (Germany) 1850-1929. Pioneer in narcotics and snake venoms.

MINKOWSKI, OSCAR (Germany) 1858-1931. Discovered relation between diabetes and the pancreas, making possible use of insulin.

MARMOREK, ALEXANDER (France) 1865-1923. Pioneer in fight against tuberculosis. Discovered a serum against streptococci.

MAGNUS, RUDOLF (Germany, Holland) 1873-1927. Discoveries in study of digitalis.

MAY, CHARLES H. (United States) 1861-. Improved electric ophthalmoscope.

MAYER, EMIL (United States) 1854-1931. Invented use of tubes in nasal operations; experiments with cocaine.

MENDEL, EMANUEL (Germany) 1839-1907. Contributions to knowledge of paralysis, tabes, mania, paranoia, and epilepsy.

MEYER, WILLY (United States) 1858-1932. New techniques in cystoscopy, appendectomy, breast operation.

METZENBAUM, MYRON (United States) 1876-. Pioneer in anesthetics. U. S. Government medal for research in radium.

MINKOWSKI, MIRCZYSLAW (Switzerland) 1884-. Contributed to knowledge of reflexes and automatic and involuntary movements.

MOSCHCOWITZ, ALEXIS (United States) 1865-1933. Operation for hernia.

MOSZKOWSKI, MAX (Germany) 1873-1939. Discovered cause of and cure for beriberi.

MUNK, HERMANN, 1839-1912. Researches in cerebral and nervous physiology and function of the thyroid gland.

NEISSER, ALBERT (Germany) 1855-1916. Discovered bacillus of gonorrhea.

NEUMANN, HEINRICH (Austria) 1873-1939. Work on ulcers in the small brain and painless trepanation without narcosis. Invented operation of the labyrinth.

OPPENHEIM, HERMANN (Germany) 1858-1919. Diagnoses of the brain and spinal tumors made operations possible for these diseases.

OTTENBERG, REUBEN (United States) 1882-. Discoveries in blood chemistry.

PASCAL, JOSEPH I. (Lithuania) 1890-. Invented the Pascal photoscope, the Turville-Pascal dynascope, the Pascal balance charts.

PECK, SAMUEL M. (United States) 1900-. Test for capillary fragility; use of moccasin venom for hemorrhagic conditions.

PICK, ERNEST (Germany) 1872-. Pharmacologist.

POLITZER, ADAM (Austria) 1835-1920. Otology.

RANK, OTTO (Austria) 1884-1939. Originated psychoanalytical doctrine of "will therapy."

RANSCHBURG, PAL (Hungary) 1870-. Invented the mnemometer.

RANSOHOFF, JOSEPH (United States) 1853-1921. Pioneer in gall bladder surgery.

RANSOHOFF, JOSEPH L. (United States) 1880-. First to suggest use of lipoid in empyema.

RAVICH, ABRAHAM (United States) 1888-. Urological instruments.

REMAK, ROBERT (Germany) 1815-1865. Discovered cells which initiate the heartbeat; evolved electrical treatment of nervous diseases.

RITTER, JULIUS (Germany) 1862-. Discovered the bacillus of whooping cough.

ROGOFF, JULIUS (United States) 1883-. Discovered hormone of the adrenal gland and new therapy of Addison's disease.

ROMBERG, MORITZ, 1795-1873. Studies on physiology and pathology of nervous diseases and description of "ciliary neuralgia."

RONGY, ABRAHAM (United States) 1878-. New methods in gynecology; new theories on sterility and the process of birth.

ROSENBACH, OTTOMAR ERNST (Germany) 1851-1907. Theory of functional diseases.

ROESNAU, MILTON (United States) 1869-. Pioneer work in anaphylaxis.

RUBIN, ISADOR (United States) 1883-. Test for sterility.

SACHS, HANS (Germany) 1877-. Method for detection of syphilis from the blood serum.

SAKEL, MANFRED (Germany) 1900-. Introduced and perfected "shock therapy" for mental disorders.

SALOMONSON, CARL J. (Denmark) 1847-1924. Pioneer in antitoxin treatment of diphtheria.

SCHICK, BELA (Austria) 1877-. Test for determining susceptibility to diphtheria.

SENATOR, HERMANN (Germany) 1834-1911. Introduced concept of autointoxication. Studies on respiration and metabolism.

SCHIFF, MORITZ (Italy) 1823-1896. Pioneer in endrocrinology and experimental excision of the thyroid.

SEMON, SIR FELIX (England) 1849-1921. Laryngology.

SILVERMAN, DANIEL (United States) 1894-. Isolated and defined the Duval bacillus as a cause of endemic and sporadic dysentery.

SOLIS-COHEN, JACOB DA SILVA (United States) 1838-1927. Laryngology.

STEKEL, WILHELM (Austria) 1868-1940. Theory of "authority complex."

STILLING, BENEDICT (Germany) 1810-1879. Pioneer in surgery and research on the spinal cord and ovariotomy.

STRICKER, SALOMON (Austria) 1834-1898. Discovered cellular formation of living tissue; vasomotor center of abdominal viscera; syntheses of the cornea, contractability of the capillaries.

SURE, BARNETT (United States) 1891-. Pioneer in vitamin research. Discovered, independently, vitamins E and B.

SWICK, MOSES (United States) 1901-. Discoveries in urography.

SZONDI, LIPOT (Hungary) 1893-. Among first to investigate influence of glandular secretion on mental processes.

TESCHNER, JACOB (United States) 1858-1927. Pioneer in orthopedic surgery, especially in cure of curvature and paralytic conditions.

TRAUBE, LUDWIG (Germany) 1816-1876. Founded experimental pathology. First exact research on digitalis in heart disease. Began taking exact temperature of sick.

UNGER, LESTER (United States) 1888-. Devised Unger blood transfusion method used internationally.

UNNA, PAUL GERSON (Germany) 1850-1929. Founder of modern skin pathology; discovered origin of soft chancre.

VALENTIN, GABRIEL G. (Switzerland) 1810-1883. Studies on blood circulation, digestion, elasticity of muscles and nerves.

VON LICHTENBERG, ALEXANDER (Germany) 1880-. Invented uroselectan, facilitating diagnosis of and operation on urinogenital system.

VERONOFF, SERGE (France)
1866-. Research and experiments in gland grafting.

VOLTERRA, MARIO (Italy) 1901-. First to recognize psittacosis in Europe and to prevent its spread.

WARBURG, OTTO (Germany) 1883-. Awarded Nobel prize in 1931 for researches on assimilation and oxidation of substances in the body.

WASSERMANN, AUGUST VON (Germany) 1866-1925. Test for syphilis.

WEIGERT, KARL 1849-1904. First to stain bacteria; author of Siva theory of tissue pathology.

WERTHEIMER, MAX (Germany) 1880-1943. Evolved Gestalt theory of psychology.

WIDAL, GEORGES (France) 1862-1929. Created serum diagnosis of typhus.

WOLBARST, ABRAHAM (United States) 1872-. Inventor of test for diagnosis of urethral discharges.

WOLFF, JULIUS (Germany) 1836-1902. "Wolff's law" of orthopedics.

ZONDEK, BERNARD, 1891-. Codiscoverer of first reliable pregnancy test.

MUSIC

ACHRON, JOSEPH (Russia, United States) 1886-. Composer and violinist. *Hebrew Melody; Suite Bizarre; Salome's Dance.*

ADLER, GUIDO (Austria) 1855-. Musicologist. Founder of Austrian School of Musical Science. *Richard Wagner; Handbuch der Musikgeschichte.*

ALKAN, CHARLES HENRI (France) 1813-1888. Pianist and composer. *Trois Grandes Études.*

AUER, LEOPOLD (Russia, United States) 1845-1930. Violinist. Teacher of Jascha Heifetz, Efrem Zimbalist, Mischa Elman and Toscha Seidel. *Violin Playing as I Teach it; Violin Master Works and Their Interpretation.*

BARNETT, JOHN (England) 1802-1890. Composer. Operas: *Mountain Sylph; Fair Rosamund.*

BAUER, HAROLD (England) 1873-. Pianist.

BAUER, MARION EUGENE (United States) 1887-. Composer. *Red Man's Requiem; Four Poems; Pan.*

BERLIN, IRVING (United States) 1888-. Song writer. *Oh, How I Hate to Get Up in the Morning; Alexander's Ragtime Band; God Bless America; This Is the Army.*

BLITZSTEIN, MARC (United States) 1905-. Composer. *The Cradle Will Rock; Cain; Triple Sec.*

BLOCH, ERNEST (United States) 1880-. Composer. *Hiver-Printemps; Hebrew Rhapsody; America*; Opera: *"Macbeth."*

BRUCH, MAX, 1838-1920. Composer. *Violin Concerto in G Minor.*

CASTELNUOVO - TODESCO MARIO (Italy) 1895-. Composer. *Fioretti; La Mandragol; Prophets.*

CHASINS, ABRAHAM (United States) 1903-. Composer. *Three Chinese Pieces.*

COPLAND, AARON (United States) 1900-. Composer. *First Symphony; Music for the Theater; Dance Symphony.*

COWEN, SIR FREDERIC HYMAN, 1852-1935. Conductor and composer. Opera: *Pauline*; Cantata: *The Rose Maiden; Scandinavian Symphony.*

DAMROSCH, LEOPOLD (United States) 1832-1885. Conductor and composer. Vital force in elevation of musical standards in this country.

DAMROSCH, WALTER JOHANNES (United States) 1862-. Conductor and composer. Dean of American conductors.

DIAMOND, DAVID LEO (United States) 1915-. Composer. *Sinfonietta for Orchestra.*

DUKAS, PAUL (France) 1865-1935. Composer. *Sorcerer's Apprentice.*

ELMAN, MISCHA (Russia) 1891-. Violinist.

FUERMANN, EMANUEL (Germany, United States) 1902-1943. Violoncellist.

FRANCHETTI, BARON ALBERTO (Italy) 1860-. Composer. Operas: *Asrael; Germania.*

FRIEDLANDER, MAX (Germany) 1852-. Music critic. Discovered more than one hundred lost lieder of Franz Schubert. *Das Deutsche Lied im Achtzehnten Jahrhundert.*

GABRILOWITSCH, OSSIP (United States) 1878-1936. Pianist. Conductor, Detroit Symphony Orchestra.

GARDNER, SAMUEL (United States) 1891-. Violinist and composer. *Quartet in D-Minor; From the Canebrake.*

GEDALGE, ANDRÉ (France) 1856-1926. Composer. Taught Ravel and Milhaud. *Treatise on the Fugue.*

GERSHWIN, GEORGE (United States) 1898-1937. Composer. *Rhapsody in Blue; Porgy and Bess; Concerto in F; An American in Paris.*

GODOWSKY, LEOPOLD (United States) 1870-1938. Pianist and composer. *Java Suite; Renaissance Suite.*

GOLDMARK, KARL (Austria-Hungary) 1830-1915. Composer. *Die Konigen von Saba; Merlin.*

GOLDMARK, RUBIN (United States) 1872-1936. Composer. *Requiem; Hiawatha; The Call of the Plains; Negro Rhapsody.*

GRUENBERG, LOUIS (United States) 1883-. Composer. *Emperor Jones; Jack and the Beanstalk; Daniel Jazz.*

HALEVY, JACQUES (France) 1799-1862. Composer. *La Juive; L'Éclair.*

HARRIS, CHARLES K. (United States) 1865-1930. Song writer. *After the Ball is Over; Break the News to Mother; Louise.*

HAUSER, EMIL (Hungary) 1893-. Violinist. Organized and directed Budapest String Quartet.

HEIFETZ, JASCHA (United States) 1901-. Violinist.

HELLER, STEPHEN (Austria) 1815-1888. Pianist and composer.

HERTZ, ALFRED (Germany, United States) 1872-. Conductor. Noted for readings of Wagner. Conductor, Metropolitan Opera Co., 1902-1915; San Francisco Symphony Orchestra 1915-1930.

HILLER, FERDINAND (Germany) 1811-1885. Composer. *Die Zerstorung Jerusalems.*

HOLLANDER, VICTOR (Germany) 1866-. Conductor and composer. *The Bay of Morocco; Der Sonnenvogel; Der Regimentspapa.*

HOROWITZ, VLADIMIR (United States) 1904-. Pianist.

HUBERMANN, BRONISLAW (Europe, United States) 1882-. Violinist.

JACOBI, FREDERICK (United States) 1891-. Composer. *Indian Dances.*

JOACHIM, JOSEPH (Hungary) 1831-1907. Violinist.

JOSEFFY, RAFAEL (United States) 1852-1915. Pianist. Edited Chopin's complete works; also *School of Advanced Piano Playing.*

KERN, JEROME D. (United States) 1885-. Composer. *Show Boat; Music in the Air; Roberta.*

KLEMPERER, OTTO (Germany, United States) 1885-. Conductor. Berlin State Opera until 1933; now Los Angeles Symphony Orchestra.

KOUSSEVITSKY, SERGEI (United States) 1874-. Conductor. Boston Symphony since 1924.

KREISLER, FRITZ (United States) 1875-. Violinist and composer, *String Quartette; Apple Blossom.*

KREYN, JULIEN (France) 1913-. Composer. *Five Orchestral Preludes; Spring Symphony; Orchestra Symphonique.*

LASSEN, EDUARD (Belgium) 1830-1904. Composer and conductor. Operas, orchestral works, incidental music for Goethe's *Faust.*

MAHLER, GUSTAV (Austria) 1860-1911. Composer and conductor. Nine symphonies.

MENDELSSOHN - (BARTHOLDY), FELIX (Germany) 1809-1847. Composer. *Midsummer Night's Dream; Italian Symphony.*

MENUHIN, YEHUDI (United States) 1916-. Violinist.

MEYERBEER, GIACOMO (JAKOB LIEBMANN BEER) 1791-1864. Composer. O p e r a s: *Les Huguenots; L'Africaine; Le Prophète.*

MILHAUD, DARIUS (France) 1892-. Composer. *Le Boeuf sur le Toit; La Creation du Monde; Salade; La Brebis Égarée.*

MONTEUX, PIERRE (France, United States) 1875-. Conductor. San Francisco Symphony since 1930.

MANA-ZUCCA (United States) 1894-. Pianist and Composer. *I Love Life; Nichovo.*

MOSCHELES, IGNAZ (Germany) 1794-1870. Pianist and composer. *Études; Allegri di Bravura.*

MOSZKOWSKI, MORITZ (Germany) 1854-1925. Composer. *Spanish Dances;* Opera: *Boabdil.*

OFFENBACH, JACQUES (France) 1819-1880. Composer. *Tales of Hoffman.*

ORMANDY, EUGENE* (Hungary) 1899-. Conductor. Minneapolis Symphony Orchestra from 1931 to 1936. Philadelphia Philharmonic since 1936.

REMENYI, EDUARD (Hungary) 1830-1898. Violinist and composer. *Violin Concerto.*

ROMBERG, SIGMUND (United States) 1887-. Composer. *Student Prince*; *Blossom Time*; *The Desert Song*.

ROME, HAROLD JACOB (United States) 1908-. Composer and lyricist. *Pins and Needles*.

ROSSI, SALAMONE (Italy) 1587-1628. Composer. Earliest successful efforts at instrumental writing and groundwork for chamber music.

RUBINSTEIN, ANTON (Europe, United States) 1829-1894. Pianist and composer.

RUBINSTEIN, ARTUR, (Poland, United States) 1886-. Pianist.

RUBINSTEIN, NIKOLAI (Russia) 1835-1881. Pianist. Founded Moscow Conservatory.

RUSSELL, HENRY (England) 1812-1900. Composer. *Cheer Boys, Cheer*; *A Life on the Ocean Wave*.

SAMINSKY, LAZARE (United States) 1882. Composer and conductor. *Pueblo*; *Tree Shadows*.

SCHINDLER, KURT (United States) 1882-1935. Conductor and Editor. Organized Schola Cantorum. *Folk Music and Poetry of Spain and Portugal*.

SCHNABEL, ARTUR (Austria, United States) 1882-. Pianist.

SCHONBERG, ARNOLD (Austria) 1874-. Composer. *Pierrot Lunaire*; *Verklarte Nacht*; *Pelléas et Mélisande*.

SCHUMAN, WILLIAM HOWARD (United States) 1910-. Composer. *Three Symphonies*.

SHILKRET, NATHANIEL (United States) 1895-. Conductor and composer. *I Dream of Lilac Time*; *Skyward*.

TANSMAN, ALEXANDER (Poland) 1897-. Composer. *La Nuit Kurde*; *Sextuour*.

TAUSIG, CARL (Poland) 1841-1871. Pianist and composer.

TOCH, ERNST (Germany) 1887-. Composer. *The Juggler*; *Piano Concerto*; *Pinnochio*.

WALTER, BRUNO (Germany) 1876-. Conductor.

WEILL, KURT (Germany) 1900. Composer. *Dreigroschen Opera*; *Lady in the Dark*; *The Songs of the Free*.

WEINBERGER, JAROMIR (Czechoslovakia) 1896-. Composer. *Schwanda der Duddelsackpfeifer*; *Wallenstein*.

WIENIAWSKI, HENRI (Russia) 1835-1880. Violinist and composer. Concertos, polonaises; *Fantaisie sur le Prophète*.

ZIMBALIST, EFREM (United States) 1889-. Violinist and composer.

PHILANTHROPY

BARNARDO, THOMAS* (England) 1845-1905. Founded Barnardo's Homes for Orphan Children.

HIRSCH, BARON MAURICE DE (Germany) 1831-1896. Contributed over one hundred million dollars to Jewish and non-Jewish charities.

GUGGENHEIM, DANIEL (United States) 1856-1930. Contributed over four million dollars to Daniel Guggenheim Fund for Promotion of Aeronautics.

GUGGENHEIM, SIMON (United States) 1867-. Established John Simon Guggenheim Foundation ($3,500,000) for aiding scientists, scholars, and artists without discrimination on account of race, creed, color or sex.

LEWISOHN, ADOLF (United States) 1849-. Donated School of Mines to Columbia University and Lewisohn Stadium to the College of the City of New York.

MONTEFIORE, SIR MOSES (England) 1784-1885. Contributed to many causes for raising material and moral standards of both Jews and non-Jews.

ROSENWALD, JULIUS (United States) 1862-1932. Donated over sixty million dollars for Negro welfare and other charities.

ROTHSCHILD FAMILY (England, France, Germany). Contributed large sums to all forms of human endeavor.

SASSOON, DAVID (India) 1797-1864. Contributed large sums to further education among all races in the Far East.

STRAUS, NATHAN (United States) 1848-1931. Established centers for distribution of sterilized milk to poor children in New York.

TOURO, JUDAH, 1775-1854. Founded Touro Hospital in New Orleans; donated funds for erection of Bunker Hill Monument.

PHILOSOPHY, SOCIAL AND POLITICAL SCIENCE

ACSADY, IGNACE (Hungary) 1845-1906. Historian. *The History of the Hungarian Nation.*

ADLER, FELIX, 1851-1933. Philosopher. Founded Society for Ethical Culture. *Creed and Deed; The Reconstruction of the Spiritual Ideal.*

ADLER, VICTOR (Austria) 1852-1918. Leader of the Social-Democratic party in Austria.

ALEXANDER, SAMUEL (England) 1859-1938. Philosopher and Metaphysician. *Moral Order and Progress; Space, Time and Deity.*

ASKENAZY, SIMON (Poland) 1867-1935. Historian. *Danzig and Poland.*

ASSER, TOBIAS MICHAEL (Holland) 1838-1913. Jurist. Arbitrator on international law in disputes between important powers. Awarded Nobel Peace Prize in 1911.

BENJAMIN, JUDAH P. (United States) 1811-1884. Statesman. Secretary of State of the Confederacy. *Law of Sale of Personal Property.*

BERGSON, HENRI (France) 1859-. Philosopher. Awarded Nobel prize for literature.

BOAS, FRANZ (United States) 1858-1943. Anthropologist. Pioneer American anthropologist. *The Mind of Primitive Man; Anthropology and Modern Life.*

BRANDEIS, LOUIS DEMBITZ (United States) 1856-1941. Jurist. United States Supreme Court Justice. 1916-1939. *Other People's Money; Business as a Profession.*

BRUNSCHVICG, LEON (France) 1869-. Philosopher. *Spinoza; Les Ages de l'Intelligence.*

CARDOZO, BENJAMIN (United States) 1870-1938. Jurist. Justice of United States Supreme Court 1932-1938. *The Nature of the Judicial Process* and *Law and Literature.*

COHEN, HERMANN (Germany) 1842-1918. Philosopher. Founded Marburg school of Neo-Kantian philosophy.

CRÉMIEUX, ISAAC ADOLPHE (France) 1796-1880. Statesman. Member of Chamber of Deputies and Minister of Justice. Abolish capital penalty for political offenses.

DISRAELI, BENJAMIN (EARL OF BEACONSFIELD) (England) 1804-1881. Prime Minister and author.

DURKHEIM, DAVID EMILE (France) 1858-1915. Philosopher. Founded modern French sociological school.

EDMAN, IRWIN (United States) 1896-. Philosopher. *Philosopher's Holiday; Human Traits and Their Social Significance.*

EZEKIAL, MORDECAI J. (United States) 1899-. Agricultural economist. Methods of statistical analysis; also price forecasting for farm products.

FLEXNER, ABRAHAM (United States) 1866-. Educator. *Medical Education; Universities; A Modern School; A Modern College.*

FRIED, ALFRED H. (Germany) 1864-1921. Pacifist. Founded German League for Peace. Awarded Nobel Peace Prize (with Tobias Asser) in 1911. *Handbook of the*

Peace Movement; *My Journal of the War.*

FRIEDBERG, EMIL VON (Germany) 1839-1910. Jurist and historian. Principal adviser of Bismarck during the *Kulturkampf* and authority on ecclesiastical history.

FRIEDENTHAL, KARL (Germany) 1827-1890. Statesman. Formulated constitution of the German empire.

FRIEDLANDER, LUDWIG (Germany) 1824-1909. Historian. *Roman Life and Manners Under the Early Empire.*

GODEFROI, MICHAEL (Holland) 1813-1882. Jurist. Author of Dutch code of judicial procedure.

GOLDENWEISER, ALEXANDER (United States) 1880-1940. Anthropologist. *Totemism*; *Early Civilization*; *The Making of Mankind*; *Anthropology.*

GOLDSMID, SIR JULIAN (England) 1838-1896. Statesman. Member of Parliament and of the Privy Council.

GOMPERS, SAMUEL (United States) 1850-1924. Labor leader. First president of the American Federation of Labor and retained that office (except in 1895) until his death. Important in fight for eight-hour day; began movement for Pan-American labor unity.

GUEDALLA, PHILIP (England) 1889-. Historian. *The Second Empire*; *Wellington*; *The Hundred Years.*

GRAETZ, HEINRICH (Germany) 1817-1891. Historian. *History of the Jews.*

GROSS, CHARLES (United States) 1857-1909. Historian. *The Guild Merchant*; *Sources and Literature of English History from Earliest Times to 1485.*

GUMPLOWICZ, LUDWIG (Germany) 1838-1909. Sociologist. One of founders of science of sociology.

HERSKOVITSE, MELVILLE JEAN (United States) 1895-. Anthropologist. *The American Negro*; *The Economic Life of Primitive Peoples.*

HUSSERL, EDUARD (Germany) 1859-1938. Philosopher. Founder of the theory of phenomenology.

JAFFE, PHILIPP (Germany) 1819-1870. Historian. *Geschichte des Deutschen Reichs Unter Lothar Dem Sachsen*; *Bibliothetic Rerum Germanicarum.*

JESSEL, SIR GEORGE (England) 1824-1883. Jurist. Solicitor-General, Privy Counsellor. Founded Court of Chancery as it exists today.

LASKER, EDUARD (Germany) 1829-1884. Political scientist. Founded German National Liberal party.

LASKI, HAROLD J. (England) 1893-. Political scientist. *Parliamentary Government in England*; *A Grammar of Politics*; *The State in Theory and Practice.*

LASSÁLLE, FERDINAND (Germany) 1825-1864. Founder of German socialism.

LEIPZIGER, HENRY M. (United States) 1853-1917. Educator. Pioneer in vocational education.

LENEL, OTTO (Germany) 1849-1935. Jurist. *Geschichte und Quellen des Romischen Rechts.*

LEVI, LEONE R.* (England) 1821-1888. Jurist. Largely responsible for codification of international commercial law.

LEVY-BRUHL, LUCIEN (France) 1857-1939. Philosopher.

LOEWENBERG, JAKOB (Germany) 1856-1929. Pedagogue.

LOMBROSO, CESARE (Italy) 1836-1909. Criminologist.

LOW, SIR SIDNEY (England) 1857-1932. Historian. *The Governance of England.*

LUBIN, DAVID (United States) 1848-1919. Agrarian reformer. Founder of International Institute of Agriculture.

264

LUZZATTI, LUIGI (Italy) 1841-1927. Statesman. Prime Minister of Italy, 1909-1911.

MANNHEIM, KARL (Germany, England) 1893-. Sociologist. *Introduction to the Sociology of Knowledge.*

MARCZALI, HENRIK (Hungary) 1856-1940. Historian. *"Hungary in the Eighteenth Century; World Politics and World Economics.*

MARX, KARL 1818-1883. Philosopher and economist. Founder of scientific socialism. *Das Kapital.*

MAUROGONATO, ISAAC (Italy) 1817-1892. Statesman. Vice-President of Italian Chamber of Deputies.

MEYERSON, EMILE (France) 1859-1933. Philosopher. *"Identity and Reality."*

MYERS, GUSTAVUS (United States) 1872-1943. Historian. *The History of Tammany Hall; History of the Great American Fortunes.*

OPPENHEIMER, FRANZ (Germany) 1864-1943. Sociologist. *System der Soziologie; Die Soziale Frage un der Sozialismus.*

PREUSS, HUGO (Germany) 1860-1925. Jurist. One of the framers of Weimar Constitution.

RAOIN, MAX (United States) 1880-. Jurist-historian. *Law as Logic and Experience; The Law and Mr. Smith.*

RATHENAU, WALTHER (Germany) 1867-1922. Industrialist and cabinet minister. *The New Economics; In Days to Come.*

READING, RUFUS, First MARQUESS OF (England) 1860-1935. Administrator. Lord Chief Justice of England and Viceroy of India.

RICARDO, DAVID (England) 1772-1823. Economist. *Law of Rent* and *Labor Theory of Value.*

RIESSER, GABRIEL (Germany) 1806-1863. Deputy in German National Assembly and member of Hamburg High Court.

SAMUEL, VISCOUNT HER-BERT (England) 1870-. Statesman. Served as English Secretary for Home Affairs and High Commissioner to Palestine.

SAPIR, EDWARD (United States) 1884-1939. Anthropologist. *Time Perspective in Aboriginal American Cultures; Language.*

SELIGMAN, EDWIN ROBERT ANDERSON (United States) 1861-. Political economist. *Essays in Taxation; The Shifting and Incidence of Taxation; Economic Interpretation of History.*

SMITH, SIR ARCHIBALD (England) 1836-1901. Jurist. Judge in Court of Appeals and Master of the Rolls.

SPINOZA, BARUCH (Holland) 1632-1677. Philosopher.

STAHL, FRIEDRICH JULIUS (Germany) 1802-1855. Founded the German Conservative party and was its recognized leader.

PHYSICS

BOHR, NIELS* (Denmark) 1885-. One of creators of the modern atomic theory. Nobel prize for physics in 1922.

BORN, MAX (Germany) 1882-. Work in connection with relativity, quantum theory and dynamics of the crystal.

EHRENHAFT, FELIX (Austria) 1879-. Discovered Brownian movement of gases and positive and negative photophoresis.

EINSTEIN, ALBERT (Germany) 1879-. Nobel prize in 1921 for work on photo-chemical equivalents; theory of relativity.

EPSTEIN, PAUL SOPHUS (United States, Russia) 1883-. Theory on surface composition of the moon.

FRANCK, JAMES (Germany, United States) 1882-. Nobel prize in physics (1925) for work in kinetics of electrons (with Herz). Proved atomic structure theory of Bohr; first proof of Planck's quantum theory.

GOLDSTEIN, EUGENE (Germany) 1856-1930. Investigation of cathode rays; discovered "second helium spectrum."

GOUDSMIT, SAMUEL ABRAHAM (Holland) 1902-. Collaborated in the discovery of the "spin of the electron."

GRAETZ, LEO (Germany) 1856-. Method of converting alternating current into direct current.

GUTENBERG, BENO (Germany) 1889-. Determination of the radius of the earth's core.

HERTZ, GUSTAV* (Germany) 1887-. Awarded (with James Franck) the Nobel prize in 1925 for work on electro-kinetics of ions and gas molecules.

HERTZ, HEINRICH* (Germany) 1857-1894. D i s c o v e r e d "Hertzian" (radio) waves.

HEVESY, GEORG VON (Germany, Denmark) 1885-. Collaborated in discovery of seventy-second element, thereby proving Bohr's theory of elements.

KAPLAN, JOSEPH (United States) 1902-. Discovered nature of iridescence of northern lights.

LIPPMANN, GABRIEL (France) 1845-1921. Process of color photography in 1891. Awarded Nobel prize for physics in 1908.

MAGNUS, HEINRICH GUSTAV (Germany) 1802-1870. Physicist and chemist. Discovery of first of platino-ammonium compounds; also "magnus effect" on projectiles.

MEITNER, LISLE (Germany) 1878-. Discovered the element protactinium with Otto Hahn.

MICHELSON, ALBERT ABRAHAM (United States) 1852-1931. Determined the velocity of light; invented interferometer. Awarded Nobel prize for physics in 1907.

SCHUSTER, SIR ARTHUR (England) 1851-1934. Work in spectroscopy.

SHORE, HENRY, (United States) 1903-. Invented constant frequency variable dot system of transmitting pictures through radio.

VOLTERRA, VITO (Italy) 1860-1940. Physicist and mathematician. Founder of "mathematical biology"; theories of integral equations.

THEATER

BARNAY, LUDWIG (Germany) 1842-1924. Actor. Founded Berliner theater.

BELASCO, DAVID (United States) 1854-1931. Playwright and theatrical producer. Noted for the creation of revolutionary stage effects. *Madame Butterfly*; *Girl of the Golden West*; *Rose of the Rancho*; *The Return of Peter Grimm*.

BERGNER, ELIZABETH (Germany, United States) 1899-. Stage and cinema actress. *St. Joan*; *The Last of Mrs. Cheney*; *Escape Me Never*.

BERNHARDT, SARAH (Europe, United States) 1844-1923. Actress.

FIELDS, LEW (United States) 1867-. Comedian and manager. Team of Weber and Fields.

FROHMAN, CHARLES (United States, England) 1860-1915. Producer. *Peter Pan*; *Chanticleer*; *Charley's Aunt*; *Second Mrs. Tanqueray*.

GRAU, MAURICE (United States) 1849-1907. Impresario.

HAMMERSTEIN, OSCAR (United States) 1847-1919. Impresario.

HARRIS, JED (United States) 1900-. Producer and director. Chekhov's *Uncle Vanya*; Gogol's *Inspector General*; and Ibsen's *A Doll's House*.

MUNI, PAUL (United States) 1895-. Stage and cinema actor. *Scarface*; *The Good Earth*; *Louis Pasteur*; *Emile Zola*.

NAZIMOVA, ALLA (United States) 1879-. Actress. *The Doll's*

House; *Mourning Becomes Electra*.

RACHEL (Elisa Rachel Felix) (France) 1820-1858. Actress.

RAINER, LUISE (Germany, United States) 1919-. Actress. *Saint Joan*; *Escapade*; *The Good Earth*.

REINHARDT, MAX (Austria, United States) 1873-1943. Producer. Originated impressionistic school of production. *The Miracle*; *Midsummer Night's Dream*.

SONNENTHAL, ADOLPH (Austria) 1834-1909. Actor. *Faust*; *Wallenstein*; *Nathan the Wise*; *Henschel*.

WARFIELD, DAVID (United States) 1866-. Actor. *Music Master*; *The Auctioneer*; *The Return of Peter Grimm*.

WEBER, JOSEPH (United States) 1867-1942. Comedian. Team of Weber and Fields.

APPENDIX

II

JEWS IN THE AMERICAN ARMED FORCES IN WORLD WAR II

This information is from the Bureau of War Records of the National Jewish Welfare Board, and represents figures compiled to June 30, 1945.

Upwards of 500,000 men of Jewish faith are serving in the armed forces of the United States; or, in military terms, more than 33 divisions.

More than 8200 Jewish men in uniform have received citations for valor and merit, many of them posthumously. Among the 8200 are 78 Jewish men who each have to their credit ten or more awards for valor, holding an aggregate of 881 such decorations. The Distinguished Service Cross, the second highest army award for heroism, has been earned by more than 50 men of Jewish faith.

Of the 500,000 Jewish men in uniform, the Bureau of War Records has a comparative figure of more than 30,000 Jewish casualties in all branches of the armed services.

At least one-third of the Jewish physicians of the nation are serving with the armed forces.

Thousands of Jewish families have given three or more sons to the service; 1059 of these families have contributed a total of 3594 members to the armed forces; 81 of these families have given 448.

There are 266 rabbis serving as chaplains, representing one-fourth of the total American rabbinate. Fully 50 percent of all rabbis in America have volunteered for duty as chaplains. *Three Jewish chaplains have lost their lives serving overseas.*

APPENDIX

III

NOTES

"January 22, 1942

"Mr. J. A. Colescott, Imperial Wizard,
Knights of the Ku Klux Klan,
P. O. Box #1204
Atlanta, Georgia.
Dear Sir:

"My attention has been directed to one of the pamphlets reprinted and published by your organization and captioned 'The International Jew.' It recites that it is 'the first reprint of a series of ninety-six articles originally appearing in the Dearborn *Independent*, publication of Henry Ford.'

"As the legal representative of Mr. Henry Ford, I request that your organization desist from the further publication and circulation of the above-named pamphlet and also any reprints of other articles related to this subject matter that appeared in the Dearborn *Independent*. The manner in which this reprint has been presented to the public amounts to a deliberate and intentional misrepresentation. It is a malicious attempt to mislead the public into believing that these articles were and still are an expression of Mr. Ford's opinions and sentiments, whereas as you well know, Mr. Ford retracted these articles in 1928 and at th' time disclaimed them as being an expression of his views and se - ments.

"Your conduct in this matter manifests a definite dispositi   to cause injury to the name of Henry Ford by a deceitful and mis ding republication, and your perseverance in this regard will necessitate legal action on our part.

"Therefore, in the interests of everyone concerned, I hope that you will heed this request.

Yours truly,

I. A. Capizzi."

"Senor Miguel Aleman,
Secretario de Governacion,
Mexico City, Mexico
Dear Sir:

"On behalf of Mr. Henry Ford, as his legal representative, I write you relative to the alleged circulation in Mexico City and Pueblo, of a pamphlet entitled, 'El Judio Internacional por Henry Ford.'

"I understand that this is the pernicious work of the German Propaganda Department attempting to undermine the esteem which the Mexican public has for the United States Government, by circulating a misleading and deceitful republication of articles that were retracted by Mr. Ford in 1928 and at that time disclaimed by him as being an expression of his sentiments.

"Although a copy of this pamphlet is not at our disposal, I understand that it indicates that Mr. Henry Ford is the author. This is a gross misrepresentation, because Mr. Ford in 1928 publicly denied that these articles were approved by him before their original publication, and denies that they were an expression of his views or opinions.

"In the intervening years, Mr. Ford has been diligent in his efforts to suppress any attempt to renew the circulation of these articles. Therefore, in this instance, any assistance which your office can render in effecting the cessation of this harmful exhibition of deceit and misrepresentation will be greatly appreciated.

Very truly yours,

I. A. Capizzi."

APPENDIX

IV

PRISONERS IN NEW YORK STATE PENAL INSTITUTIONS

YEAR	TOTAL PRISONERS	JEWISH PRISONERS	PERCENTAGE
1940	13,085	290	2.22
1941	12,624	246	1.95
1942	11,263	210	1.86
Total	36,972	746	2.02

POPULATION OF NEW YORK STATE:

TOTAL	JEWISH	PERCENTAGE
12,959,000	2,234,400	17.24

These tabulations are from the following detailed statistics:

STATE OF NEW YORK	Total	Jews	Percentage
Committed to State Prisons			
1940.........................	2109	182	8.62
1941.........................	1997	163	8.16
1942.........................	1814	139	7.66
	5920	484	

Committed to Reformatories			
1940			
Men	686	40	5.8
Women	284	7	2.46
	970	47	
1941			
Men	1061	30	2.83
Women	266	5	1.88
	1327	35	

271

1942

Men	1046	11	1.05
Women	285	15	5.26
	1331	26	

Committed to Institutions for Defective Delinquents

1940

Men	148	4	2.7
Women	46	–	
	194		

1941

Men	162	7	4.32
Women	35	–	
	197		

1942

Men	165	8	4.85
Women	32	1	.03
	197	9	

Committed to Penitentiaries

1940

Men	9421	56	.59
Women	391	1	.025
	9812	57	

1941

Men	8741	39	.594
Women	362	2	.55
	9103	41	

1942

Men	7632	36	.47
Women	289	–	
	7921		

The statistics available for eight states, namely, New York, Connecticut, Illinois, Maryland, Michigan, New Jersey, Ohio, and Pennsylvania, which contain 80 per cent of the total Jewish population of the United States, show that the Jewish population is 7.56 per cent of the whole. The percentage of Jewish prisoners in all these states is 2.09 per cent and covered the following years:

New York (1933, 1934, 1935) . . . 2.07 per cent; Connecticut (1929, 1930) . . . 4.15 per cent; Illinois (1930, 1931) . . . 1.41 per cent; Maryland (1933) . . . 1.14 per cent; Michigan (1928) . . . 1.28 per cent; New Jersey (1928, 1929) . . . 4.8 per cent; Ohio (1929, 1930) . . . .078 per cent; Pennsylvania (1928, 1929, 1930) . . . 1.43 per cent.

These are the latest statistics upon this point available for the above-named states, except that of New York, which is given above. It is fair to assume that the percentage of Jewish prisoners was not any greater in subsequent years, as is indicated by the later statistics of the state of New York detailed above. Thus, in the eight states which contain 80 per cent of the total Jewish population of this country, if the Jewish prisoners in state penal institutions equaled the percentage of Jewish population, then the prisoners would be 7.56 per cent of all prisoners, when in fact it is only 2.09 per cent, a record to which the Jews may point in reply to these criticisms.

BIBLIOGRAPHY

V

A History of the Christian Church—George P. Fisher.

A History of Political and Religious Persecution—Fernando Garrido and Charles Y. Cayler.

America's 60 Families—Ferdinand Lundberg

Anti-Semitism—Hugo Valentin

Anti-Semitism, Its History and Cause—Bernard Lazarre

Anti-Semitism Yesterday and Tomorrow—Lee Levinger

Anti-Semitism Throughout The Ages—Count Heinrich Coudenhove-Kalergi

Aspects of Jewish Life and Thought—(The Letters of Benammi)

Behemoth—Franz Neumann

Catholicity of Philadelphia—J. L. Kirlin

Conflict of Christianity with Heathenism—Gerhard Uhlhorn

Daniel Deronda—George Elliot

Ezekiel to Einstein—Francis J. Oppenheimer

For The Honor of the Nation—Compilation by Samuel W. McCall and Charles W. Eliot

Group Movements Throughout the Ages—Robert H. Robert

History of the Jews—Heinrich H. Graetz

History of the Jewish People—Max L. Margolis and Alexander Marx

History of the Jews—A. L. Sachar

History of the Rise of the Huguenots of France—Henry M. Baird

History of the Jews—Henry Hart Milman

History of Puritans—Daniel Neal

History of the Crusades Against The Albigenses—Jean C. L. de Simonde

History of Bigotry in the United States—Gustavus Myers

History of the Jews in America—Peter Wiernik

Hoaxes—Curtis D. MacDougall

Israel Among The Nations—Anatole Le Roy Beaulieu

Israel and the Nations—Joseph S. Bloch

Intolerance—Winfred E. Garrison

Inquisition and Liberty—George G. Coulton

Jews in a Gentile World—Isacque Graeber and Steuart Henderson Britt

Jewish Contributions to Civilization—Joseph Jacobs

274

Jewish Pioneers and Patriots—Lee M. Friedman
Nobel Prize Winners—Flora Kaplan
Organized Anti-Semitism in America—Donald S. Strong
Outlines of Jewish History—Lady Magnus
Public Opinion—Walter Lippmann
Prejudice Against the Jew—Phillip Cowen
Religious Thought and Heresy in the Middle Ages—Frederick W. Bussell
Religious Persecution—E. S. P. Haynes
Shakespeare and the Jew—Gerald Friedlander
Sufferance is the Badge—A. L. Sachar
Social and Religious Heritage of Five Centuries—Carl Heath
Selected Essays—Ahad Ha-'am (Asher Ginzberg)
The Jew In The Literature of England—Frank Modder Montagu
The Universal Jewish Encyclopedia—Vol. 1, p. 341
The Nazarene—Sholem Asch
The Answer—Ludwig Lewisohn
The World Crisis and Jewish Survival—Abba Hillel Silver
The History of Quakerism—E. Russell
The Huguenots—Otto Zoff
The Story of American Catholicism—Theodore Maynard
The Reformation of the Sixteenth Century in its Relation to Modern Thought and Knowledge—Charles Beard
The Voice of Jerusalem—Israel Zangwill
The Mind in the Making—James Harvey Robinson
The Jewish Contribution to Civilization—Cecil Roth
The Christian-Jewish Tragedy—Conrad Henry Moehlman
What I Believe—Sholem Asch
Why We Behave Like Human Beings—George A. Dorsey

Index

Aaron, Jonas, 136
Abbott, Dr. Lyman, 88
Abraham, Noah, 140
Abravanel, Don Isaac, 130
A Child's History of Civilization, 6
Achron, Isidor, 161
Adams, John, 138
Adler, Julius Ochs, 209
Agobardus of Lyons, 36
Agudath Harabbanim, 102
Ahad Ha-'Am, 79
Akademie der Bildenden
    Künste, 110, 111
Albigenses, the, 174, 182, 183
Aleman, Senor Miguel, 49
Alexander I, Emperor of Rus-
    sia, 31
Alschuler, Judge Samuel, 80
Altgeld, Governor John Peter, 96
American Christian Defenders, 120
American Mercury, the, 146
American Vigilant Intelligence
    Federation, 61, 120
Anabaptists, the, 171, 172
Andreyev, Andrew, 67
Annius of Viterbo, 51
Anti-Semitism,
    accusations of ritual murder, 21
    and "The Black Death," 22
    articles in Dearborn *Independ-
        ent*, 45
    as an emotional attitude, 77
    Benjamin Franklin prophecy, 57
    charges of Communism and Bol-
        shevism, 60
    corrective of, 231
    Count Heinrich Coudenhove-
        Kalergi on, 17

Dreyfus case, 52-56
    effect of, 125-128
    during the Crusades, 16
    in conflict with Christianity, 202
    injected into the child mind, 2, 3
    in juvenile literature, 4-9
    in Marlowe, 13-16
    in Shakespeare, 12-16
    Kishinev massacre, 29, 68
    libels concerning the Talmud,
        33-37
    Nazi propaganda, 114-123
    pogroms in Russia, 29-32
    "Protocols," the, 39
    reaction of the Jew, 197
    Sunday school instruction in, 9,
        10
    versus American unity, 124
Archivo General de India, 131
Aristotle, 155
Arnstein, Karl, 152
Arnstein, Sam, 209
Aryans, characteristics of, 185, 186
Ascoli, Max, 145
Asser, Tobias Michael Carel, 148
Auer, Leopold, 161
Auerbach, Berthold, 160
Augustine, 23
Aurelian, 182
Aurelius, Marcus, 182
Avila, Miguel, 52

Baer, Clarence, 209
Bailie, Earle, 87
Baker, Newton B., 97
Bancamerika-Blair, 86
Bank of International Settlements,
    100

276

277

278

279